NEVER AT THE OFFICE

AN ITALIAN ADVENTURE

Mike Clegg

To: Sir Michael
I'm sure you'll identify
with some of those experiences
Book 2 will cover much of
the time you, too, were
serving in Naples.
Best Wishes,
Mike

Never at the Office: An Italian Adventure

Mike Clegg

Copyright © 2020

ISBN: 978-0-9954823-6-4

Published by Mike Clegg in conjunction with Writersworld. This book is produced entirely in the UK, is available to order from most book shops in the United Kingdom, and is globally available via UK-based Internet book retailers and www.amazon.com.

Copy edited by Ian Large

Cover design by Jag Lall

www.writersworld.co.uk

WRITERSWORLD
2 Bear Close Flats
Bear Close
Woodstock
Oxfordshire
OX20 1JX
United Kingdom

☎ 01993 812500

☎ +44 1993 812500

The text pages of this book are produced via an independent certification process that ensures the trees from which the paper is produced come from well managed sources that exclude the risk of using illegally logged timber while leaving options to use post-consumer recycled paper as well.

In memory of my dear friend

Serhan Sevim

Who sadly died before this book was written.

CONTENTS

PROLOGUE: SEE NAPLES AND DIE!..7

1   THE RETURN...15
2   MOVING IN – HOME AND OFFICE..................................23
3   THE COLD WAR...35
4   NATO'S STRUCTURE...41
5   MY FIRST DAY AT WORK...44
6   FRIENDS, NEIGHBOURS AND ACQUAINTANCES.......50
7   THE LOCAL AREA...58
8   DEFENDING THE SOUTHERN REGION.......................69
9   *I CAMPI FLEGREI* – THE FIERY FIELDS.....................75
10 PLANNING NATO EXERCISES......................................78
11 THE REAL FIERY FIELDS...90
12 COMMAND POST EXERCISES......................................95
13 UNDERGROUND AGAIN..101
14 REAL EXERCISES – LIVEXES.......................................108
15 NAPLES – THE NEW CITY...119
16 BACK TO SCHOOL...131
17 HILO TOURS..144
18 THE BRITISH WAY OF LIFE..151
19 ALL AT SEA...158
20 LIGHTHOUSE OF THE MEDITERRANEAN...................168
21 AN ITALIAN INTERLUDE...177
22 IN THE SHADOW OF VESUVIUS..................................180
23 THE INTERNATIONAL ARCHAEOLOGICAL SOCIETY...193
24 THE ASCENT OF VESUVIUS..201
25 THE SLEEPING GIANT..207
26 MY OWN VILLA...212
27 DIGGING AT THE GLORIOUS ROCK.............................217
28 NIGHTS AT THE OPERA...221
29 LIFE IN THE BAY OF NAPLES – CAPRI........................225

30 FRIENDS AND ALLIES...236
31 LIFE IN THE BAY OF NAPLES – ISCHIA.......................239
32 EXERCISE ABLE ARCHER..245
33 BEWARE GREEKS BEARING GIFTS 249
34 FINAL THOUGHTS 254

PROLOGUE

SEE NAPLES AND DIE!

Vedi Napoli e poi muori, 'See Naples and Die'; so said Johann Wolfgang von Goethe in 1787. He meant that there is nowhere in this world as beautiful as Naples so once you have seen it you may die in a state of sublime happiness. My introduction to this fabled city was, however, almost literal. Let me explain.

At the time I was serving as a pilot in the Royal Air Force as a member of 203 Squadron based in Malta. We were equipped with the antiquated but still capable Shackleton Mark III, the last big, piston-engined aircraft operated by the RAF whose pedigree included the Lancaster and Halifax bombers of Second World War fame. It was often described as 'forty thousand rivets flying (noisily) in close formation' and was not renowned for its reliability. But, we did have two small jet engines in addition to our four Rolls Royce Griffons – the jet age had not bypassed us completely. Even so, the aircraft was underpowered.

The Shackleton was designed to carry out long patrols over the sea to seek out enemy warships and to hunt submarines. It carried a crew of ten: five officers and five senior non-commissioned officers (SNCOs). 203 Squadron had been moved to Luqa in Malta from Ballykelly in Northern Ireland at the beginning of 1969 to counter the expanding Soviet naval presence in the Mediterranean. On 9th May that year my crew was briefed to carry out a routine exercise with one of Her Majesty's submarines in an area a few miles to the west of Naples. As the last of the daylight faded we located our playmate running at periscope depth, its masts throwing up a feather of spray, tell-tale white against the wine-dark sea, and clearly visible from our height of one thousand feet. On the eastern horizon Naples was preparing for the night, its twinkling lights contrasting starkly with the dark and threatening mass of Vesuvius looming over the city. We exchanged UHF radio messages with the submarine before opening out to ten miles to carry out a radar homing, the precursor to dropping a pattern of active and passive sonobuoys with which to track our friendly target underwater. Isolated in the darkness of his curtained tent the radar operator adjusted his set and concentrated on maintaining contact with the submarine masts; he was the key to initiating the exercise.

'Captain – Radar contact 260 degrees, ten miles.'

'Action stations, action stations – turning on. Co [pilot], call "Comex"' (the radio message to commence the exercise).

I felt the usual surge of adrenaline as I heaved the aircraft round towards the reported contact. Behind me in the cramped, noisy and dimly lit fuselage my crew prepared for the forthcoming exercise: the routine navigator left his seat and moved quickly to the bomb aimer's position in the nose; the tactical navigator prepared his tactical plot; the sonics operators manned their CRTs ready to look and listen for acoustic contact on the submarine and one crewman manned the tail lookout position. I set the rpm to 2,600, increased speed, descended to 500 feet and followed the radar operator's terse instructions, homing us in to his small intermittent contact. At five miles the contact was lost; the submarine had gone deep. The tactical navigator took over the conn, calling for 'bomb doors open' at four miles. Shortly afterwards our sonobuoys left the bomb bay (each buoy reputedly costing the same as a mini!). I called for the bomb doors to be closed and turned back towards the centre of our sonobuoy pattern. We waited for the first sonar contact. In the cockpit all was normal, the many instruments glowing faintly red in the now subdued lighting. Behind the two pilots the tactical team – ghostly figures in the half-light – leaned over their equipment and became engrossed in the complex task of tracking the submerged submarine, a familiar routine for these experienced aviators. The sonar operators were soon in contact and reporting active fixes to the tactical navigator. Following the tacnav's directions I positioned the aircraft for a simulated attack on the target. As we ran in the co-pilot opened the bomb doors and the navigator selected a Signal Underwater Sound (SUS) that he would release to simulate a torpedo attack. If accurate the submarine would mark the attack with a smoke float. (In theory. Submariners being a devious bunch were just as likely to claim that no sound was ever heard, even if the SUS bounced off the sub's hull!)

Suddenly there was an ear-splitting bang followed by a terrifying banshee wail. The aircraft lurched violently to the right and, looking down at the instruments, I saw that our number three engine was accelerating through 3,600rpm.

'Crew – Captain Overspeed number three engine – feather number three.' We had suffered one of the most feared airborne emergencies, with the engine turning almost a thousand rpm more than the normal maximum. Because of a serious mechanical component failure the contra-rotating propellers had become physically disengaged from the engine and were now acting like a giant child's windmill, but in a wind of over 120 miles an hour! The engine, meanwhile, racing way above its maximum rotation speed was in serious danger of tearing itself apart.

I'm sure I wasn't alone in having the thought flash through my mind that the last two overspeed incidents in Shackletons had resulted in the loss of the aircraft concerned, together with most of the crew members. We had but little time, seconds only, in which to stop the rampaging engine before it disintegrated and severed the hydraulic lines, the only means by which we could stop the mad rotation of the propellers and prevent them flying off to smash into the fuselage. More seriously, if the hydraulic lines were to be severed the resultant spray of fluid onto the hot engine would almost certainly result in a fire, the worst nightmare of all airmen.

Even before I'd completed my warning to the crew my co-pilot, Mike Thompson, and flight engineer, Ray Donovan, had begun the feathering procedure as I struggled to control the violently vibrating aircraft. Gradually both engine and propellers came to rest. The quick reactions of the co-pilot and engineer had saved the day. Now, with a very sick aircraft and with adrenaline flooding our bodies we had only one option – an emergency landing at the nearest airfield, Naples Capodichino.

With increased power on our remaining three piston engines to maintain flying speed the aircraft gave voice to a deafening roar of defiance to which was added the jarring but reassuring whine of our two jets that the flight engineer had started up as part of a well-rehearsed emergency drill. The next few minutes seemed interminable and our state of mind was not helped by the starboard lookout reporting in a somewhat strangled voice that the right wing was on fire. Fortunately this turned out to be nothing more than the reflection of our revolving red, anti-collision light in the oil from our damaged engine rippling across the surface of the wing.

The airport staff at Naples had been alerted by radio to our plight and, in addition to passing us instructions in highly excited English, most of which were incomprehensible, had positioned all the crash vehicles by the side of the runway – not necessarily a reassuring sight, but with the numerous flashing lights, certainly a colourful and dramatic one. There was one advantage, though: no air traffic delays. In fact our landing was entirely uneventful and, leaking oil like a wounded elephant trailing blood, we taxied to our allotted parking area and took stock. You could almost hear the sighs of relief throughout the aircraft whilst the silence that greeted the shutting-down of the engines was almost tangible. The drama over, we left our aircraft – a forlorn, grey creature from another age – dripping oil onto the pristine concrete of the parking area. See Naples and die? Not this time!

Airfields, or airports, are much the same the world over. However, if blessed with a military side, life is much easier for a military crew. And so it was in Naples where the United States had, and still has, a military presence. A very obliging duty officer – Torricelli by name but American by birth, citizenship and navy – quickly arranged, in Italian or English as the occasion required, communications with our base in Malta, transport to what he called 'downtown Napoli' and accommodation in the Hotel Vesuvio. Our aircraft wasn't going anywhere for a while so we left it in a slowly expanding pool of oil and climbed on board a crew coach for the journey into the city, a journey almost as exciting as our recent experience in the air. The volume of traffic, the frenetic driving that regarded every empty space as a challenge, not to mention the pavements thronged with people of all ages spilling over into the road like an incoming tide, appeared more a chaotic film set than a major European city. Before long, though, and to our great relief, we were, the ten of us, sitting in the hotel bar steadying our nerves and celebrating our arrival in Naples with a glass or two of Nastro Azzurro; no beer had ever been better received. It was a somewhat inebriated crew that retired that night – but we couldn't help wondering what the submarine crew thought when they came to periscope depth and found us, gone!

We assembled at what passed for breakfast in downtown Napoli – dry toast in cellophane wrappers and strong coffee – to learn that it would be a few days before our damaged aircraft could be restored to flying and fighting trim, so what to do? The first requirement was money and here we learnt to appreciate the benefits of Her Majesty's Diplomatic Service. Without turning a hair, albeit insisting on a signature or two, HM Consul General's staff handed over a veritable fortune – or so it seemed – in the form of millions of Italian lire. Next, those of us confined to flying suits, a change of dress seemed to be in order. I should explain that transport-trained aircrew, who were used to flying from their home base to other airfields, always took a change of clothing on board with them, usually uniform which could be adapted as civilian attire. However, those of us brought up in the maritime tradition, in which the landing generally took place many hours later at the same airfield as the take-off, tended not to bother. This, of course, did have its drawbacks when unscheduled stopovers occurred. Flying suits were ideal in the air but had considerable limitations on the ground; apart from attracting too much attention, they stank! So it was that the malodorous pilots and flight engineer ventured into the old quarter of Naples. This turned out to be an error of judgement. As the buildings closed in on us threateningly on either side, so did a crowd of urchins who, whilst apparently friendly, attempted to relieve us of anything removable, dodging with alacrity any attempts to beat them off. Fortunately our plight was noted by a shopkeeper who dispersed the youthful muggers with some well-rehearsed Neapolitan oaths accompanied by the extreme gestures that seem to be an essential part of communicating in southern Italy. He was also able to escort us to a family member who just happened to deal in just the sort of attire we were seeking – cheap and cheerful. Soon, proudly arrayed in red shirts and brown trousers, probably the last remaining stock of Garibaldi's uniforms, we returned to the comparative calm of the hotel. A valuable lesson had been learnt: when entering that area known as *Spacca Napoli* do not draw attention to oneself, either by wearing a flying suit or indeed by looking like a tourist, a lesson that is as valid today as it was then.

The following day, still at a loose end, we decided on a crew outing. We began by visiting the Archaeological Museum, a veritable treasure house of things Roman. We wondered at marvellous mosaics, wall paintings, statues and various artefacts in quick succession, until a shady looking custodian rose from his bored contemplation of nothing in particular and stopped us with a hissing noise and a hand gesture at waist level. Looking furtively around, he asked if we would like to see the 'special' room. Taking a huge key from his pocket he unlocked an imposing door and ushered us, with many a backward glance, into a dimly lit room. Around the walls were arrayed a series of sexual images complemented in the centre of the room by a number of statues on the same theme. This collection has recently been opened again to the public but in the late '60s it was thought by the church to be too corrupting for general display. As a final comment on the content, one of the crew on leaving the room said in what was clearly a disappointed tone: 'I thought I was going to learn something new.' Some human activities apparently never change.

Our next stop was Pompeii, at that time in much better condition than today. Exposure to the elements, earthquakes, too many tourists, poor site management and disastrous preservation techniques have all taken their toll. So, if you have not yet visited this unique survival of a bygone age, go now before it is too late. We dutifully tramped the streets, amazed at the sheer size of the town, until overcome by fatigue and hunger. We lunched in the open air, next to the Forum Baths, under a canopy of vines. At a table close by sat a middle-aged English couple – clearly identifiable by their bizarre clothing: a shapeless, flowery frock for her; baggy shorts and sandals, with socks, for him. They took an unusually close interest in our group. Finally the husband nodded to himself and voiced his opinion loudly and in the unmistakable accent of Yorkshire: 'Appen it's institute outing. Them in't red shirts must be t'offenders and them in't blue t'warders.' It took a long time to live down those red shirts.

The next morning, fortified only by another miserable Neapolitan breakfast, we decided to scale the west face of Vesuvius – not on foot as is necessary today, but by the much less strenuous and more enjoyable long-gone chair lift. We were transported noiselessly up the cindery cone, the sterility of the immediate surroundings being more than compensated for by the magnificent panorama of the Bay of Naples, guarded by the islands of Capri and Ischia, shimmering in the brilliance of an early summer's day. Vesuvius itself was boringly quiet – not even a decent burst of steam nor a puff of smoke were in evidence. In fact the volcano had been sleeping since 1944. In the eruption of that year a lava flow had destroyed half the town of San Sebastiano. Had it not been for the saint, perhaps the whole town would have been engulfed; and had the saint not felt peeved at the presence of Saint Gennaro, the patron saint of Naples, who was being held round a corner in reserve, perhaps he might have stopped the lava flow outside the town. The British author, Norman Lewis, then serving in the army, wrote an excellent account of the event in his book *Naples '44.*

All good things come to an end, as did our stay in Naples. The next day we climbed aboard our repaired aircraft and took off for Malta. As we climbed noisily away we were able to take one last look at Vesuvius and the vibrant but chaotic city placed so vulnerably at its foot. We had truly seen Naples, and we had not died. I did not expect to return.

[As a sad post script to this adventure Mike Thompson was later to lose his life when his Lightning XP753 crashed into the sea off Scarborough during a flying display on 26th August 1983.]

1

THE RETURN

Fifteen years later a bright, sunny March day found me driving southwards towards Rome. The *Autostrada del Sole* stretched before me, winding its way through the hilly countryside of Tuscany, in and out of tunnels each with its exhortation to *accendere i fari* (use headlights), and overlooked by little hilltop villages. My destination – Naples! I had been assigned to a North Atlantic Treaty Organisation (NATO) post in the Alliance's Southern Region. 'Ah, Never At The Office' quipped my friends, out of cynicism perhaps, but more likely out of jealousy. Even the staff of our local Italian restaurant in Northwood had something to say and implored me not to venture south of Rome. 'Is no good. Full of *mafiosi* and criminals [as if there were a difference!] and drivers are *cretini*,' they informed me, adding, '*Napoli è un casino*.' (a description translating roughly as the city is the embodiment of chaos – a sentiment I could readily believe). They were from Milan, however, and northern Italians are ever unflattering in their opinion of their southern countrymen. My explanation that I had no choice in the matter moved them almost to tears. However, those colleagues who had experience of Naples assured me that, although the driving was chaotic, major accidents were rare; and despite a prevalence of bag-snatching youths on motor scooters, violent crime against the person was virtually unknown. It was armed with this somewhat more comforting information that I had left the security of familiar England and set out on what was to be not so much a job, more an Italian adventure.

I spent my first night in Italy at a motel by the side of the *autostrada*. Surrounded by scaffolding and concrete mixers, it appeared unfinished and there were no other guests in sight. But the hotel management seemed happy to accommodate me. The evening was cold and the central heating in my spartan room hardly kept the chill off. I tried a few words of Italian at the reception desk. *'Troppo caldo,'* I explained. 'Too cold.' The receptionist, a short, darkish man of middle years dressed impeccably in a grey suit, accompanied me to my room. He felt the radiator. I gave a convincing display of shivering to add emphasis to my complaint. *'Allora,'* said my friend, raising his hands, an expression of deep understanding lighting up his face. *'Non troppo caldo; troppo freddo!'* A quick glance at the dictionary proved him correct, though why *caldo* should mean hot instead of cold defeated my sense of logic.

A little later I went in search of dinner, this time forearmed with the correct Italian word *cena*. The receptionist's reaction to my query was quite remarkable. He picked up the telephone and proceeded to shout into the instrument, held in his left hand, whilst waving his right hand in an agitated fashion. After a few seconds of this alarming diatribe he replaced the telephone, smiled at me and said a single word: 'Soon.'

Some five minutes later a small battered red Fiat drew up in a cloud of dust outside the glass-panelled back door of the hotel. A short, thick-set man aged around 40 leapt out, almost ran into the hotel, grabbed my arm, propelled me to the Fiat and indicated that I should climb in. This I did, though not without some trepidation. We set off at an alarming pace along a dirt road liberally dotted with potholes. The road seemed to lead nowhere and I began to think that perhaps I had been abducted. As I was still pondering this possibility, my driver braked to a sudden stop outside an isolated single-storey, white-painted building. Was this to be my place of incarceration? No. It turned out to be a *trattoria*. Soon I was seated in splendid isolation in a brightly lit, barn-like room of about 20 tables, enjoying my first genuine pizza and a bottle of remarkably good wine from Montepulciano. Somewhat to my surprise my driver returned an hour or so later and returned me, again at breakneck speed, to the hotel where I spent a comfortable

– and warm – night. Next morning, after a disappointing breakfast of pre-wrapped toast and lukewarm coffee (a disappointment which stirred memories of my first visit to Italy and to which I was to become accustomed) I headed south again.

Some miles south of Rome the traffic, which had not been unduly heavy except on the diabolical *Grande Raccordo Anulare* around the Eternal City, came to a complete standstill. After several stationary minutes drivers and passengers forsook the increasingly oppressive heat of their vehicles and started to amble in and out of the lines of cars and trucks. The more innovative among the men, young and old alike, patrolled their immediate vicinity seeking likely talent. Soon a number of budding liaisons were under way. To my surprise no-one seemed at all impatient. *'Incidente,'* a truck driver told me. 'Accident,' translated my dictionary. And so it proved to be when we eventually got under way. Seven blanket-covered shapes lay by the side of the road under the fascinated gaze of a hundred or more people crowded on a bridge across the motorway. So much for the rarity of major accidents!

As I neared the Naples tollbooth (most Italian *autostrade* are toll roads) I became aware of a change in driving habits and a difference in the appearance of the cars. Drivers lacked any lane discipline, wandering from lane to lane at random and even straddling the lane markers as if frightened of getting lost. Flashing indicators seemed to have only an historical significance: rarely did they signal any intent on the part of the driver. The cars themselves were somewhat battered, old and new alike. Like the armour of some medieval knight fresh from a hard-fought battle, bodywork was dulled, dented and scratched; bumpers were bent and wing mirrors hung uselessly down or were absent altogether. Yet even the smallest, meanest vehicle was driven with all the passion of a Formula One ace. Clearly this new driving environment would take some getting used to. However, for now I was content merely to reach the Naples tollbooth safely; here I was to meet a colleague, Flight Lieutenant George Gale, a navigator by profession, who would escort me to his house. George was to be my 'sponsor', a task established to guide new arrivals in Naples through the astonishingly different and difficult arrival procedures. He was there as planned and, taking up a trail position behind him, I began my first circumvention of Naples on the *Tangenziale*. Imagine a racetrack packed with cars of different performance, driven by drivers of varying ability but with a common lack of any lane discipline, and you may sense something of this exhilarating experience. But there is no substitute for the real thing.

A little to my surprise, but hugely to my relief, I emerged north of Naples unscathed physically albeit a trifle scarred mentally. George and his wife, Val, lived in an apartment block set scenically in a cherry orchard against a backdrop of the thickly wooded slope of Monte Sant'Angelo, the outer face of an extinct (it was hoped) volcano. In fact, long dead volcanoes and still active volcanic phenomena abound in this area, known to the ancients as *Campi Flegrei*, the Fiery Fields. Here it was that Aeneas descended into the Underworld in search of his father – you can still see the point of his entry, Lake Avernus. Within the sleeping crater of Monte Sant'Angelo the Americans have their main rest and relaxation, R&R, centre named Carney Park after a former commander of the United States Sixth Fleet in the Mediterranean. As is normal wherever there are American servicemen and their families, the US government had provided a plethora of facilities for their people, in contrast to the niggardly treatment meted out by successive British governments. Carney Park boasted baseball diamonds, a large outdoor swimming pool, a golf course, barbecue areas, holiday chalets, a restaurant and picnic sites all set in a well-maintained oasis of green surrounded by thickly wooded slopes – a piece of continental USA set down in the hustle and bustle of the Naples area. This complex ensures that US servicemen and women and their families can, if they wish, believe themselves back home. Shielded by the towering walls of the crater, and immersed in an Americans-only society with a dollar economy, Italy can for many Americans still be a continent away.

George's apartment block, on the other hand, was definitely in Italy, overlooking the small, undistinguished village of Monterusciello. A single, dusty street pockmarked with substantial potholes curved through a disparate collection of buildings – shops and private houses. Most prominent were a filling station, a small supermarket and a row of small businesses: a greengrocer's, a butcher's, a hairdresser's, a baker's and a clothier's. More interestingly, on one corner stood an establishment selling roast chickens, not the KFC variety but whole chickens skewered head to tail on a multi-pronged spit rotating slowly over a glowing wood fire. Their still living companions scratched around underneath, quite oblivious to their impending fate. On the opposite corner Roberto's *Pizzaria* was gearing up for the evening's trade, wood-smoke pouring from the pizza oven. As we looked down on this typical Italian scene, the doorbell rang imperiously. George opened the door to an excited-looking man who almost ran into the room. 'Have you heard; Ian and Margaret McPhearson have been shot!' he blurted out. He then filled in some of the details. Apparently the couple, an RAF officer and his wife, had been walking on the beach at the foot of the ancient acropolis of Cumae when they were approached by a youth with a pistol. He demanded that Margaret hand over her handbag and, to emphasise his demand, fired a shot close to them. Unfortunately, as it transpired, Margaret was convinced it was a blank and set about the youth *à la* Margaret Thatcher. He promptly shot her and ran. Ian set off in pursuit, and was shot in turn. As luck would have it the pistol was a .22 calibre and the wounds were not life-threatening, but serious enough for all that. Listening to this story, the second of my props – that of the basic non-violence of the people of southern Italy – collapsed. Perhaps my Milanese friends had been right after all!

As daylight faded we were joined by another RAF couple and soon, after a few stiff gin and tonics, my confidence began to return. Indeed, the way of service life in Naples as described by my new friends appeared more and more attractive. Suddenly the pleasant conviviality of the moment was disrupted by a violent shaking. Ornaments on the sideboard shivered, as if cold, before falling over and the chandelier in the centre of the ceiling swung wildly. No-one moved and only I seemed to be concerned. 'Gosh, that was a big one,' said Val.

'A big what?' I countered.

In reply Val introduced me to the phenomenon of bradyseism. This part of the Italian coast has, since time immemorial, gone up and down as the two major tectonic plates of Europe and Africa move in relation to each other. Accompanying this movement is a shaking of the ground, known as *terremoto*, a mild form of earthquake. At this point in history, March 1984, the ground was rising at a geologically phenomenal rate of several millimetres a week and every day brought a number of earth tremors, some unnervingly severe. These were having a devastating effect on the town of Pozzuoli, the port where St Paul had once landed on his way to Rome and execution. Indeed, the old harbour was being left high and dry, the fishermen having to climb down ladders to reach their boats, whilst round about them the old town crumbled, building by building, to take on the appearance and condition of a bomb-site.

Close to the harbour lies the so-called Temple of Serapis, so named from a statue found in the ruins. In fact the structure was the main market, or *macellum*, of Roman Puteoli. At its centre are marble pillars, each one disfigured by the borings of marine molluscs indicating that once these pillars were largely submerged, such has been the movement of the ground here since antiquity. However, this time the local authority appeared to have little confidence that Pozzuoli would survive this latest manifestation of nature's power and had begun to construct a new town at nearby Monterusciello. In the short term traffic was being excluded from the centre of the old town by the simple expedient of blocking all access roads with walls of tufa stone. The populace, operating by day as best they could amid the growing rubble, were required to depart at night and seek a safer refuge for sleep. Despite the obvious danger, no-one I ever spoke to in Pozzuoli wanted to move to the new town; human nature was, perhaps, ever thus! For example, across the other side of the bay looms Vesuvius, which in a cataclysmic eruption in AD 79 buried the Roman towns of Pompeii, Herculaneum and Stabiae and extinguished the lives of many. Yet the people living on the volcano's slopes and in its menacing shadow completely ignore the fact that one day it will erupt again, wreaking havoc, destroying properties and claiming many thousands of lives. No; far better to turn one's face from the danger, site one's house to look across the beautiful Bay of Naples and push any thought of disaster to the back of one's mind.

We British, unaccustomed to living with the ever-present threat of natural disaster, were not so pragmatic; we sought the advice of an expert in these matters – Dr John Guest of the University of London – 'to allay the fears of the British community'. Dr Guest duly flew out to Naples and, having met numerous Italian volcanologists and 'walked the ground' as it were, delivered his verdict to the community, assembled for the occasion in the grand reception room of the Deputy Senior British Officer's villa. The expectant throng wore varied expressions: anticipation, excitement, concern or downright fear. Dr Guest's opening statement did not, however, inspire confidence. 'Well,' he said, 'I wouldn't live here.' So much for allaying our fears! He went on to explain that the chief danger was an explosive eruption with its origin somewhere near the centre of Pozzuoli. Everyone within a radius of about 10km would probably die, while damage to property would be extensive out to about 20km. Armed with this information we returned home to work out how far we were from the assumed epicentre. The MOD, in its usual parsimonious fashion, decided that it would pay for a move to safer territory for anyone living in the 'kill zone'; others within 20km or so were advised to move – at their own expense! It turned out that the house that was to be my new home was just outside the 10km zone; I was not to move. I was, however, to see evidence of local fatalism. At the projected epicentre of the eruption – Zone Alpha the local authority named it – an establishment quickly opened up: *Zone Alpha Pizzeria.*

Happily, Dr Guest's worst fears were not realized. In November 1984 the ground gave one final shudder – 4.7 on the Richter Scale – and relapsed into its more stable phase. The inhabitants returned to Pozzuoli, houses were rebuilt or restored, the temporary walls came down and traffic returned to its usual chaos. Normality reigned once more, although the fishermen still had to climb down ladders into their boats: the land had risen some two metres in two years.

Back at George and Val's, the shaking passed and was not repeated. Normal conversation resumed and more duty-free drink flowed. As the evening progressed I learnt much about the social life of the British community, a life that always has a particular significance whenever and wherever servicemen and women, and their families, find themselves far from home. I learnt rather less about the work of NATO in Naples. But there would be plenty of time for that. Much later I retired to bed, reflecting on my new experiences and pondering a future quite different from that I would have enjoyed in the UK.

2

MOVING IN – HOME AND OFFICE

The following morning George took me to see the house I had undertaken to rent. We drove through Monterusciello and entered a landscape of small farms and orchards. On the outskirts of the village, two unsightly groups of large metal skips at the roadside intruded on the rural charm. These were for the deposit of household rubbish – no door-to-door collections here! Under normal circumstances these sufficed but in the anarchical regime of 20th century local government in southern Italy the refuse men were often on strike – *sciopero* is the Italian term. Mountains of rubbish soon accumulated, attracting a veritable menagerie of mice, rats, cats and stray dogs, until some public-minded citizen fired the lot, the resultant pyre then smouldering for days like the aftermath of some barbarian invasion. In fact, despite the almost total disregard for public cleanliness, southern Italians are fastidious in their own homes. Rubbish is carefully bagged and taken to the ubiquitous skips on – not in – the car. Should the bags fall off en route – well, that's someone else's problem.

The house I was to rent was on a private housing estate named *Parco Azzurro*, Blue Park, situated just off the old Roman road to Rome, the *Domiziana*. This road was built on the orders of the Emperor Domitian around AD 90 to link Rome with the then major port of Puteoli, now Pozzuoli. It served as the main road to Rome for many centuries, in fact until the construction of the *Autostrada del Sole* after World War II. *Parco Azzurro* was built by a group of retired Italian Air Force officers, one of whom, *il generale*, still controlled the estate. An old jet trainer aircraft parked just above the main gateway evoked memories of his former occupation.

The way into the *parco* was barred by a substantial blue and white metal gate overlooked by the glass-fronted custodian's office. George pulled up alongside a post and inserted a key; the gate rolled slowly aside and we drove through. Clearly security was part and parcel of *parco* life. Indeed, just before I had arrived in Italy the then custodian had been sitting in his office when a car had driven up and stopped just outside the barrier. A young man in a dark suit and wearing dark glasses had climbed slowly out. Leaving his office to see if help was required, the custodian approached the newcomer. Asked his name, the custodian gave it – and was shot dead! The young man climbed back into the car and drove off towards Naples. All this was observed by *il generale* from his own office by the gate; an execution by the *Camorra*, the Neapolitan version of the *Mafia*, for which no-one was brought to justice. Under the towering umbrella pines which shaded us from the bright sunlight of the southern Italian morning it was difficult to imagine that such a horrific scene could have been enacted here. I shuddered, mentally at least, as we continued uphill along a narrow road that wended its way between white-painted villas of different design and degree of grandeur, their gardens alive with the bright red of hibiscus and vivid purple of bougainvillaea. We passed the *parco*'s own *pizzeria*, the open-air swimming pool, closed at this time of the year, and finally arrived in Via Eolo and the villa – Number 5 – that was to be our home for the next three and a half years. Like many of the houses here it was built on a slope with a small, terraced garden – mostly of grass – and accommodation on two levels with a cellar-cum-garage underneath. Our arrival was greeted by the frenzied barking of three dogs – an Alsatian and two of more doubtful parentage – in the garden just across the road; not for nothing was the estate known as '*Parco Barco*'! The landlord, Eduardo, was waiting for us at the top of the small flight of steps that led to the front door. He was by profession a lawyer but, like many hundreds of lawyers in Naples, had never practised; it was enough in Neapolitan society for him to be called *avocato*. Just beyond normal retirement age, Eduardo was tall and thin and had short iron-grey hair and an unhealthy complexion. His looks, serious expression and dark suit gave him the air of an unsuccessful undertaker. His wife, Leila, was as plump as Eduardo was thin. Short and dark-haired she was much more animated and, as a teacher of English, a useful go-between as her husband spoke only Italian, and atrocious French. Fortunately the formalities were brief as George had already completed the necessary paperwork for this essentially private rental. Eduardo had already been paid one month's rent in advance and would not be calling for another three weeks. According to George, Eduardo was wont to arrive with a pistol very much in evidence, but whether this was a sign of an extortionate rent, fear of the *Camorra* or merely image, George was unable to say. After the introductions and a short tour of the house Eduardo and I parted on what seemed like good terms – and, indeed, throughout our time in the house we remained friendly; and he never visited with a gun!

The arrangement into which I had entered was a peculiarity faced by the serviceman in many places overseas. As there were no military quarters available, each family had to enter into a private agreement with a local landlord. This agreement was semi-official in that each serviceman had a rent allowance, dependent on his rank. The precise figure was not supposed to be known by the landlords but, this being Naples, all knew very well. They also knew that the allowance was generally increased each year so they invariably sought a rent just above the official rental ceiling, working on the assumption that the newcomer would be happy to pay over the odds for a short time secure in the knowledge that the allowance would soon catch up. My landlord, Eduardo, was no exception and I had already agreed, by proxy, to take on the house at a monthly rent some 500,000 lire more than my allowance. It seemed an enormous amount but was only about £210. In the event, the allowance was raised by 500,000 lire just after I moved in!

The house itself was quite different from the normal RAF Married Quarter. From the outside it was quite plain, a green-painted box-like structure set in a small garden with several umbrella pines, a couple of palm trees and, most usefully, an especially prolific tangerine tree. By the front door, accessed by a short flight of steps, was a sad-looking bougainvillaea bush – a bush which, after being fed and encouraged by my wife, flourished dramatically and eventually covered the whole of this side of the house with a riot of purple. Inside, the rooms were high-ceilinged and light, having just been painted white. The main living room had as its focus a centrally-positioned, brick-built, open fireplace. As we were to discover, the winters in southern Italy are not always warm and, although the house did have a rather primitive central heating system, the open fire often proved a welcome refuge from the chilly Neapolitan nights. In summer, though, the house kept remarkably cool. The kitchen was nothing special, except that it had a small balcony from which we could pick tangerines from the tree outside. So many fruit did this tree produce that we eventually grew fed up with them and they became merely decoration or an attraction for visitors used to paying supermarket prices for this fruit.

On the floor above, reached by a rather grand marble staircase, were the three bedrooms, a bathroom and a WC – of no particular note. However, up here was the most attractive feature of the house – a rooftop patio from which we enjoyed a magnificent view over Cumae, the first Greek colony on mainland Italy, to the island of Ischia beyond. On certain days, when atmospheric conditions were just right, we could see the mysterious island of Ventotene, which appeared as if by magic only to disappear again overnight as if swallowed by the sea like some modern day Atlantis. But the greatest sight of all was the sunset. A combination of high clouds and clear air resulted in spectacular displays of changing colours as the sun, growing ever larger, sank slowly into the sea whilst overhead the clouds turned a fiery red. You almost expected the sea itself to boil around the shrinking sphere which, just before it disappeared for the night, took on the appearance of an alien spacecraft, looking to be almost within touching distance. Very occasionally, as the disc vanished, a green flash appeared fleetingly. In all my years in Italy, though, I saw this phenomenon twice only.

The house was partly furnished, thanks to the Ministry of Defence system in force that required incoming families to purchase a 'job lot' of items from the family being replaced. The purchase was made with a proportion of a grant and loan from public funds (i.e. from the taxpayer) handed over on arrival, the remainder being used to buy new furniture and household goods up to a standard that would be expected back home in the UK. The sale of household effects at the end of one's tour of duty was then used to pay off the original loan element. Unfortunately the system was open to abuse! For example, outgoing families often overpriced items thus making more money on the sale of the 'job lot' than was required for their loan repayment. Furthermore, it was not unknown for items that had been agreed as forming part of the 'job lot' to have been replaced with items of inferior quality when the incoming family finally took up residence. Incomers were routinely told, albeit unofficially, that the remainder of the grant/loan money could best be used to finance a second car (admittedly more of a necessity than a luxury). Of course, items purchased outside the 'job lot' had to be approved and supported by a valid receipt; but there were ways around this. A television set (not an approved item) became an approved 'glass fronted cabinet'. And receipts could be obtained from accommodating tradesmen for any amount, regardless of the actual price paid. So, the system designed to ease the newcomers' life in Naples was not quite working as planned. It was to be another ten years before the system was applied correctly. However, as I surveyed my new home, I was content. The *parco* was smart, the house agreeable and affordable, and the in-place furnishings acceptable. I hoped that my wife would be of the same mind.

Having taken over the house it was time to drive to the base, about six miles west from the centre of Naples, where the United Kingdom National Support Unit was located. This organisation, as its name implied, would be responsible for providing administrative support to me during my stay in Naples. The drive proved to be interesting. Shortly after we had set off we came across a barricade of burning car tyres behind which stood a group of ordinary-looking men, happily chatting to each other and to drivers of cars forced to a halt by the barrier. George explained that this was a protest at the government's lack of action in re-housing local people following the big earthquake of 1980. The epicentre had been in the Abruzzi Mountains but the effects had been felt down here in Campania. The acropolis and amphitheatre of Pozzuoli had been completely closed, as had large areas of Pompeii, due to the severe damage caused by the earthquake. Many of the inhabitants of the Pozzuoli area had been given temporary accommodation in prefabricated huts on a waste site just north of the town. Four years later they were still there, refugees in their own land.

We were able to take an alternative route and so bypass the protesters. Shortly thereafter we passed the temporary accommodation: lines of small, grey huts between which ran dirt tracks where small children were playing and growing ever more dusty. Lines of washing added a little colour but it really did look like a scene from the Third World. No wonder the men were out protesting.

Just beyond this depressing example of bureaucratic incompetence we joined the *Tangenziale* towards Naples. At this time of the day – mid morning – it was remarkably quiet and, on this occasion being driven, I was able to look around, an activity I had not dared to do on the previous afternoon. Initially the road ran at the foot of an extinct volcano; high up on the left-hand side was the angular block of the monastery of *San Michele*, festooned with communications aerials. This foundation was down to its last inhabitant who kept the small chapel neat and tidy. As I found later access was by a terrible dirt road, partially washed away and suitable only for four-wheel drive vehicles. Notwithstanding this challenge, locals would drive up in their little Fiats for picnics on feast days, the youngsters to play football on the flat area behind the monastery, their elders to enjoy the marvellous views towards Capo Miseno, once the base of the Roman Fleet. From here the Fleet Commander, Pliny the Elder, set sail towards Pompeii on a rescue mission following the terrible eruption of AD 79. He never returned, but his fate was recorded for posterity by his nephew, Pliny the Younger, in a letter to the Roman historian, Tacitus. The description he gave of the eruption is so vivid that it could have been the film-script of the Mount Saint Helen's eruption of 1980. We'll hear more of this story later.

A few miles further on the road entered a tunnel. Up on the right-hand bank, and rather hard to discern, were the remains of a Roman structure, significant enough to delay the construction of the motorway for several months. Of course, in this area any construction work is likely to uncover Roman remains. Therefore, many are not reported to avoid delays that, because of the sheer volume of such traces of the ancient world, may run into years. As we approached the end of the tunnel a magnificent view of Vesuvius emerged, the cone of the volcano framed dramatically in the exit. At some 4,000 feet in height, the summit is sometimes capped with snow, but not at this time of the year. The smoke that was once its trademark is no more, the eruption of 1944 putting paid to that. In fact, such is its apparent present benevolence that much (illegal) building has taken place on its slopes in recent years, the inhabited portion of the mountain growing ever closer to the top. One day, perhaps soon, these new settlers will regret their folly; the volcano is not dead, it merely sleeps and there are now signs of its reawakening. It will almost certainly wake with explosive force as the build-up of pressure under the plug of rock in the caldera bursts forth. However, on our journey the mountain looked benign, a picturesque backdrop to the scene ahead.

We were now descending into the crater of another extinct volcano, that of Agnano. To our right steam issued from the hillside, yet another reminder that volcanic activity was still present and that the *Campi Flegrei* of the Greeks was not just an historical oddity. Ahead of us, on the flat floor of the original crater, was the sanded oval of the Agnano *ippodromo*, a racetrack used for trotting races, a sport popular in Italy. Now, a few trotting horses were being put through their paces in the warm, spring sunshine. At this point we left the *Tangenziale* and joined a queue of vehicles. Actually 'queue' is not the right word for these vehicles stretched across the whole road, occupying any available space regardless of lines. The goal was one of four tollbooths, for in Italy few motorway-type roads are free; this one belongs to the *Banco di Napoli* and, as it is one of the busiest roads in Italy, it must be a profitable side-line for the bank. On the far side of the tollbooth, the chaos seemed even worse. 'Squeeze Alley,' remarked George. 'If you think this is bad, wait till you hit it in the morning rush hour – which you will every day you go to the office.'

The term was coined by the Americans, who have a gift for succinct descriptive terminology. As we approached the 'alley' concerned, I could see how apt the description was. Three lanes of traffic from the tollbooths were joined by another two lanes from the right; all were squeezed into the single lane of the alley, millimetres only between each vehicle. Progress seemed impossible, and yet we did move forward, albeit slowly. There was even a protocol; no eye contact with other drivers, and the car with its bumper even a fraction of a millimetre ahead had right of way. The chaos was not helped by a set of traffic lights at the end of the alley; fortunately, no-one took any notice of them! I could now see why so many cars in the Naples area had missing wing mirrors and wore so many battle scars.

Safely through Squeeze Alley we drove past the turning to the American Naval Support Activity (NSA) where I was to work and continued towards the main NATO base. Climbing a hill, the side of the original crater, I noticed a strangely-dressed woman sitting on a wall on the left-hand side of the road. An extremely short skirt almost met an excessively low-cut sweater, a delight on a young girl but with not quite the same impact on an overweight woman of advanced middle years. 'Humpty Dumpty,' George enlightened me. 'She is the oldest prostitute in Naples and has been sitting on that wall since the Allies took Naples in 1943; or so it is said. Her real name is Pasqualina.'

And so I became acquainted with another of the daily journeys' landmarks. Just beyond Humpty's patch we came to another set of traffic lights. They were on red, but George ignored them. 'This is called "Chicken Corner",' said George. 'No-one actually stops, but you have to be careful as another main road comes in from the right.'

This practice was, in fact, common in Naples and had the effect of speeding the traffic flow with the occasional dramatic meeting of vehicles or, alternatively, causing complete logjams. I soon learnt that the only safe way to deal with Neapolitan traffic lights was to adopt a modified form of behaviour: traffic lights red – proceed with caution; traffic lights amber – proceed with caution; traffic lights green – proceed with extreme caution! This seemed to work remarkably well. However, if the rules were ignored, the result could be disastrous. On a later occasion I followed an Italian car to the lights on red. The driver slowed, looked and continued. I did likewise. The driver behind me – an American serviceman – knew only that one could ignore lights on red. He slowed, didn't look – and was promptly hit amidships with such force that his car was bowled over and deposited, on its side, beyond the road junction. A noisy crowd quickly gathered amidst the broken glass and spilled petrol and hauled the cars' occupants out of their battered vehicles. Fortunately, nobody was seriously hurt but the incident brought home to me the dangers of Neapolitan traffic lights.

Having survived my first experience of Chicken Corner, I was relieved to discover that at the next set of traffic lights we turned right; the excitement of traversing lines of traffic would come on our return journey. Now the entrance to the base lay a couple of hundred yards straight ahead identified by security barriers either side of a white-painted guardroom over which was writ, large and in colour, the identity of the base in both Italian and English. *Carabinieri*, smart in their blue, winter uniforms, manned the barrier and after checking our service identity cards in a somewhat cursory manner, allowed us through. At first sight the base was impressive. A group of five, three-storeyed white buildings arranged in an open square flanked a partly grassed central space complete with a ceremonial parade ground (used, needlessly to say, as a car park). A monumental marble staircase led up to the main headquarters building at the far end. At its foot rose an art-nouveau tower, representing a rudder, surmounted by a flagpole from which the NATO flag hung limply. In fact the whole complex, now rented by NATO for a vast sum, was originally built as a home for 5,000 Neapolitan orphans and funded by the *Banco di Napoli*. Construction was completed in 1939 and the art-nouveau rudder was, at that time, surmounted by the Fascist symbol of fasces and axe. As a link with this quite different usage, one of the base's busiest traders – Tony, of Tony's Garage – had once spent some time on one of the Fascist Youth camps, drilling with a wooden rifle. The outbreak of war put paid to the idea of housing orphans; the site was occupied by the Germans from 1941 to 1943, the Allies from 1943 to 1947, and refugees from 1947 to 1952. In 1952 an agreement was reached to rent the site to NATO and a number of headquarters moved in shortly afterwards.

The base was not, however, dedicated solely to NATO's military activity. To feed the inner man there were a number of dining facilities open to all: the Allied Officers' Club, the Flamingo Enlisted Men's Club, an Italian Mess, and an American All-ranks Mess were all open at lunchtime. The Allied Officers' Club also provided fine dining in the evenings sometimes with entertainment by international artists; I particularly remember an excellent piano recital by Mussolini – not Benito the Dictator but Romano his youngest son and well-known jazz pianist – and a lively performance by The Platters. Apart from these facilities that are normally found on a base there were also many others: library, church, gymnasium, sports facilities including an Olympic-sized swimming pool, bowling alley, theatre and a complete range of shops. Newspapers, magazines, shoes, clothing, artwork, souvenirs, furniture and household goods could all be purchased, as could a haircut and beauty treatment, while banking and insurance services were also available. The social focus of all this capitalist activity was Rizzo's Bar which, as well as providing a meeting place for underemployed NATO personnel and their families, served probably the best cappuccino in the whole of Italy. It was here that I first saw demonstrated the way in which Neapolitans circumvent rules, regulations and laws. According to the law every purchase in Italy must be supported by an official receipt, a *ricevuta fiscale*. In Rizzo's, as in most Italian bars, the procedure was to order at the cash desk, pay, receive a receipt and then move on to the counter. Here you exchanged your receipt for the goods ordered – *cappuccini*, *pasti* and so on. The receipts were then placed in a box – and every 15 minutes or so the box was returned to the cash desk for the same receipts to be recycled. A very neat way of reducing income, and all this under the eyes of the *carabinieri* who were regular clients of the bar. However, perhaps this was not surprising as it is the *guardia di finanza* who are responsible for policing financial transactions, not the *carabinieri* who are a para-military force and were present on the base for security matters and, I suspect, ceremonial occasions as their uniforms were by far the most spectacular.

My destination, the UK Support Unit, occupied a less than impressive office over the ground-floor shopping centre in one of the buildings – L Building. As is normal on a military unit there were many forms to complete with information I had filled in on many previous occasions. It occurred to me, not for the first time, that perhaps the Services were concerned that my number, rank, name, date of birth etc. might somehow have changed over the years. There followed the issue of ration cards for duty-free petrol, cigarettes, liquor and electrical goods. This is quite normal practice in NATO appointments. Under Status of Forces Agreements, Host Nations undertake to provide certain perks for foreign personnel during their stay in the country concerned. In fact, if you were to smoke all the cigarettes and drink all the liquor to which you were entitled; at best you would become a chain-smoking alcoholic, at worst you would not live to see the end of your tour of duty. I never did determine why this particular practice was continued and, indeed, continues to this day. On the credit side, cigarettes were useful in Naples even for the non-smoker as they could be used as a form of currency for a variety of services rendered by local artisans – gardeners, maids and the like. Regrettably, some personnel succumbed to temptation and sold on most of their ration to the local economy, an action that had an impact on the sale of smuggled cigarettes in the vicinity of the base. I should add here that most of the cigarettes sold around Naples were brought in clandestinely, at night, by fast motor-boats from across the Adriatic Sea. These were then distributed by the *Camorra* and sold at certain vantage points by the side of the road, especially at the *autostrade* tollbooths. Their price was closely linked to that of the duty-free cigarettes on base and to the number being transferred to the local economy.

My seemingly endless form-filling complete, and now equipped with a multiplicity of ration cards, I moved on to the Security Department to be photographed, and issued with a NATO identity card. This unit was jointly manned by Italian *carabinieri* and American security personnel with a total disregard for client status; it was first come, first served, be you general or private. As in most NATO units, there were far more chiefs than Indians so the process was somewhat protracted. Nevertheless, half an hour later I was the proud possessor of an Allied Forces Southern Europe identity card, a document essential for access to innumerable NATO perks where one's own service identity card was as much use as an out-of-date passport.

3

THE COLD WAR

Having completed the important personal aspects of my official arrival in Naples I could turn to the subject of work. However, at this point perhaps I should say something about the Cold War, NATO's *raison d'être*.

It now seems a long time ago but after the end of the Second World War the western powers were afraid that the Soviet Union was intent on spreading its control and communist ideology across the whole of Europe. It had already seized control of many East European states and the 1948 Berlin blockade and coup in Czechoslovakia gave ample credence to this fear. To counter further expansion 12 western nations – Belgium, Britain, Canada, Denmark, France, Iceland, Italy, Luxembourg, the Netherlands, Norway, Portugal and the United States of America – signed the North Atlantic Treaty in April 1949 based on Article 51 of the United Nations Charter, which states that independent states have the right to individual or *collective* (my italics) defence. Lord Ismay, NATO's first Secretary General, put the alliance's purpose more simply, it was 'to keep Russia out, America in, and Germany down'. From a military perspective, the most important article was Article 5: '...an armed attack on one or more shall be considered an attack on all... and members will take such action as deemed necessary, including the use of armed force, to restore and maintain international peace and security.' To achieve this a complex military organisation was formed to take control of member states' forces should the need to use armed force ever arise.

In 1952 both Greece and Turkey joined the Alliance and, despite Lord Ismay's words, West Germany became the 15th member in 1955, an event that led to the formation of the Warsaw

Pact, an alliance of the Soviet Union and eight East European states. Not everything was plain sailing, though. In 1966 President De Gaulle withdrew France from the Integrated Military Structure in protest at what he saw as American dominance. Then, as a result of the Turkish invasion (or 'intervention' depending on which side of the argument you're on) of Cyprus in 1974 Greece, too, withdrew from the Integrated Military Structure and did not re-join until 1980. The 16th member, Spain, joined the Alliance in 1982 and this number stayed the same until the end of the Cold War.

But what was the Cold War, the military thinking of which was to determine my work? Along with my colleagues I had served my career to date in this period of warfare that was termed 'Cold' because there were no direct hostilities between NATO and the Warsaw Pact. However, although an uneasy stability had fallen on Europe after Churchill's Iron Curtain had descended, elsewhere in the world the seemingly disparate concepts of colonialism and communism were leading inexorably towards military conflict. It was not long in coming and soon NATO nations' forces – though not NATO itself – were to become involved in proxy wars.

Military thinking had of course changed after atomic bombs were dropped on Hiroshima and Nagasaki to end World War II and the whole world had viewed with horror the awesome power and destructive capability of these weapons. So had warfare changed forever? These proxy wars were soon to provide the answer, for in 1950 the Korean War broke out.

Immediately after the end of World War II Korea had been freed from Japanese colonial rule and divided at the 38th Parallel with the Soviet Union administering the north and America the south. To no-one's surprise negotiations on unification were unsuccessful and in June 1950 North Korean communist troops invaded the south. Advised and supplied by the Soviet Union the North Koreans advanced rapidly and drove US and South Korean forces somewhat ignominiously into a small area in the extreme south east of the country. It looked very much as if a communist victory was on the cards. To avoid this humiliating outcome the US sought a United Nations Security Council resolution asking member nations to assist South Korea. Fortunately for the US the Soviet Union, which would almost certainly have blocked the resolution had it been represented, had boycotted proceedings because of the UN refusal to accept Mao's communist regime as the official government of China. So the resolution was passed and, although NATO was not directly involved, several key members answered the call: the US (about 90% of the total troop number), the UK, France, Canada, the Benelux countries and, later, Turkey and Greece.

Having successfully carried out a massive amphibious landing behind enemy lines the UN forces commanded by General MacArthur quickly advanced to the Yalu River, the Korean border with China. For reasons that are not entirely clear, but which might have reflected China's concern about an invasion of its territory, a massive Chinese army crossed the border in October 1950. Forced to retreat MacArthur requested the use of atomic weapons, a request that was seriously considered by the US government. However, after much debate the request was finally denied. This was a defining moment in military history: it clearly demonstrated that nuclear weapons were a political not a military tool. Warfare had not, after all, changed forever. The war, fought conventionally, dragged on until 1953 when an armistice was signed confirming the 38th Parallel as the dividing line between North and South Korea.

Another proxy war was that in Vietnam, which had its origins in the conflict between the French and the communist Viet Minh under Ho Chi Minh in the French colony of Indo China. Although this had been ongoing since 1946 the turning point came in 1950 when Ho Chi Minh's government was recognised by both China and the Soviet Union. This immediately resulted in a flow of weapons to the communist forces. The French were finally defeated at Dien Bien Phu and subsequent agreements made at the Geneva Conference of 1954 stated that France would relinquish all territorial claims in its former colony and that Vietnam would be divided, north and south, at the 17th Parallel. However, neither the US nor South Vietnam signed the agreements, thus setting the stage for the disastrous Vietnamese War in which the Americans and South Vietnamese forces, supported by Australia and other anti-communist nations, faced the North Vietnamese who were trained and equipped by China and the Soviet Union. Significantly both these communist nations had developed nuclear weapons: Russia in 1949 and China in 1964. However, despite there being several occasions when the use of atomic weapons could have given either side a significant advantage they were not used; the war was, as in Korea, fought conventionally. It did not end until 1975.

As General MacArthur had indicated in Korea the tactical use of atomic weapons was considered, at least by some, a legitimate military course of action. This became less valid, however, in 1952 when the US successfully tested a thermonuclear hydrogen bomb – a fusion device a thousand times more powerful than the earlier fission weapons. A year later the Soviet Union tested a similar device. Coupled with advances in Intercontinental Ballistic Missiles (ICBM), Submarine Launched Ballistic Missiles (SLBM) and bombers equipped with stand-off missiles the concept of MAD – Mutual Assured Destruction – an apocalyptic event that would devastate the entire world, was now a real possibility. These were the weapon systems that became the cornerstone of NATO's deterrent policy. But was the world more or less safe? Would anyone consider the first use of these horrifying weapons? In 1962 these questions were answered.

I was in my first year's training at the RAF College, Cranwell, where most of the time was taken up with parades and drill practice, lectures on military matters and academic studies. Oh, and one afternoon a week we flew the aged Chipmunk trainer – to keep our interest going before we began formal flying training in the second and third years. In October 1962 we became aware that a situation had developed on the other side of the Atlantic: it became known as the Cuban Missile Crisis. Our military tutors briefed us as events unfolded and I recall discussing the likely outcome with my colleagues. Were we worried? I don't think we were – but we should have been. In fact, we thought perhaps our training would be accelerated and we could move straight on to flying training without the burden of aerodynamics, thermodynamics, electronics, mathematics and war studies. But what was the crisis and how serious was it?

In October 1962 a US reconnaissance aircraft over Cuba photographed Soviet short and medium range ballistic missiles being assembled at a number of launch sites on the island. As the sites were within one hundred miles or so from the American mainland almost the entire continental USA was within range. The decision to install these weapon systems was in large part a direct result of the ill-fated US-sponsored invasion of Cuba in the Bay of Pigs in 1961 and was intended to prevent any such action in the future. Clearly the US could not accept these weapons so close to its shores.

After considering a number of options, including a full-scale invasion and subsequent removal of Cuba's President Castro, President Kennedy imposed a naval blockade and insisted that President Khrushchev remove all missiles from the island immediately. Throughout the next few days and weeks tensions rose dramatically as back-door exchanges between Kennedy and Khrushchev took place. Reconnaissance flights continued over Cuba and one U-2 was shot down. Nuclear-armed American bombers went on airborne alert while others were dispersed on 15 minutes standby. ICBMs were readied for launch and nuclear-armed air defence fighters took to the skies. Khrushchev responded to Kennedy by telegram, stating his view that the blockade was a clear act of aggression; he also ordered submarines armed with nuclear-tipped torpedoes to break the blockade. NATO, although not directly involved in the diplomatic standoff, would be immediately drawn in should hostilities break out. World War III was but a button push away.

Finally resolution came with a quid pro quo. In 1961 the US had deployed Jupiter Medium Range (1,500 miles) Ballistic Missiles to Turkey. These posed a similar threat to the Soviet Union as the Cuban missiles posed to the USA. In a secret deal Kennedy agreed to remove the US missiles from Turkey in exchange for the removal of missiles from Cuba. The world gave a collective sigh of relief – and I was to complete my full three years at Cranwell – academics included. However, the proximity to Armageddon had rattled everyone, not least Kennedy and especially Khrushchev. In 1963 a bilateral agreement between the US and Soviet Heads of State established a direct communications link for use in times of emergency; 'better late than never' you might think. Furthermore, over the succeeding years a number of arms control treaties came into effect in an attempt to reduce the threat of nuclear war. However, despite these worthy measures the threat never disappeared. In a later chapter I'll explain what happened in two NATO exercises that nearly brought us to the brink once again.

What the above events had demonstrated was that the availability of nuclear weapons had not actually changed the face of warfare. Nuclear weapons were political rather than military and their main purpose was as a deterrent, the concept of Mutual Assured Destruction putting an almost overwhelming constraint on their use. However, to avoid any misunderstandings it was clearly necessary to ensure that robust channels of communication were maintained between the heads of state of nuclear powers. It would seem that if wars did break out conventional warfare was as likely as it had ever been. And so it has proved; there has not been a year since 1945 when armed conflict has not occurred and all have been fought conventionally.

4

NATO'S STRUCTURE

Given the pattern of post-WWII armed conflicts it seemed axiomatic that any war with the Soviet Union would, at least initially, be fought conventionally. My work, therefore, was to be concerned predominantly with conventional warfare and specifically with the involvement of maritime patrol aircraft in NATO plans and exercises. However, to understand where I fitted in to the organisation I need to describe its Cold War command structure so please bear with me as I unravel its complexities. And don't worry too much about the acronyms: NATO was, and still is, an organisation of this type of abbreviation.

The highest level of NATO consisted of three Major NATO Commands (MNCs): Allied Command Atlantic (ACLANT), commanded by an American Admiral, Supreme Allied Commander Atlantic (SACLANT); Allied Command Europe (ACE), commanded by an American General, Supreme Allied Commander Europe (SACEUR); and finally, so that we British were not side-lined, a British Admiral, Commander-in-Chief Channel Area (CINCHAN) commanded the important sea lanes through British waters.

Under the three MNCs were a number of Major Subordinate Commands (MSCs); in Europe these were Allied Forces Northern Europe (AFNORTH); Allied Forces Central Europe (AFCENT); and, you may have guessed, Allied Forces Southern Europe (AFSOUTH). We are moving closer to my humble role, but there are still more levels to learn.

Below the MSCs came the Principal Subordinate Commands (PSCs); I'll just highlight the five in the Southern Region. These were: Allied Air Forces Sothern Europe (AIRSOUTH) commanded by an American 3-star general; Allied Land Forces Southern Europe (LANDFORSOUTH) commanded by an Italian 4-star general; Allied Land Forces South East (LANDSOUTHEAST) commanded by a Turkish 4-star general; Naval Striking and Support Forces Southern Europe (STRIKFORSOUTH) commanded by an American 3-star admiral, who was also Commander of the Mediterranean-based US Sixth Fleet; and finally Allied Naval Forces Southern Europe (NAVSOUTH) commanded by an Italian 3-star admiral.

The final level of this somewhat convoluted organisation was the one in which I was to work: a Functional Command, under NAVSOUTH, headed by an American 1-star admiral, Commander Maritime Air Forces Mediterranean (COMARAIRMED). In fact my place of work was neither at the main AFSOUTH base, nor on NAVSOUTH's island but, as I mentioned earlier, in the nearby American Naval Support Activity (NSA) complex at Agnano. Here American servicemen and women, and their dependants, could pretend that they had never left the good ol' US of A; American stores selling American food, books, clothes and other items abounded and the dollar was the only currency in use. Quite why it was necessary to fly into Italy such items as fresh milk, bread and meat was initially something of a mystery to me. Later I discovered that, for many Americans, Naples was one of the worst postings they could be given. To help make it more acceptable, they were given the opportunity to live in an exported American environment and were offered advantageous treatment when they returned home. I was subsequently fascinated to meet Americans who had never spent a lira, never visited Naples, never travelled anywhere else in Italy, and had never spoken a single word of Italian despite having lived in the country for anything up to three years. And yet there were others – some of whom we shall meet later – who made the most of their stay in this wonderful country. I should point out that most of the Americans in Naples were not part of NATO; the Support Activity was responsible for providing all the support necessary for all the American forces in the Mediterranean, the major elements of which were the Carrier Battle Groups, the nuclear submarines and the maritime patrol aircraft that were deployed to the Mediterranean from the United States on lengthy detachments. Usually under American national control, these forces would be transferred to NATO control in periods of heightened tension, a military option practised regularly in NATO exercises. Almost without exception, though, the NATO commanders involved were also American so no real transfer took place. With so many personnel in support of these forces it was perhaps not surprising that the US government provided so many facilities. In addition to the shopping complex, which also included a cinema and a restaurant, there was a large naval hospital, elements of several American universities, a high school, an elementary school and a number of hobby and recreational clubs. And, of course, there was the Rest and Relaxation, R&R, retreat of Carney Park. In comparison we British had a small medical and dental clinic, and a primary school.

5

MY FIRST DAY AT WORK

Having completed the initial administration that enabled me to work as a NATO officer it was time to join the MARAIRMED team at the NSA. (See, you're probably picking up NATO-speak already!) Not surprisingly the most important event on my first day in office was an arrival interview with COMARAIRMED, an American admiral, Ben Hacker. Ben was the first Naval Flight Officer (NFO) in the United States Navy to achieve this rank and was a great character. He had a gift with words and was a tremendous public speaker, able to make the most mundane subject sound absolutely fascinating with much flowery phraseology. In fact I had known Ben for a number of years, from the time he had commanded a maritime patrol squadron. Perhaps his greatest unpublished claim to fame was the undetected removal of three RAF squadrons' standards and their transfer to the US base at Keflavik in Iceland where Ben's squadron was on detachment. This remarkable feat was carried out after a formal dinner at the RAF maritime patrol aircraft base at Kinloss in Scotland at which Ben and his squadron officers were guests. Coincidentally, a fire was discovered just after the dinner had ended and the RAF police were convinced that the Americans had started it as a diversion. In fact this was never likely as the duty officer was supposed to check on the safety of the standards in such a situation. In fact, he did not do this at the time. (Several weeks later another fire was started deliberately in the mess; the culprit was a disaffected corporal steward.) The standards were duly returned, in an aircraft of the United States Navy, their removal having been in retaliation for our purloining of the American squadron commander's 'Batcape', worn on 'formal' occasions and a reflection of the squadron's emblem, 'Batwoman'. This event had taken place some months previously at the 'First Annual Traditional VP21 Guest Night' (sic) held in the Officers' Club at Keflavik on Iceland and to which Commander (as he was then) Hacker's friend, Wing Commander Win Harris, Officer Commanding 201 Squadron, and squadron members had been invited. The fact that RAF standards are presented by Royalty and treated with appropriate honour was, of course, not fully appreciated by the Americans involved in the retaliatory raid. The story was, however, a useful starting point in my arrival interview with my new boss!

This proved to be particularly interesting. After the initial pleasantries, Admiral Hacker presented me with a document marked 'SECRET US/UK EYES ONLY' and asked me to explain certain elements. I explained that, as a NATO officer, I no longer had the level of security clearance needed to view such a document. 'But you wrote it,' continued the admiral, and I had to admit that this was partly true. In my previous appointment as Wing Commander Operations at the RAF's maritime headquarters at Northwood I had spent considerable time in the United States and in Sicily working with my opposite numbers on an operational plan involving RAF Nimrods operating in the Mediterranean under American rather than UK control. Our aircraft would be deployed to Sigonella in Sicily and join the United States Navy P-3 Orions in the search for and tracking of Soviet nuclear submarines entering the Mediterranean from the Atlantic. These operations were always covert and other NATO countries in the theatre were neither involved nor, indeed, aware of them; hence the security classification. It had taken a long time for the British authorities to agree the transfer of operational control but the fact that the Americans were keen to promote this co-operation reflected the high regard in which they held the maritime element of the Royal Air Force. Fortunately I was able to clarify the elements in question and, as a result of this initial meeting I was appointed 'unofficial' adviser on USN/RAF co-operation and was even invited to the Admiral's 'US Eyes Only' morning briefing.

A few days after this meeting I flew with Admiral Hacker in an American Orion P-3C maritime patrol aircraft to Gibraltar for a formal Dining–In Night at the RAF Officers' Mess. The host was Admiral Hacker's NATO counterpart, Commander Maritime Air Gibraltar, Air Commodore John Pack. We both knew Air Commodore Pack as he had been the Station Commander at RAF Kinloss at the time of the 'stolen squadron standards' incident. The dinner itself was a great success and the following day the admiral asked me to pilot the P-3 back to Naples; he would be navigating. I had flown the aircraft several times before so shortly after take-off from the Rock I took control from the left-hand seat. All went well until approaching Carbonara, on the southern tip of Sardinia. I was using the flight instrument system tuned in to the Carbonara VOR radio beacon; Admiral Hacker was using the aircraft's inertial navigation system – and there was a discrepancy between the heading I was on and that required by the aircraft's system. The conversation went something like this:

'Pilot – Navigator; where are you going?'

'Navigator – Pilot; to the Carbonara beacon; where are you going?'

Within microseconds the aircraft commander, a lieutenant commander of the United States Navy, came racing onto the flight deck looking ashen. He leant over and said in a strangled voice: 'Do you know who is navigating the aircraft?'

'Yes,' I replied. 'But don't worry, I know where we are.'

The commander retired, probably thinking his career had just taken a turn for the worse. Fortunately, when we arrived back in Naples the admiral laughed at our exchange and went on to invite my wife and me to dinner at his residence later in the week. The aircraft commander then came over and asked if I actually knew the admiral. I was able to assure him, to his great relief, that I had known Admiral Hacker ever since he had been a lieutenant commander.

As is often the case in NATO, senior officers may have national responsibilities in addition to their international ones. Admiral Hacker was no exception and actually wore three 'hats': as the US commander responsible for the support of all US naval aircraft in the Mediterranean area; as the operational control authority for US maritime patrol aircraft deployed to the theatre; and last (and least demanding) as the commander of NATO maritime patrol aircraft, which in peacetime remained under national control – the UK's Nimrods sometimes being an exception. Each of the 'hats' had an associated staff, the NATO one being the smallest, all located in the same building close to the American shopping complex.

My immediate superior was a US Navy captain, Paul Pedisich, whose experience was in carrier-borne anti-submarine warfare aircraft. He was an easy-going but professional officer with a real interest in Italy and the Italian way of life. Under his command was a small international staff, not all members of which were maritime aviators. The unit's administration was in the hands of Lieutenant John Christman USN, a P3 aviator, who had married an Italian girl, much to the benefit of the other MARAIRMED officers; I'll explain how later. The Operations Officer was an Italian Navy commander, Giorgio Massi, a man of exceedingly short temper. His favourite trick was to let down two tyres of any car that parked in his designated parking space. He was also wont to refer to the Americans as the 'army of occupation' thus exhibiting an attitude hardly conducive to good international relations.

Later he was replaced by a charming Italian, Commander Italo Marinari, who became and still is a close friend. The Weapons Officer was another American, Commander Dick Barnum, a helicopter pilot who had seen service in Vietnam and one of the nicest guys I have ever met. He and I were to do a lot of archaeological exploring in the following years. Responsible for 'Intelligence', almost a non-job in NATO, was a Greek Navy Commander, Captain Stinis. The final international staff member was a Turkish Navy Lieutenant Commander, Serhan Sevim, a surface navy officer who was my deputy and who became, and remained until his sad death of cancer in 2012, another very close friend. (I am still in touch with his family.)

The British officer contingent comprised Flight Lieutenant George Gale, whom you've already met and who had the misfortune to work for Commander Massi; Flight Lieutenant John Fraser, who ran the communications centre; and myself – Staff Officer Plans and Exercises. My job was to plan the involvement of maritime patrol aircraft in NATO exercises, a number of which were routinely planned each year, and to ensure that the maritime air element of NATO war plans was kept up to date. As I was to discover, the workload was not too onerous; like most NATO jobs it was much less demanding than an equivalent job back home and could have been done quite adequately by an officer one rank lower. You will have noted that with the exception of the three British RAF officers the other members of the MARAIRMED staff were navy. This was not unusual as the majority of the world's maritime patrol aircraft are controlled and operated by the individual nation's navy whereas in the UK, Australia, New Zealand, South Africa and Canada (before unifying their military) these functions are the responsibility of the air force.

The building in which we worked, the grandly named Building 70, had a restaurant in the basement and the admiral's office on the seventh floor. A variety of US Navy staffs lived on the intervening floors, access to which was controlled by a US Marine guard. Our NATO space, shared with our submariner colleagues of COMSUBMED, was on the fourth floor, my office having a splendid view of the car park where, as a senior officer, I rated a personal parking space. This was a particularly valuable privilege as American servicemen and women are early risers and were wont to arrive in the car park looking for a space from around 6am onwards; by 7am there was not space even for a pushbike.

Building 70's entrance hall was in reality 'The Quarterdeck' and was given all the honours due to such a prestigious part of a ship. Two lifts served the upper floors which, in the style of American terminology, started at the second floor (for those who have not visited America, the ground floor is, to them, the first floor). One of the lifts was reserved for the admiral. Shortly after starting work and following one of Admiral Hacker's briefings I entered this special lift on the seventh floor by mistake. I was a trifle embarrassed when I reached the ground/first floor to be met with the shouted exhortation 'Attention on deck', an order that was accompanied by some discordant piping. I muttered a quick 'Carry on', and made good my exit. Fortunately, Americans generally have no idea of other nations' rank structure so nobody thought to question my splendid arrival. I was wise enough not to repeat the mistake though.

Thanks to George I now knew something of the main NATO base, my place of work and the international staff with whom I would be working for the next three years or so. It was now time to sort out my domestic arrangements.

6

FRIENDS, NEIGHBOURS AND ACQUAINTANCES

For the first few days I had stayed with George and his wife, mainly because Val felt sorry for my having to move in on my own to a house that was but sparsely furnished. I have to admit that their kindness was much appreciated but, in due course, I felt that I had to take the plunge. So later in the week George duly dropped me off and I stood in the garden of Number 5, Via Eolo, looking up at the house that was to be my new home. From the outside it looked a bit bleak and I had to admit to feeling a touch of homesickness and a sense of loneliness. As I slowly climbed the front steps an aged Volkswagen campervan drew up at the front gate. An American voice hailed me: 'Hey, you must be our new neighbour. Jump in, we're going for ice cream.' I did so and met the Isaac family for the first time. Jerry was a dentist in the United States Navy and with him were his wife, Renee, and two of his daughters, Valerie and Carolyn.

We drove down to the nearby town of Arco Felice, a sort of seaside resort with a single main street running parallel to the sea and a long strip of uninviting sand; maybe it would look more inviting in the summer. As in other towns in this part of Italy, parking was merely a case of stopping in a convenient (for us) unoccupied bit of road. Despite the traffic chaos caused by the apparent abandonment of vehicles, including our own, on the highway, no-one seemed to mind in the least. We strolled down to a small *gelateria* – ice-cream parlour – where Jerry was greeted as a most-favoured-status customer. We were ushered to white plastic seats at a white plastic table under a multi-coloured awning and overlooking the main road. The traffic was phenomenal. Everyone seemed to be in a hurry, yet the sheer number of cars made rapid progress impossible. This didn't stop the drivers trying though. Jerry ordered ice-cream and we sat back to enjoy that best of activities – watching the world go by. Valerie and Carolyn, both amply endowed, ensured that the service was swift, Italian males of all ages being greatly appreciative of a well-formed bosom. The ice-cream was excellent, as is most ice-cream in Italy, and the action on the street beyond absolutely hectic. There was a theory amongst the non-Italians that the driving habits were based upon the need to project the image of 'a person of consequence'. Thus, if one drove a gleaming red Ferrari, one was clearly a POQ; however, if one could afford only a battered Fiat 500, one had to drive it as though one were a POQ. The Fiat driver, therefore, would drive as though at the wheel of a Formula One car, go where no-one else would (on the pavement for example), park in the middle of the street, stop anywhere to talk to friends and never mind the traffic behind, and generally impose his (this seemed to be a male-only trait) character on every other road user. By so doing, others would clearly recognise a POQ despite his status not being heralded by his mode of transport. The impact of being a POQ was later demonstrated to me many times on the *autostrade* where even the most aggressive drivers would smartly pull into the nearside lane at the first sighting of a scarlet Ferrari coming up from far behind.

Arco Felice was not a place to observe many Ferraris, but there were many drivers attempting to impress as POQ; it made for fine entertainment, spoilt only by the realisation that I would soon have to become part of the driving scene, Neapolitan-style. I put that thought out of my mind and concentrated on the many car-free citizens strolling past our table. Unlike their car-borne compatriots, few seemed to be in a hurry. All ages were represented and all were engaged in animated conversation with much elaborate gesturing, an essential part of Italian communication. I was to learn that, so important is this aid to speech, it is used even when speaking on the telephone. Many gestures can actually be used in place of words. For example, a clenched index finger with the second joint pressed against the right cheek near the mouth and partly rotated back and forth indicates that something is good; a clenched thumb used likewise indicates that something is very good. A raised arm is similar to the American use of the middle finger and can be used to assuage frustration when driving; however, it must be used with caution as it is a rather more robust equivalent of our two-fingered gesture.

In conversation I learnt that Jerry and Renee had a house in Charleston, South Carolina, and that they had two other children: a daughter, Bess, and a son, Billy, the youngest member of the family. Jerry was of Syrian extraction – a fact highlighted by Renee whenever Jerry did or said something she thought irrational – and he worked at the United States Naval Hospital just up the road from the NSA complex where I would be working. He was a great lover of Italy and of all things Italian. Renee had a gentle personality and was very family orientated; she was also particularly concerned about the spread of communism, as I was to discover later. By the time darkness had fallen and the temperature had dropped too far for us to remain *al fresco*, I knew that the Isaacs were going to be great friends and neighbours. In this I was to be proved correct. (Now, more than 30 years on, we still stay with the Isaacs every year on the island of Ischia where they rent an apartment from a lady who was once Jerry's secretary.)

Before leaving we shook hands with the proprietor and his two teenaged sons who were obviously smitten with the Isaacs' daughters. We stepped out onto the street and joined the promenading early evening crowd; even in this provincial, out-of-season, seaside town, the *passeggiata* was clearly the thing to do. As I was to discover later this activity was widespread in southern Italy and, whilst it appeared less formal here than in Naples for example, it was still very much part of the social scene for people of all ages. The older generation was represented mostly by husbands and wives identifiable by sober dress, discrete greetings to friends and acquaintances and a rather stately progression. The younger generation, in contrast, tended to move in noisy, animated single-sex groups, their dress an advertisement for all that was currently fashionable. In between the two extremes, newly married couples seemed content to show off each other, or their new offspring. The scene, with its backdrop of impatient ever-flowing traffic, seemed to capture the whole essence of southern Italian society, a society moulded by the Mediterranean climate, thereby having the good fortune to live much of its life out of doors, an aspect generally denied we northern Europeans. One element, however, was missing: there was none of the overt public displays of affection that are so much part of the British scene. This is not to say that Italians do not do their courting in public; it is just that the *passeggiata* is rather too formal an occasion for such intimate exchanges. For these a less formal ambience and a less public venue are required. To meet these demands there are certain areas that traditionally host this activity. As I was to learn later, one of the favourite areas for Neapolitans is on the Posillipo Hill to the north of the city. Here, in the Municipal Gardens many of the techniques of courting can be observed. For the even more intimate moments, the car is used, all activity being hidden from public gaze by newspaper-screened windows. This venue for private, amorous exchanges is essential in a society in which most young men and women, until marriage, live with their parents.

After a few days in my new home I met the family who occupied the house on the other side of us from the Isaacs. Head of the household was Gerardo, one-time Director at the San Carlo Opera House in Naples. This appointment was abruptly terminated mid-contract and, when Gerardo objected, he was visited by a couple of unsavoury characters who warned him that further dissension would not be in his best interests. Wisely, Gerardo sought another job. Living with him was a woman, Elena, I assumed to be his wife, an attractive thirty-something with shortish black hair, dark eyes and a very pale complexion who was expecting their first child. It was not until later that I discovered that Gerardo was still married, but separated, and had grown-up daughters. Also living with Gerardo and Elena was Elena's younger sister, Rosa, similar in build and colouring to her sister and with classically beautiful features. Although Gerardo spoke a little English, I saw him rarely and neither Elena nor Rosa spoke anything other than Italian. Given my limited command of their language, communication could, and often did, lead to misunderstandings. Another member of their household was an attractive and friendly, but very nervous, dog named Katie. Little did I know at the time how large a part in my life this little animal would play.

One very important family did not live on the *parco* – they collected its rubbish! Every day father, mother, son and daughter arrived in and on their ancient and battered red truck. Clambering over a mountain of neatly stacked refuse they carefully loaded the bags that were hung outside each gate. Not a piece of rubbish was spilled. We were indeed favoured; elsewhere householders had to transport their garbage to the nearest roadside skip where it was (sometimes) collected by the local authority's dustcart.

Around this time there was apparently a dearth of dustcarts to be seen in Naples. Crews were reporting for duty before placing their vehicles unserviceable with a variety of faults. Eventually the authorities visited the garages where these unglamorous but vital workhorses were being repaired; there they found their crews enjoying their second jobs – as garage mechanics working on their own vehicles.

Another family vital to the smooth day-to-day operation of the *parco* ran a hardware store a little way down the *Via Domiziana*. However, apart from being the supplier of the usual household necessities, Eddie Russo and his son delivered and collected the gas *bombole* that we all used for our cookers and portable heaters. We mere mortals struggled to lift these squat, grey, gas-filled cylinders but Eddie and his son strode into house or garden with cheery smiles and greetings, each carrying a heavy *bombola* effortlessly on one shoulder. Interestingly, each *bombola* (despite the object's shape and contents, the word means 'cylinder' not 'bomb') came with a certificate costing around £10 – the Neapolitan equivalent of a 'penny on the bottle'. When taking over a house, therefore, one also took on half a dozen or so of these certificates, which would be passed on in turn; in fact, I still have my original one. One drawback of the ubiquitous *bombola*'s use for cooking is that southern Italian families, once restricted to what was in fact a healthy diet, are now able to dine like the rest of us on unhealthy fried food. A plate of chips – *patate frite* – unknown but a few decades ago, is now as commonly seen on Neapolitan menus as pasta.

A rival to the Russo family hardware store was that owned and run on base by Tony Fierro. He sold just about everything you wanted in the hardware line, and many things you didn't even know you wanted. His shop, entered down a short flight of steps, was an Aladdin's Cave infused with that now rare real ironmonger's smell. At the counter sat Tony's mother, a charming old Neapolitan lady with a beautiful smile; she did not otherwise participate in the business though. Tony was another of the local people who became – and remains – a good friend. He was an active sailor, participating in many of the local regattas in his own yacht, and a keen and accomplished tennis player and skier.

I mentioned above that our new next-door neighbours owned a dog, Katie, a very attractive looking animal, a sort of cross between a sheltie and an Italian greyhound. Because of her size and colouring, the Italians thought she was a fox. She had been rescued by Rosa from a group of ragamuffins who had been tormenting her with fireworks. Not surprisingly this behaviour had made Katie somewhat wary of human beings and she always kept her distance, while giving every appearance of wanting to be friends. Eventually, though, Katie ventured into our garden and gradually lost her nervousness around us. At this point I should have perhaps have read the warning signs and seen the direction in which our relationship was heading. The next step came when my wife gave Katie a piece of raw steak. Having been fed on pasta, served on a plastic bag, this must have been the equivalent of *haute cuisine* for the dog who, not unnaturally, returned on a daily basis for such fine dining. 'That dog is not to come into the house,' I recall telling my wife. Needless to say, Katie ignored this and was soon a regular visitor indoors. And, to cut a long story short, although I took Katie back home each evening, eventually Gerardo handed her back to me and said, with a trace of relief I fancied: 'I think Katie wants to live with you!' And so she did.

Having joined the family, as it were, Katie joined us in our many activities. She sailed, water-skied (well, sat in the speed boat), swam in the sea, joined in excavations and accompanied us on trips out and about and even to Oberammergau in Germany, home of the NATO School. Generally we encountered no problems but, on one occasion, we had booked to go on a ski trip to nearby Roccaraso. Sadly, though, the hotel did not accept dogs. I asked our organiser, 'Clubs', the Royal Navy physical education NCO, if he could put in a word for Katie. Having ascertained that she was a 'small' dog, he made a case for her and she was given special dispensation. On the day we travelled to the resort I was sitting on the front seat of the car putting on my ski boots; Katie was lying on the back seat. While I was fastening my clips an enormous Abruzzi mountain dog appeared, just as Clubs was driving past. Nothing was said at the time but later, in the hotel, he saw Katie and asked if she were my dog. I answered 'Yes,' whereupon he breathed a sigh of relief and told me that he had seen the giant animal by my car and had been wondering all day how he could explain to the hotel owner how the small dog had become something closer in size to a donkey!

Katie became more confident as time passed – except when thunderstorms were in the offing. Naples experiences many of these, and they normally occur at night. Katie had ignored my order: 'That dog is not to come upstairs,' and slept on a beanbag by the side of the marital bed. Slept, that is, until she heard the thunder of an approaching storm – about half an hour before it arrived. My warning was a dog sitting on my head, breathing heavily, and drooling onto my face. No matter how hard I tried to share the burden, Katie always chose to sit on me – never on my wife. And this could go on for an hour or more!

However, apart from giving me the odd sleepless night, Katie was little trouble and was a constant and lovable companion. She stayed with us throughout our tour and, finally, travelled to the UK. We were concerned that she would not fare well on an aircraft and took pains to discover what options were available. Having travelled ourselves on Alitalia, we chose Lufthansa although this required an overnight stop in Germany. We need not have worried, though. Katie was met in Manchester by the kennel staff who took her to her place of incarceration for the mandatory six month quarantine period. Happily she accepted this without any noticeable adverse effects, helped by weekly visits from my sister-in-law and parents-in-law. Six months later she joined us for a spell in Lincolnshire, a place she seemed to enjoy. Her favourite pastime there was to chase – but never catch – the brown hares that lived all around us. After seven years of UK living we all returned to Naples for a second tour. But again, that's another story.

7

THE LOCAL AREA

Of course, one of the main advantages of a posting to this part of Italy – apart from the weather and the food – was that there was an abundance of historical sites to visit. Some, like Pompeii and Herculaneum, were world famous, but there were many others less so and I had decided I wanted to explore as many as I could. So having more or less settled in at both home and office I thought it time to start. And where would be better than the first Greek colony on the mainland of Italy – Cumae, Cuma in Italian? In fact I could look down on the distant acropolis of the city, a darkly wooded and isolated hill, from the roof of my new home. The drive to the site was short but nonetheless interesting. Climbing aboard any car in and around Naples, whether as driver or passenger, was always the prelude to an interesting experience! Still inexperienced in Neapolitan driving my leaving the *parco* was a challenge. Traffic from the left was travelling downhill, usually in excess of the speed limit, while to the right was a blind corner. And, of course, I had to cross to the far lane. Not for the first time, nor the last, I took a deep breath, executed a very satisfying racing start, and joined the action.

A mile or so along the 'Doh-mitts' (as all non-Italians called it) I turned off right towards Cuma. Ahead lay the steep and wooded ridge of Monte Grillo, apparently barring the way. However, on rounding a slight bend I could see that a cutting for the road had been made in the ridge. Passage was through an enormous, 60-foot high Roman arch of brick and tufa stone, the road itself being the original Roman surface of shiny, black, irregular blocks of volcanic basalt; it was a trifle bumpy, but still eminently serviceable. This archway, *Arco Felice* (Happy Arch) was built to commemorate the completion of the *Via Domiziana* at the end of the first century AD and was the main exit from the city of Cuma on the road to Puteoli, the Roman name for the modern Pozzuoli. Just beyond the arch to the left of the road I caught a fleeting glimpse of the entrance to a tunnel linking Cuma with Lago Averno, part of the military works undertaken around 35 BC by the future emperor Augustus' admiral, Agrippa, during the civil war. A little further on amidst fragrant orchards and scabby stray dogs and round a couple of exciting bends, I arrived at the gently sloping approach road to the acropolis, the 'upper city' standing guard over the mainly Roman lower city. At the top I found a small car park guarded by an ancient man and a host of dogs. I gave the guardian half of what he asked (a good rule of thumb anywhere in Naples) and walked over to the ticket office to pay the admission fee. Within, a noisy game of cards was in progress. As I was to learn, 'custodians' of sites in this part of Italy are far more likely to be found in the office than on the site itself: the rationale seems to be 'why wander alone with only the spirits for company when comradeship is so close?' Anyway, I did eventually obtain my ticket and headed into the seemingly deserted site. The long approach road was bounded by tufa-stone walls and shaded on the left by dark green fir trees while to the right a common wire fence was beautified by brilliant white and blue convolvulus flowers. Through the fence I could see across an orchard to the imposing bulk of the acropolis hill, its near-vertical face made even more inaccessible by defensive walls, their Greek origin evident in the massive blocks of stone. In the stillness and solitude I could almost believe I was walking back through the centuries, back to the time of Cuma's first foreign settlers who, unlike me, were seeking a permanent home in this alien land.

Cuma was founded around 750 BC by Greeks from Euboea led, according to legend, by Hippocles and Megasthenes who followed a dove sent by Apollo. In fact, the area must have been known to the Greeks well before this time as they had earlier established a trading post on the nearby island of Ischia, which they called

Pithekoussai. To the north lay the iron-rich land of the Etruscans, and of the soon-to-emerge Romans. With its trade, horse-breeding, metal-working and agriculture Cuma soon became a prosperous city. However, relations with the neighbours were not always cordial. The Etruscans attacked the city on a number of occasions, a final battle taking place at sea in 474 BC when the Cumaeans, with the help of Greeks from Syracuse in Sicily, defeated a large Etruscan fleet. I remember seeing one helmet from this battle in the British Museum and a second in the Museum at Olympia, both identified by an inscription – *Hieron, son of Deinomenes, and the Syracusans dedicated to Zeus Etruscan spoils from Cumae.* In 470 BC prosperity was such that the Cumaeans were able to found a second colony that they named, with singular lack of imagination, Neapolis – New City – now known as Naples. The good times were not to last, though, as the city was shortly afterwards captured by the Samnites, a warlike, mountain people who clearly wanted a share of the Greeks' prosperity. Despite this change of rule there does not seem to have been any significant destruction; Cuma continued to prosper and, what is more, decided to throw in her lot with Rome when this new power came onto the Campanian scene. This alliance, which remained strong during Rome's struggles against firstly Pyrrhus of Epirus then the Carthaginian, Hannibal, served Cuma well as the city grew ever larger, reaching its maximum extent in the second century AD.

It was with this fascinating history in mind that I began my lonely tour; I seemed to be the only visitor on the site. Cuma was famous throughout the ancient world for its Sibyl. Virgil, who knew this area well and was buried just outside Naples (though not in the structure now known as 'Virgil's Tomb') wrote about the Sibyl in his marvellous epic poem, the *Aeneid*. In this Aeneas visits the Sibyl in her grotto and she escorts him down into the underworld where he meets and speaks with his father, Anchises. For centuries the Sibyl's grotto remained hidden until in 1932 the great Italian archaeologist, Amedeo Maiuri, uncovered what he and most others considered to be the site itself. It was this I wished to see first.

I soon found the entrance, cut into the bedrock of the acropolis and marked by a Latin quotation from the *Aeneid*. The tunnel stretched ahead of me, its dark interior relieved only by faint light entering through small openings cut through the rock on the right side. I walked in and was immediately enveloped by the silent and eerie atmosphere, although physically there was ample room either side of and above me. The far end was, at this point, invisible and, as I walked further and further towards the Sibyl's place of consultation, I relived something of the awe and gathering fear that ancient supplicants must have felt as ever-increasing darkness slowly closed in on them. Such individuals would have paid a fee and have been escorted to the Sibyl by Priests of Apollo. The passage itself and the associated ritual must have been designed to instil a proper sense of piety and respect for the god – terror would probably be a more likely result. Virgil described it as being a cavern with a hundred mouths whose voices carried the responses of the mysterious unseen Sybil.

Footsteps echoed in the gloom, as if someone were following me. I looked behind. No-one was there; the footsteps were mine alone. At last I reached the end of the tunnel; here it opened out into a chamber, its axis at right angles to the approach passage. To the left an arch framed a smaller chamber. At its entrance, to left and right, were stone benches while holes in the vertical faces suggested the original presence of a door or curtains. Perhaps this was the 'holy of holies' where the now terrified supplicant would have come face-to-face with the Sibyl. Virgil's description gives us a terrifying image of a frenzied woman who appeared larger than life, her hair unkempt, her face transformed by passion and speaking in an unearthly voice. Apart from being petrified the supplicant would not understand any of the Sibyl's rantings but fortunately these would have been 'interpreted' by the priests.

Maybe a satisfactory interpretation depended on the size of the fee! So, was I standing before the holy of holies? Emotion said 'yes', but on inspecting the layout of this end-chamber more closely I thought an alternative explanation more likely. The shape of the chamber, facing the 'holy of holies', reminded me of a church – with nave, transepts (one extending down the approach passage) and a chancel beyond the arch. Given that there were other signs of an early Christian presence here, perhaps co-existing with pagan worship associated with the temples above that I had yet to see, a chapel physically underground seemed a possibility. Indeed, until the emperor Theodosius banned paganism in AD 397 Christians often held services underground; the catacombs in such places as Rome, Malta and nearby Naples provide evidence. However, regardless of the exact purpose of the Sibyl's Grotto, the very atmosphere was heavily charged with mystery and things spiritual. Archaeologists are always quick to assign a ritual purpose to sites they cannot otherwise explain; here, I believe them to be correct.

The grotto is actually below the level of the acropolis proper and the next part of my tour was up a long and curving stone stairway, the steps broad and shallow. The entrance to the upper city was once guarded by two towers. Only one remains, and that dating to the Byzantine period; the other collapsed into a Roman crypt during a siege by the Byzantine general, Narses, in AD 552 when the Goths held the city. The entrance to the upper city was up five wide, shallow steps, the topmost of gleaming white marble, the well-worn surfaces bearing witness to the countless number of people that had travelled in and out over the centuries. Just beyond the ceremonial gateway, on the left, a belvedere gave onto a stunning view along the coast to Lago Fusaro and the high ground of Monte di Procida beyond. Out to sea lay the islands of Procida and Ischia, barely visible in the hazy conditions. Just below, now a sea of green orchards and vegetable crops, once lay Cuma's harbour, an isolated outcrop of ruined masonry now marking the site of the Roman lighthouse. When the Greeks first arrived they would have pulled their boats up onto the sandy beach right at the foot of the acropolis, just below where I was standing. Here, too, the Trojan Aeneas landed having abandoned the Libyan queen, Dido, to her sad end at her own hands. Virgil describes how the ships moored stern first using their anchors to hold their positions, a technique known as Med-mooring. While some of his men prepared camp and others explored the local area Aeneas climbed the nearby hill alone and entered the cave of the 'Sybil feared by men'.

Musing on this I left the belvedere and continued along the so-called 'Sacred Way', a road paved with the same irregular blocks of basalt I had driven over at Arco Felice. On either side the dense vegetation strove to reclaim the ancient way laid so bare by the archaeologists. A few hundred metres on a narrow side-road led to a sacred area – *temenos* in Greek – thought to be dedicated to the god, Apollo. According to Virgil, the inventor Daedalus landed here after fleeing, on home-made wings, the court of King Minos of Crete. You'll recall that his son, Icarus, flew too close to the sun, his wing fastenings melted and he fell to his death in the sea that now bears his name. His wiser father avoided such a fate and in relief at his safe arrival dedicated his wings to Apollo and built a spacious temple to the god. To me the sacred area was something of a disappointment. The remains of a temple filled most of the site but only the base of the original Greek building was visible. Above were traces of Roman *opus reticulatum*, a building technique that used square-based, conical pieces of tufa set in concrete and arranged in a diagonal, net-like pattern. Concrete was invented by the Romans and in this area the abundance of a volcanic material known as *pozzolana* made a particularly enduring version. So hard is it that, over the centuries, the tufa stone has weathered away leaving a picturesque concrete honeycomb. Other signs of Roman usage were the columns, not of expensive marble but of cheap tiles in the shape of slices of pie and placed one on top of another to form the column drum. Originally the brickwork would have been covered with plaster and painted; in fact, I could see quite a lot of the painted plasterwork still in place.

I climbed the steep steps of the temple base and found that there were many body-sized holes in the floor – the graves of the city's great and good when Christianity became the official religion of the Roman Empire. From this vantage point I had a grandstand view of the lower city, its remains mainly Roman in character – a temple, a baths complex and a forum area. Beyond I could see the ridge of Monte Grillo and, piercing it triumphantly, Arco Felice. Turning my attention to the other fragmentary and confusing ruins of the sacred enclosure, I realised that more research would be needed before I could make more than a guess as to their purpose; a few explanatory notice boards would have been useful but these did not appear for several years. So, leaving these puzzles for another day I re-joined the Sacred Way and headed ever upwards. The thick and luxurious greenery on either side eventually gave way to a grove of trees, and the gently-inclined road to a steep flight of stone steps. At the top of the steps stood another massive temple. Again, only the base of the Greek structure remained to bear witness to the skill of the Greek builders. Roman *opus reticulatum* was much in evidence as were (reconstructed) Roman brick arches. As in the temple of Apollo, graves had been carved into the base when the structure had become a Christian basilica dedicated to Saint Massimo. His remains and those of Saint Giuliana were once interred here but were translated to Naples at the final destruction of the city by the Duke of Naples in 1207. By that time Cuma had apparently become a den of bandits and other ne'er-do-wells. Looking around I could see that at one time this basilica, the cathedral of the city, had been lavishly decorated; traces of rich marble flooring and wall panelling clung tenaciously to the underlying stone and brick as if anxious to inform the modern viewer that here, once, all was far different from the rather sad ruins of today. One remarkable survival impressed me: a splendid font, its stepped interior for total immersion baptisms still retaining much of the luxurious marble facing. The archaeologists who excavated this temple in 1927 named it for Jupiter, but on no particular evidence other than its position at the summit of the acropolis. Personally, in the peace and quiet of this rather gloomy spring afternoon, alone among the ruins with only the trees and the occasional lizard for company, I could not help but be seduced by the spirit of the place; what human tragedies, triumphs and even everyday events had been enacted on this now deserted spot, sacred for so long. On balance, though, I sensed more of a Christian presence here – the old deity, whoever he or she was – must have been banished more than a millennium and a half ago.

I sat and mused for some considerable time before the spring chill brought me back to the present and reminded me that I still had one more remarkable engineering project to see, this time a Roman achievement – the *Crypta Romana* – once thought to be the Sibyl's Grotto. In the civil war following the assassination of Julius Caesar in 44 BC, Octavian, the future emperor Augustus, was struggling for mastery of the Roman world. One powerful adversary was Sextus Pompeius, the son of Pompey the Great, who had gained control of Sicily and of the surrounding seas. Octavian's lieutenant and son-in-law, the general Marcus Vipsanius Agrippa, was tasked with reversing this situation and, to help him achieve this, he constructed a number of road-tunnels and canals to link the port of Cuma with a new harbour, *Portus Julius*, in the Bay of Pozzuoli. The *Crypta Romana* was the first element – a tunnel driven right through the centre of Monte Cuma, under the ancient acropolis. To see this impressive work I had to retrace my steps down the Sacred Way almost to the foot of the acropolis hill. There a green iron railing marked the near edge of the crypt, the far side being the honey-coloured, sheer rock face of the hill itself. I looked down into the chasm, its floor some 50 feet below me. Originally there would not have been a chasm; the siege works of Narses had caused one of the two gate-towers above to collapse into the tunnel beneath. Looking up I could see where the tower had once guarded the entrance to the acropolis while below me was what looked like a grand entrance hall with four enormous niches built into a wall of tufa blocks against the cliff opposite. Moving around the railing I could see the opening of the tunnel – a large, dark and forbidding doorway framed by shadows given an ephemeral substance by the late, hazy afternoon sun. It did not look at all inviting; indeed, I felt almost relieved when I noticed a hand-written sign on a rickety fence blocking access to a very overgrown stone staircase, presumably leading to the original entrance to the crypt. The sign stated unequivocally: 'DIVIETO d'ENTRATA', ENTRY PROHIBITED. It looked as though I would not have to brave the perils of the crypt after all!

As I turned to leave I heard the sound of much laughing and shouting coming ever nearer from the direction of the site entrance, round the corner from where I was standing. A minute later three Italian youths appeared, pushing and shoving each other in a friendly but boisterous manner. They were in their late teens I guessed and looked, as do many Neapolitans, somewhat menacing: shortish, dark of hair and complexion, and with designer stubble. They were clearly in high spirits. On seeing me they fell silent and one said, quizzically but politely: 'Salve', a greeting I hadn't come across before but one that I was to hear time and time again in the Naples area. The lads spoke reasonable English and initially identified me as an American and seemed pleased when I told them I was English. They then asked me what the gaping chasm was. I told them about the Roman crypt, which seemed to interest them as they decided it must be investigated more closely. I pointed out the prohibiting sign to them but one of them overcame this slight bureaucratic difficulty by pulling the sign from the fence and casting it into the undergrowth. They then climbed over the fence and invited me to join them. Well, I did want to explore the tunnel and I hadn't seen a custodian all afternoon, so, why not?

We forced our way down the overgrown staircase and found ourselves on a pile of rubbish amongst which was a football, of all things, a great find for my new Italian friends who – like all Neapolitan youths – saw themselves as Maradona, then the star of the Naples football team. On the far side of the rubbish we entered the entrance hall I had earlier looked on from high above. This seemed to be an ideal venue for an impromptu game of football with the tunnel entrance serving as a goal. Somehow I don't think Agrippa would have approved. Eventually, and not surprisingly as the entrance was about 20 feet high, the ball disappeared deep into the tunnel. We followed, my new-found companions making enough noise to waken the dead. It took some time for our eyes to become accustomed to the gloom but I soon realized that this tunnel was on an altogether grander scale than that of the Sibyl's Grotto; it was wider, higher and probably of a size to allow the passage of loaded carts. We went ever deeper into the hill, led on not by Apollo's dove but by the football that was kicked onwards whenever we found it. Light from the entrance grew ever fainter, but there were some light wells far above us, cut through the rock. After about 150 metres a rounded doorway on our right invited us to enter an enormous cave-like chamber. My eyes were drawn towards an eerie, shining and somewhat diffuse column in the centre of the chamber, looking for all the world like one of Star Ship Enterprise's transporter beams. It took me a few moments to realise what it really was: a column of light shining down through a deeply cut light well. My friends amused themselves by standing in the column of light, then stepping back into the darkness and complete invisibility – quite an impressive trick. Another hundred metres or so further on we came to a bend in the tunnel; continuing round to the left we saw the tunnel exit ahead of us, but closed by a barred metal gate. There was nothing for it but to play football back down the tunnel and into the fresh air. My friends invited me to accompany them around the rest of the site but I decided I had had enough excitement for one day. The last I saw of them they were racing each other down the Sibyl's Grotto – she must have been turning in her grave!

8

DEFENDING THE SOUTHERN REGION

Although surrounded by the past, it was in the present that my work lay. Each day therefore saw me nervously negotiating the perils of Squeeze Alley to my office at the Naval Support Activity, Agnano. As I mentioned earlier I was fortunate in having an assigned parking space especially as the majority of those working at the NSA did not enjoy such a facility; for them, finding a space required an early – a very early – arrival. Our working day began nominally at 8am. The American members of staff were invariably in long before this time, the Brits (as we called ourselves) five minutes before time, the Turks on time, the Italians often late, the Greeks sometimes not at all. The Maritime Air Forces Mediterranean – always known by its acronym, MARAIRMED – operations room, where we all assembled each morning, was manned 24 hours a day, the night shift being covered by either an Italian Air Force warrant officer or an RAF corporal. And despite the disparity in ranks our corporals more than held their own with their more senior colleagues. Their main tasks were to collate the incoming message traffic and to plot on a large chart of the Mediterranean the reported positions of Soviet warships and submarines using special red tokens. One night a particularly strong *terremoto* shook the building; the warrant officer on duty attempted to flee, only to find the exit doors jammed. He spent an uncomfortable night sitting under the operations desk and, to add insult to injury, all his carefully plotted Soviet ships and submarines ended up in a heap on the floor.

As staff officers our initial task was to review the overnight 'messages', the NATO term for the paper copies of electronically transmitted information known as 'signals' in our own services. The maritime forces throughout NATO used specialised formatted messages known as the RAINFORM system. For example, the tasking message to a maritime patrol aircraft (MPA), telling it where to go and what to do, was known as a Form Green. The report on its mission was a Form Purple and in-flight sightings of Soviet contacts were sent as Forms Red. These forms furnished the bulk of our daily reading material and were tedious in the extreme. Unfortunately, we had to plough through these in order to discover the odd gem – such as a request for a staff officer to visit Athens, for example. This chore completed we adjourned to our respective offices for a well-deserved coffee and whatever routine work required our attention. For the majority of staff this seldom amounted to very much.

Once a week we attended the main briefing at our superior headquarters, Naval Forces Southern Europe (NAVSOUTH) in which MPA usually had a cameo role. This headquarters was housed in the former Italian Air Force Academy building on the small island of Nisida, an extinct volcano, which was connected to the mainland by a causeway. The route from Agnano to Nisida was full of interest. It bypassed the AFSOUTH headquarters and plunged into the chaos that was Bagnoli. Originally a rather genteel seaside resort, this town of decaying grandeur had its most appealing feature, a splendid beach area, totally disfigured by an enormous steel mill with its associated docks. According to some, the plant was erected by Mussolini to provide employment for Neapolitans; to others, the plant was deliberately sited to spoil the area, many of whose inhabitants had opposed him. The road through the steel mill complex was probably the worst in Italy. So bad was it that it was essential for the preservation of tyres and suspension to know the exact location of all manhole covers, of which there were many, any one of which could – and frequently did – cause damage which, if not irreparable, was exceedingly expensive to fix. Having survived Steel Mill Road, there the causeway to negotiate under the watchful gaze of the ancient female offenders' prison high above on the crater wall. Despite the causeway being extremely narrow, locals would insist on parking along the whole length as it gave access to the last vestige of Bagnoli's beach. As long as nothing was coming the other way there was enough room to drive down what remained of the roadway; however, if you met an oncoming vehicle, there was nothing for it but to manoeuvre in the odd space between parked cars or gaps in the wall, accompanied by the shouts and gestures of numerous helpful onlookers. The final hurdle was the single-storey office block of the *Guardia di Finanza*, the grey-uniformed paramilitary force responsible for matters financial, including the pursuit and apprehension of smugglers. This latter activity was especially popular in Naples; in fact, most of the cigarettes bought on the streets at traffic lights, street corners and *autostrade* tollbooths came courtesy of the smugglers. So endemic was this trade that the sellers of smuggled cigarettes even went on strike to draw attention to what they saw as harassment by the forces of law and order. Suddenly smokers had to pay the (excessive) official price to feed their habit; this was clearly not acceptable. There was no change in the law but before long the cigarette vendors were back at their traditional posts. A crisis had been averted. At Nisida the officers of the *Guardia di Finanza* seemed to spend most of their time lounging against their flashy Alfa Romeos, smoking what one could only assume were duty and tax paid cigarettes. Immediately beyond was the main and only land gate to NAVSOUTH, a place with which I was to become very familiar.

Apart from the weekly briefing I visited Nisida on other occasions, to discuss plans with my naval colleagues and, less frequently, to visit the Senior British Officer in Naples, an admiral, whose NATO post was Chief of Staff to the Commander Allied Naval Forces Southern Europe – COMNAVSOUTH – an Italian admiral. It was while wandering the corridors of power on these visits that I became struck by the level of British presence in the headquarters: Royal Navy and Women's Royal Navy Service officers, petty officers and ratings seemed to permeate the entire building. I soon learnt, too, that the UK exercised an influence out of all proportion to its naval force contribution in the region, the British not having had any warships stationed permanently in the Mediterranean for some years. Now, although COMNAVSOUTH was an Italian admiral, it was the British Chief of Staff who was responsible for the day-to-day running of the headquarters. Furthermore, Royal Navy officers at captain, commander and lieutenant commander level held many of the key staff posts. A further anomaly was that security of the headquarters was provided largely by Royal Air Force police. The reason for this unexpected level of British participation was, as often the case in NATO, an historic one and, to understand it, we need to go back to the early 1950s.

Shortly after NATO was formed the first NATO naval force in the region, Allied Forces Mediterranean (AFMED) was created with Admiral Lord Louis Mountbatten as its Commander-in-Chief (CINCAFMED). He held this NATO post in addition to his national position as Commander-in-Chief Mediterranean (CINCMED). In those far off days we maintained a significant Mediterranean fleet based in Malta so, not surprisingly, the majority of personnel in the headquarters, just outside Valletta were British with security provided by RAF police. There was, however, a second naval command, Allied Naval Forces Southern Europe (NAVSOUTH) based in Naples and commanded by Admiral Robert Carney, who was also Commander-in-Chief Allied Forces Southern Europe. Having two naval commands caused a certain amount of friction aggravated by the fact that the major component of NAVSOUTH was the United States Sixth Fleet with its nuclear-capable carrier aircraft. Clearly the US was not going to hand over control of these assets to a Brit! After much acrimonious discussion NAVSOUTH was disestablished and its assets, excepting the US Sixth Fleet, were transferred to AFMED. A new headquarters, Naval Striking and Support Forces Southern Europe (STRIKFORSOUTH) was created in Naples to exercise, when required, NATO command and control of the Sixth Fleet.

This NATO compromise solution never really worked because of overlapping operational responsibilities between AFSOUTH and AFMED. Then, in 1964, Malta gained its independence and AFMED found itself a NATO HQ on non-NATO territory. Thereafter, in

1967, the British military rundown continued with the disbandment of the Mediterranean Fleet. AFMED's demise followed, its functions being assumed by a new headquarters with a familiar name: Allied Naval Forces Southern Europe (NAVSOUTH). Manning levels stayed much the same, though, and the HQ remained in Malta. However, in 1971, Dom Mintoff of the Malta Labour Party came to power and requested (probably a NATO euphemism!) the closure of NAVSOUTH. The Italian government stepped in with the offer of a home for NAVSOUTH and later in the year the headquarter's predominantly British staff, the RAF police – and even a fleet of Bosun sailing dinghies – moved into their new premises on the seafront in Nisida. And this explains why the British presence was so marked in NAVSOUTH.

Influence, though, does not depend exclusively on 'presence'. One of the reasons why some, usually jealous, individuals deride NATO as standing for 'Never at the Office' is that its headquarters are, or were in the 1980s, overmanned; this gave many individuals ample opportunity for being out of the office. The situation arose because each member nation wanted to have a presence at the highest possible level in all areas of the various commands. Also, in the 1980s we were well into the Cold War and everyone knew, or at least thought they knew, where NATO stood in relation to the Warsaw Pact. Consequently staff work was largely routine and followed a set pattern, a pattern that could be applied rigidly by unimaginative commanders. Let me give you just one example of this trait.

As I mentioned above my particular responsibilities were the maritime patrol aircraft elements of NATO plans and exercises. In the 1980s, of course, the Cold War had been in existence for many years and few changes were required in our main war plans: the potential capability of the enemy, the Warsaw Pact, was well known, its likely courses of action identified and NATO's response clearly defined. Unfortunately I found the MARAIRMED war plan rather difficult to follow despite it being written in my native language. It had been added to, amended and altered so many times over the years by different hands that its text was disconnected. I thought it would be a good idea, therefore, to rewrite it completely – a two-week job. My boss was happy for me to continue and I set to. As I had calculated, the actual rewrite did not take long; but then I ran into NATO inflexibility. All documents, before being finally approved, had to follow a tortuous route through various agencies each of which was given the opportunity to comment. While there were no particular comments on my rewrite, I came across a complete block when the document ended up on the desk of a Greek admiral at NAVSOUTH. He called me to his office and asked me why I had rewritten the plan for, he said, the plan's review was not scheduled for another two years. No matter how I tried to explain that the rewrite was a significant improvement, he would not accept that such staff work should be done out of normal sequence. And so the rewritten plan sat on his desk for nearly two years before it received final approval. I had learnt an interesting lesson.

The other major factor in promoting influence is the ability to write convincingly in English. British officers of middle rank and above are generally good at staff work; they have been specially trained and they are writing in their native language. My NATO colleagues from the Southern Region nations, even if they spoke excellent English – and many of them did – did not have the same command of the written word. Greek and Turkish officers had the added problem of having to comment on NATO papers that touched on sensitive national issues. Here a diplomatic response was often needed, but the officer concerned was rarely equipped with the nuances of English that permitted a response acceptable to all. At NAVSOUTH in particular, therefore, the UK was able in terms of influence to punch well above its weight.

9

I CAMPI FLEGREI – THE FIERY FIELDS

The area between my place of work and new home was called in antiquity the *Campi Flegrei*, the Fiery Fields, so named for the constant and occasionally violent volcanic activity that so impressed the ancients. I was interested to see if any such activity remained. Having once more safely transitioned from the relative safety of the *parco* to the rough and tumble of the *Domiziana*, I headed back up the hill in the direction of Naples. I stopped first in a litter-strewn lay-by overlooking the volcanic crater lake of Lago Averno, the entrance to the underworld as Virgil would have us believe. I mentioned above that Octavian's general, Agrippa, constructed a new naval base, named *Portus Julius* after Julius Caesar, and linked it to Cuma by a series of tunnels and canals. The canals linked Lago Averno to the nearby lake of Lago Lucrino and thence to the open sea. I could see no signs of this work but the ruins of a large Roman bathhouse still stood proudly on the eastern shore.

Below me the water looked dark and uninviting but the lush vegetation cascading down the steep slope and the ordered ranks of a vineyard robbed the scene of any menace. But menace there could be a-plenty. I learnt later that members of the NATO sub-aqua club, diving to investigate signs of Roman presence, had located a car with two bodies tied up inside – more of the *Camorra*'s handiwork no doubt. The lake was almost surrounded by the high walls of the crater but on the far side was a wide gap beyond which sparkled the Mediterranean-blue sea and a view along the coast. Along it I could see silhouetted against the sky a large, angular structure at the head of a small peninsular; this was the imposing medieval castle built by Don Toledo, Viceroy when the Kingdom of Naples was in Spanish hands. Although I did not know it at the time, the castle had become the refuge for many of the local population displaced by the ongoing *terremoto* activity around Pozzuoli. Beyond the castle at the end of the coast stood the strange flat-topped hill of Capo Miseno, once the location of one of the two Roman fleets in Italy at the time of Vesuvius' AD 79 eruption. Somewhere on the far right of the crater was the exit from the Roman tunnel through Monte Grillo that I'd spotted on my visit to Cuma, the *Grotta di Cocceio*, linking the city to Averno that was actually used until the 1940s. However, the tunnel exit was now hidden by dense undergrowth.

The scene before me fitted Virgil's description but I could see no sign of any fiery fields activity. To be sure, the lake was contained within the crater of a volcano, but one whose energy had long since been dissipated. Looking to my left, however, I could see a rather more promising feature – a thickly wooded hill that, I had read, was the area's newest volcano. Named imaginatively 'Monte Nuovo', New Mountain, it erupted out of the blue in September 1538 over a period of two days destroying the village of Tripergole. I thought that this might prove a more likely venue.

While I mused on this and continued to enjoy the view, two cars drew up. Out of the first stepped a bride resplendent in an elaborate white wedding dress with an enormous train that was quickly gathered up by an attendant bridesmaid. The young man in the shiny but rumpled silk suit who followed the girls out of the car I took to be the bridegroom. From the second car emerged a photographer, several expensive cameras strung round his neck, and a henchman carrying various reflecting devices. The photographer proceeded to 'arrange' the bride in a number of fetching poses, some with the groom and some without, against the spectacular scenic background of the entrance to hell, surely not a prediction of things to come. Even the rubbish scattered liberally about did not seem to be a deterrent. Was there some deep symbolism here, I wondered? In fact, as I was soon to discover, the photographing of bridal couples, usually the day after the ceremony, is very much part of the wedding tradition here and couples are to be found in all the scenic, historic or otherwise 'interesting' sites patiently submitting to their photographer's artistic creativity – draped around Roman columns, lying languidly on marble benches, peering through exotic undergrowth and generally lying about in suchlike poses. Sir Lawrence Alma-Tadema specialised in painting such scenes; he would have been in his element as a Neapolitan photographer.

Leaving the resigned-looking newly-weds to their fate I drove on to Monte Nuovo. Parking close to the foot of the not insubstantial hill, I began to climb. This was more like it! Here and there small jets of steam issued from fissures underfoot and a faint odour of sulphur permeated the still air. I climbed higher on a roughly defined pathway, stopping every so often to admire the view across the bay to the village of Baia. Once this was the holiday resort *par excellence* for Roman emperors and the aristocracy; now, despite the beauty of the view, the overall effect was somewhat spoiled by the rather down-at-heel buildings along the seafront. Over to my right there were even a number of rusting hulks abandoned just offshore to the mercies of a small shipyard. Clearly this part of the Italian coastline was no longer a watering-hole of the great and the good. Turning back to the pathway I continued my ascent, interested to learn what lay ahead.

From the top I looked down into an impressive crater. To my disappointment there were no obvious signs of volcanic activity – no smoke, no steam, no view into the bowels of the earth. Indeed, I was taken aback by the arrival in the bottom of the crater of three horses whose riders proceeded to tackle a short jumping course. Monte Nuovo had obviously been tamed. I completed my walk around the entire circumference of the crater and made my way back down the hill to my car. So far the Flegrean Fields had not impressed me; that was to come later.

10

PLANNING NATO EXERCISES

I've already mentioned that my NATO job involved plans and exercises, the latter being designed to test the former. To achieve this and to familiarise NATO nations' forces with the plans, each NATO region ran a series of exercises. These were of two types: LIVEXES, in which actual forces took part to practise their war-fighting roles using NATO procedures in co-operation with other NATO forces; and COMMAND POST EXERCISES (CPXs), which were 'paper' exercises in which the War Headquarters were manned but the forces existed only on paper. NATO forces were always BLUE; the enemy, who demonstrated remarkable similarities in equipment and tactics to the Warsaw Pact, were ORANGE. Generally speaking all exercises were 'fought' by conventional forces; nuclear weapons, being primarily political, figured only in certain CPXs, the reason being that the tactical use of these weapons would inevitably result in retaliation in kind and set in train an unstoppable escalation. As in World War II, in which the possession of poison gases by both sides prevented their use, the mutual ownership of both tactical and especially strategic nuclear weapons would, it was hoped, act as a deterrent. This is why nuclear warfare did not figure in our routine exercise activity.

The sequence of events that led up to a LIVEX was quite complicated and was effected through a series of planning meetings. In the Southern Region the first of these, the Initial Planning Conference, was held in AFSOUTH's HQ some 18 months before the scheduled exercise start date. It involved representatives of contributing nations – the US, UK, Italy, Greece and Turkey – together with NATO planning staffs, a total of over one hundred officers. You may have wondered about the absence of the French; surely they were a Southern Region nation? Of course, they were but in 1966 President De Gaulle withdrew all French forces from NATO's integrated military structure, though France remained in the Alliance itself. Although there were secret contingency plans for French forces to be absorbed into the NATO command structure should war break out they were not exercised.

The large conference room where the proceedings opened was impressive with dark blue carpets and curtains and expensive blue-upholstered chairs set before a hollow square of polished wood tables. Such opulence reflected the fact that the Commander-in-Chief Allied Forces Southern Europe, a US admiral known by the NATO acronym of CINCSOUTH, or just 'the CINC', also wore a national hat; US national money was therefore available for prestigious venues, be they conference rooms, offices or corridors. NATO equivalents were spartan in comparison. Each conference always began with an address by one of AFSOUTH's generals who invariably waxed lyrical on the solidarity of NATO and the benefits of such exercises as we were about to plan. By far the most entertaining of these welcoming speakers was General Parodi Dandini, an *alpini* officer with a belief in his own power of oratory. Unfortunately his form of English and his accent, coupled with the NATO-speak he used, made him almost totally incomprehensible. Looking around the imposing conference room it was possible to identify the visitors straining valiantly to understand what on earth was being said; the locals did not try. After this mandatory torment the conference got under way.

In the subsequent plenary session each nation was asked to allocate a certain number of units, the aim being to obtain a total that would match the requirements of the outline plan drawn up by the region's exercise planning staffs. As I mentioned above, the 'goodies' were the 'Blue' forces; the 'baddies', whose forces uncannily resembled those of the Warsaw Pact, were 'Orange'. For my part, I sought the participation of as many maritime patrol aircraft as possible, largely in the 'blue' role that was much preferred by the crews as it involved the more complex anti-submarine warfare (ASW), rather than the less challenging anti-surface unit warfare (ASUW) required by the Orange commanders. However, the forces offered initially did not often match the requirement so there followed a series of pleas from the conference chairman for nations to be a little more generous. Eventually an acceptable compromise was reached and the plenary session was adjourned for the various sub-committees to meet and discuss their particular part in the forthcoming exercise. I was a member of the maritime sub-committee.

Although the procedure was apparently straightforward, there was a major problem: that of Greece. Greece and Turkey had a number of political disagreements that spilled over into the military world. The immediate origin of these was the Turkish invasion – or intervention depending on which of the two nations you are listening to – of Cyprus in 1974. This followed the attempt by the Greek junta in Athens to oust President Makarios and install their own puppet president, Nikos Sampson. The coup failed but it did precipitate the long-planned Turkish invasion. Greece, in response, pulled out of NATO's integrated military structure and withdrew her men from NATO staffs. Eventually, when the dust had died down, Greece was permitted to re-join in 1980 under an agreement known as the Rogers Plan named after the Supreme Allied Commander Europe, General Bernard W Rogers. However, Greece and Turkey, as with many other things, interpreted the agreement rather differently. Foremost among the differences was the question of the establishment ('stand-up' in American terminology) of the Seventh Allied Tactical Air Force (7ATAF) at Larissa in northern Greece, the home of the Hellenic Tactical Air Force (HTAF). Izmir, in Turkey, was already the headquarters of 6ATAF while 5ATAF headquarters was at Vicenza in Italy. Greece claimed that the establishment of 7ATAF was part of the agreement of her re-joining the NATO flock. Not so, replied

Turkey. And here it is necessary to explain how the NATO system operates. Decisions are taken on a consensus basis; in other words, all nations have to agree on any decision before it becomes NATO policy. Clearly this presented a problem when considering any matter involving the Aegean area.

This difference of interpretation was not confined to the 7ATAF question, however; there were also the treaties of Lausanne and Paris to consider. In short, Turkey was of the opinion that the island of Lemnos should have been demilitarised under one treaty; Greece, on the other hand, interpreted the other treaty to state that this requirement had been superseded and, to prove the point, had built a major military airfield on the island. Yet another conflict concerned the transmission of flight plans between Turkey and Greece. Flight plans contain information on an aircraft's movements so that it can be identified when crossing from one nation's airspace to another's. Commercial airliners use this system as a matter of course but the International Civil Aviation Organisation (ICAO) has granted a waiver for 'state' aircraft, interpreted by most nations as 'military' aircraft. However, in most circumstances military aircraft flying between the airspace of different nations do submit flight plans. Turkey, citing the ICAO waiver, refused to pass flight plans on military aircraft movements to Greece. In normal circumstances this would not have presented too much of a problem as adjacent air defence systems automatically pass aircraft movements to each other in a procedure called 'cross-telling'. Unfortunately, due to the political differences between Greece and Turkey, this system was not in place. This led to the unusual situation of military aircraft taking off from Turkey and heading out into the Aegean area being identified, correctly according to NATO procedure, as 'unknown' by the Greek air defence system. The response was to launch armed air defence fighter aircraft to intercept these 'unknown' contacts. The Turks, knowing that they would be intercepted by armed Greek fighters, armed their own fighters. Often dogfights ensued and, although neither missiles nor guns were fired, several aircraft were lost as a direct result of these interactions during my time in Naples.

As if these differences were not enough, there was another major dispute – concerning territorial waters and national airspace. The Greeks claimed a territorial waters limit of six nautical miles but, uniquely, an airspace limit of ten nautical miles. Again NATO was unable to adjudicate, leaving it up to individual nations to determine what limits they would accept. The Turks, needless to say, not only disputed the ten-mile national airspace limit but also regularly over-flew Greek islands in the Aegean to emphasise their dismissal of Greek claims.

It may come as a surprise that two NATO members, neighbours and allies, should exhibit such enmity. To seek the reason for this we need to look at the history of these two countries. For several centuries the Christian lands that became the modern nation of Greece suffered under the rule of the Moslem Ottoman Turks and it was not until 1832 that Greece was recognized as a fully-fledged sovereign state, the outcome of the bloody War of Independence.

At the start of the First World War Greece chose neutrality, largely because King Constantine was the brother-in-law of the German Kaiser. Turkey, on the other hand, joined the Central Powers. Then, in 1917, King Constantine was forced to abdicate and Greece entered the war on the side of the Allies. After the war Greece sought to recover those parts of Turkey that, historically, had been peopled by Greeks for more than 2,500 years and still retained significant Greek populations. Thus began the Greco-Turkish War, which began with the Greek occupation of Smyrna (Turkish Izmir) in 1919. Greek forces then advanced eastwards towards Ankara. Initially they were successful but, under the effective leadership of Kemal Ataturk, Turkish forces eventually drove the Greeks back to the coast, recapturing – and subsequently burning – Smyrna in October 1922. The war ended in 1923 with the signing of the Treaty of Lausanne, a major provision of which was the traumatic exchange of populations; over one million Greeks were forced to leave their homes in Turkey while about half a million Turks travelled the opposite way. Only one island retained significant mixed Greek and Turkish populations: Cyprus.

Cyprus, too, had been part of the Ottoman Empire until Britain took over its administration, though not its sovereignty, in 1878. In 1923, under the Treaty of Lausanne, Turkey relinquished her claim to the island and it became a British Crown Colony in 1925. In the Second World War Turkey remained neutral while Greece joined the Allies. Of note, many Greek-Cypriots, and some Turkish-Cypriots, enlisted in the British Army. At the end of the war most British colonies sought, and were granted, independence. In Cyprus, however, the situation was complicated by the different wishes of the mixed population: the Greek-Cypriots wanted *enosis*, union with Greece, while the Turkish-Cypriots favoured partition. Britain was inclined to grant neither and, as a result, increased tension led to the formation of the Greek-Cypriot terrorist organisation, EOKA, in 1955. This coincided with the outbreak of Turkish riots in Istanbul directed against the Greek population. Then, in 1957, the Turkish-Cypriots formed TMT, the Turkish Resistance Organisation to serve their own interests. Terrorist attacks continued until 1959 and the following year saw Cyprus gain its independence, helped by its first President, Archbishop Makarios, rejecting the vexed policy of *enosis*. Sadly the constitution brokered by Britain, Greece and Turkey never worked and violence between the two communities broke out in 1964. Many Turkish-Cypriots left the island and those that remained were forced into defended enclosures. The situation was made worse by the formation in 1971 of EOKA-B, a terrorist organisation like its predecessor with the aim of *enosis*.

Meanwhile, in 1967 Greece had fallen under the control of a harsh and undemocratic military junta. From a NATO viewpoint this situation was unwelcome but American support of the junta ensured that NATO business continued as usual, the Cold War threat being considered overriding. However, in 1974 Athens backed a coup by EOKA-B to assassinate President Makarios and replace him with the terrorist, Nikos Sampson. But things did not go according to plan; Makarios survived and Turkey, invoking its powers of intervention as specified in the Cypriot Constitution, landed troops on the north coast of the island, supported by air and naval forces. Turkey eventually extended control over about one third of the island. As a result of the failed coup Sampson was imprisoned, President Makarios returned to office, the Greek junta fell and Cyprus became a divided island. And, as already mentioned, Greece withdrew from NATO's Integrated Military Structure. By the time I arrived in Naples the northern part of Cyprus had been proclaimed 'The Independent Turkish Republic of Northern Cyprus', a state recognized only by Turkey and a situation the Greeks found impossible to accept.

Not surprisingly, given this historical background and the resultant disagreements, exercise planning could not satisfy both the Greek and Turkish representatives who were required to act in accordance with their national political positions. Turkey had the upper hand, having NATO headquarters on its soil. Greece, therefore, withdrew from each and every exercise, having failed to have any of its positions formally accepted by the exercise planners who were, of course, bound by NATO doctrine. The climax came at the final plenary session of the planning conference when the Greek representative read a carefully prepared political statement – to which the Turkish representative replied, not without a barely disguised sense of satisfaction.

For three years I thought that the disputes between Greece and Turkey were simply political manoeuvrings designed to give us exercise planners additional headaches – as if there were not sufficient problems in the planning process as it were. Then, in

March 1987, my view changed for in this month the Turkish research ship, *Sismik 1*, escorted by Turkish warships, entered the Aegean to conduct seismic surveys of the disputed Continental Shelf. In response Greece put her armed forces on a war footing and the scene was set for a conflict between two NATO allies. Fortunately common sense finally prevailed, thanks in part to Lord Carrington, NATO Secretary General's intervention, and the two sides backed off leaving the question of the Aegean Continental Shelf unresolved.

Returning to the exercise conference, I was always intrigued to note that by the end the number of delegates had reduced considerably. Indeed, throughout the three days of the proceedings more and more of the attendees drifted off to sample the on-base shopping or the delights of the local area. Only the hard-core exercise planners remained and even these – or, at least, some of them – returned from coffee and lunch breaks at an ever-later time, much to the frustration of the various sub-committee chairmen. Another aspect that was new to me was the habit of certain delegates to read the local newspaper and discuss certain of its contents during the deliberations of each morning's plenary session.

Some months later the Main Planning Conference (MPC) was held, again at the AFSOUTH headquarters though with far fewer delegates. The format followed that of the IPC, plenary sessions being followed by sub-committee deliberations concerning the detail of each phase of the forthcoming exercise. The maritime element generally involved a carrier battle group of the US Sixth Fleet, learning what to them were the somewhat alien NATO procedures, and an amphibious group transiting the west Mediterranean into the Aegean Sea and conducting amphibious landings in Turkish Thrace (another bone of contention with Greece, which considered 'Thrace' to be simply an historic geographical area not requiring an adjective, and certainly not 'Turkish'!). We also included a convoy of merchant ships transiting from one allied port to another. As far as the maritime aircraft were concerned my job was to provide the maximum training opportunities for the crews.

The main roles of maritime patrol aircraft (MPA) are anti-submarine and anti-surface vessel warfare (ASW and ASUW). Of these, the crews generally prefer ASW and this was the aspect on which I concentrated during the planning process. MPA operated either independently, on what were known as Area Operations, or in Direct Support to a particular group of ships in which case they were under the control of a naval commander, the Officer in Tactical Command, on board a suitably-equipped warship. To ensure a high degree of interaction between 'blue' anti-submarine forces and the 'orange' exercise submarines, the naval planners routed the amphibious group and the convoy through a succession of submarine patrol areas. This also ensured that there would be detection opportunities for any MPA operating in direct support of the surface groups concerned as well as targets for the orange submarines. For Area Operations I had to liaise closely with the 'orange' submariners who, not surprisingly, were reluctant to offer unlimited detection opportunities to MPA constantly overhead their patrol areas. Although an American nuclear submarine was sometimes assigned to an exercise, generally to operate in the 'blue' role and co-operate with MPA, those operating in the 'orange' role were invariably diesel-electric boats. Of course, this was not surprising as no participating Southern Region nation possessed nuclear-powered submarines except France which did not participate in NATO exercises, for reasons I explained above. The main difference between the two types of submarine was that while nuclear boats could remain submerged indefinitely diesel-electric boats could not. For submerged operation they ran on their electric motors but the batteries that powered them needed frequent recharging and this required running the diesel engines. To do this they had to raise an induction mast, known as a snorkel or snort, to obtain the necessary air supply; this exposed mast, although small, provided a radar detection opportunity for the patrolling MPA. In addition air-dropped sonobuoys could detect the noise of the diesel engines. To avoid detection, therefore, a submarine commander had to limit the use of the diesel engines to periods when MPA did not pose a threat, a condition he could often determine by reference to his electronic support measures (ESM) equipment, which could detect MPA's radar transmissions. As submariners are, by nature, secretive and devious – characteristics necessary for their survival in wartime – it was difficult to convince them that some sacrifice on their part was essential if we were to achieve the overall aims of the exercise. Eventually we reached a compromise: the submarines were given MPA-free periods to recharge their batteries and the MPA were offered detection opportunities. As an aside you might wonder how MPA could detect submerged nuclear submarines. The answer is that the aircraft dropped patterns of sonobuoys designed to detect the noise emanating from a submarine. However, noise levels were extremely low and this type of submarine presented a very challenging target.

The planning sequence was concluded with the Final Planning Conference (FPC) held a few weeks before the commencement of the exercise itself. The aim here was to iron out any remaining difficulties, to seek confirmation of nations' assigned forces and to help resolve any issues concerning deployment bases for MPA and port facilities for naval vessels. The culmination of this process was the production of a comprehensive and exceedingly weighty Exercise Operation Order, which was passed to the operations staffs for implementation. Finally the exercise itself, with its pre-scripted series of events, took place, closely monitored by senior NATO commanders and, as far as the naval forces were concerned, by shadowing Soviet units. Meanwhile, back in the various headquarters the men and women played their minor parts in a rehearsal for a drama that no-one really expected to have a first night

This sequence of planning conferences, although tedious at times, did allow us to meet on a regular basis military colleagues from a number of nations. Despite the various differences of opinion, even those between Greece and Turkey, personal relationships were always good and there were several opportunities to meet less formally and confrontationally than was the case in the planning rooms. One such occasion was the semi-formal luncheon held on the first day of the IPC, hosted by whichever general officer was in overall charge of the conference. It was here that one aspect of the submariners' deviousness was highlighted. They exchanged the small wine glasses on the table they had been allocated for the large water glasses on the general's table. Thus the wine on the submariners' table always ran out before anybody else's and additional bottles were ordered and put on the general's account. I have to admit that, deviousness notwithstanding, the submariners' table was also popular among the MPA community! Lunches other than on the first day could be taken at a variety of venues, dependent on taste. For some, the canteen atmosphere and enormous portions of the 'dry' American Troop mess beckoned; for others, it was the Italian mess where the food was more local and, what is more, included wine. Cost was immaterial as both were incredibly cheap.

The planning process for the CPXs was similar, but generally only involved two conferences and, as no real forces were involved, participation was much reduced. In fact there was only one major CPX a year: a NATO-wide exercise code-named 'WINTEX' and a Southern Region equivalent, each held in alternate years. These exercises were designed specifically to test NATO's transition to war (TTW) procedures as well as its war plans, although WINTEX involved national governments and was much more of a political exercise. During the Cold War the associated TTW procedures, a series of comprehensive and detailed measures to be taken in response to an escalating threat, were designed to place NATO on a war footing should the situation demand. Among the many measures was the requirement for nations to hand over command of national forces to NATO. What is not generally realized is that NATO did not have many units under its command in peacetime. Therefore, to operate effectively as a war-fighting alliance, it had to take command of those forces that nations had assigned or earmarked for NATO's use. There were also many other actions required of nations and of NATO headquarters to ready the Alliance for war, responding, as far as the exercise was concerned, to a steady heightening tension – input by the exercise intelligence scenario. So Military Vigilance gave way to Simple Alert to be followed by Reinforced Alert. This process, although straightforward in theory, always caused problems in practice. Finally the exercise situation worsened and General Alert was declared; hostilities broke out and then continued for a pre-determined time, the 'enemy's' political decisions and forces' actions, and their successes and failures, being determined and controlled by a group of officers known as the exercise Directing Staff who followed the general game plan in an 'Orange' operation order.

Despite the planning problems both types of exercise did achieve their aims: NATO commanders faced a sequence of events they may have had to face in wartime, nations' forces gained valuable experience operating alongside allies and any weaknesses in the war plans were revealed. I have to say that I enjoyed the entire process.

11

THE REAL FIERY FIELDS

Returning to my initial visit to the *Campi Flegrei*, you'll recall I said that I was not immediately impressed. I thought Lago Averno and Monte Nuovo tame so in due course I decided that I would give the Fiery Fields another chance by visiting a further site to see if this were more in keeping with the area's name and reputation. The day I chose, a Sunday, was overcast with just a hint of drizzle in the air – never good for the spirits in any part of the world. However, I continued with my plan and drove the short distance to Solfatara, a little beyond and uphill from the then crumbling town of Pozzuoli. Arriving at the site I drove through an ornate arch underneath a very imposing three-storey, eighteenth-century, pink-painted villa and parked on a sort of small, rural car park – all trees, bushes and stray dogs. I collected my ticket and walked down a broad avenue lined with eucalyptus trees. On my left was a camping area, busy even this early in the season. Most of the visitors seemed to be German, in large camper vans with towels at the ready in case of brightening weather, with a sprinkling of northern Italians among them. The avenue ended at a log cabin housing a bar and, not surprisingly, a souvenir shop quite well stocked with guidebooks, postcards, jewellery and other bits and pieces made of shiny black and sparkling volcanic stone.

In front of the cabin was a sign, with an arrow: *AL CRATERE* – 'to the crater'. I walked as directed, neither climbing nor descending, and in a few yards left the green and pleasant land behind and stepped into a veritable moonscape, desolate, dramatic and awesome. The complete change of scenery took my breath away. High and jagged cliffs partly obscured by clouds of steam encompassed a circular area, completely devoid of vegetation, more than a kilometre across; the surface was dazzlingly white, flat and steaming; the smell of rotten eggs, hydrogen sulphide, overpowering. I was in a volcanic crater. This was more 'fiery fields'!

The ground was hard and warm underfoot and covered with a very fine, yellowish-white powder that flew up at every footstep. The central part of the crater was fenced off and, as I drew nearer, I could see warning signs: *Pericolo da morte* – 'danger of death' – given added emphasis by a skull and crossbones symbol. Reaching the fence I saw the reason for the warning. On the other side was a large fissure leading to a pool of black mud that writhed and bubbled ominously. I walked slowly around the fenced area between small gently steaming hillocks, keeping my eyes peeled for any additional fissures that might have escaped the fencing. In the side of one hillock I noticed a shining clump of rich, yellow crystals of sulphur. I bent to touch it – and recoiled, blowing on burnt fingers! Continuing round the crater, I came across more spectacular activity on the far side. A ferocious column of steam, like dragon's breath, was issuing from a large vent with the noise and energy of a jet engine; close by, a small brick building, shrouded in steam, looked to be on the point of collapse. This area, too, was cordoned off – not that I had any desire to move any closer, a burnt finger was sufficient for one day.

I continued my circumnavigation, climbing a little way up the cliffs every now and then to investigate small caves. All were lined with beautiful sulphur crystal formations; all were hot. Looking back towards my point of entry I could see where, in the distant past, an eruption had broken through the surrounding cliffs and allowed lava to flow towards the sea. Also, much to my surprise, I could see that several houses had been built overlooking this volcanic crater; optimism or stupidity? As I was to learn later, this same outlook applied to those living near Vesuvius, on the other side of Naples. Despite the fact that Vesuvius was overdue an eruption, the last having been in 1944, many people had built, albeit illegally, on the slopes; many millions more lived – and still live – within range of the volcano's destructive power, power to which Pompeii and Herculaneum bear startling witness.

Up to this point there had been no-one else in the crater. Now I saw coming towards me another figure. He headed towards me with a brisk but slightly stooping gait; close to I could see that he was particularly weather-beaten and appeared to be as old as the crater itself. He was wearing a colourful knitted pullover, brown jacket and a very English hat; in his hand he held a bundle of rolled newspapers. In a soft voice and in good but heavily accented English, he wished me 'good morning', told me that his name was Bruno and that he was the guide to Solfatara. He enthused about the conditions, saying that grey skies and a hint of rain were ideal for seeing the volcano in its best light. He then proceeded to reel off countless facts about the volcano, which apparently last erupted in 1198, enumerating the various gases and minerals emitted, and listing the temperatures of the several mud pools and steam vents. But his most impressive contribution came close to another brick structure housing two, arched steam rooms named, according to Bruno, 'Purgatory' and 'Hell', the latter being the hotter of the two. As we approached we saw an almost naked German sitting in Purgatory, his body streaming with perspiration. Bruno said that this was a favourite pastime of German campers – good for the chest! Bruno now demonstrated a remarkable phenomenon. Lighting his rolled newspapers then blowing out the flames, he wafted the now smoking paper close to the building. In no time an enormous quantity of steam appeared, apparently out of thin air. Our German friend disappeared in the ensuing cloud, to be followed by Bruno himself. I half expected the steam to clear, leaving me alone again in the crater. However, I need not have worried; as Bruno's wand ceased to smoke, so the steam decreased until all was as before. The phenomenon, said Bruno, was caused by water vapour condensing around the smoke nuclei.

He next picked up a large piece of rock and threw it into the air. I jumped when it hit the ground as the whole crater seemed to vibrate as though a thin crust was about to split open and hurl us into the depths. 'Not so,' said Bruno. He explained that this unnerving effect was due to the honeycomb structure of the underlying rock – a bit like the inside of a 'Crunchie bar' – formed by the continuous passage through the rock of steam and various gases. I was much relieved. Crossing the smoking crater I noticed a large cross high on the crater wall. Pointing it out to Bruno, he told me that it marked the spot where *San Gennaro*, the patron saint of Naples, had been beheaded after the lions in Pozzuoli's amphitheatre had declined to eat him. On that note we finished the tour, and returned to the bar where we enjoyed an excellent cappuccino. Over the years when I was leading tours in this area I was able to enjoy Bruno's demonstrating to various groups the phenomena that I first saw that Sunday morning; he always appeared exactly as he did all those decades ago.

So, after Solfatara I was able to revise my views on the fiery fields; but more was to come. Some time after my eye-opening visit to Solfatara I met an American professor, Michael Karris, a leprechaun-like figure with red hair and glasses, a most engaging personality and imbued with prodigious energy. He was a lecturer at the University of Rome and also at a branch of an American university on the NATO base. We soon became friends and one Saturday he said he had something interesting to show me – practical use of the Fiery Fields' thermal activity. We began our tour at a spa, the *stufe di nerone* – 'Nero's Stoves' – just along the coast from Monte Nuovo. Here the saunas and the remarkably green hot water swimming pools were heated completely naturally, the source being the same heat that had caused Monte Nuovo to put in an appearance.

These were interesting but the highlight of our visit was a short distance away. Leaving our car on a piece of waste ground at the foot of a decidedly unstable-looking cliff, we walked along the busy coast road for a few hundred metres with the sea on our left until we came to a series of houses built into the cliff itself. We climbed the few stone steps carved out of the bedrock and knocked on a gaily-painted door. This was opened by one of the fattest ladies I have ever seen. She clearly recognized Michael (most people did) for she invited us in with a broad smile and words of welcome. Having listened to a litany of her medical complaints and news of her far-flung family, Michael asked to see the *galleria*. Our hostess waved a podgy arm in the direction of the back wall on which hung a large purple velvet curtain. Moving it to one side revealed a dark passageway leading downwards and to the right, deeper into the hillside. From the hidden depths wafted a warm, damp current of air. Armed with torches we started to descend. As we descended, treading slowly and carefully, the temperature rose markedly and the air became ever more humid. Eventually we arrived at the end of the passage, or at least the end as far as we were concerned for here the passageway was flooded. In the yellowish, artificial light of our torches the water looked dark and forbidding with wraithlike tendrils of steam writhing above the flat-calm surface. I almost expected Charon to appear with his boat; could I also hear the barking of the many-headed Cerberus or was my imagination running riot? I was persuaded to put my hand in the water; it was hot! As we made our way back to the light of day, Michael explained that this heat provided free central heating for the lady of the house. In the winter proper the curtain was pulled back and the natural heat flowed into the house. In the summer the curtain and a dresser were placed over the passage opening and another vent was opened to the outside world, allowing the unneeded hot air to add to global warming. Back inside the house, and now absolutely dripping with sweat, we gratefully accepted the offer of a long, cold drink. Suitably refreshed, we took our leave and returned to the outside world.

12

COMMAND POST EXERCISES

The Stoves of Nero were not my only experience of cave-like dwelling; my job also involved periods of subterranean activity – during Command Post Exercises (CPXs). In these war games NATO commanders and HQ staffs came closest to planning and conducting actual war, albeit on paper, for in Livexes we knew where the enemy were whereas in CPXs we didn't. As we've seen Livexes involved real forces but there were no real casualties. In CPXs, on the other hand, the paper forces acted as they would in wartime and both Blue and Orange 'simulated' losses occurred as decided by the ever-vigilant Directing Staff. For those of us in the Southern Region the other major difference was that Livexes were controlled from our peacetime locations while CPXs were fought from our war headquarters. This establishment, known as 'Proto', was located deep in a mountain some 35 miles north west of Naples and had been constructed by the Germans in World War II. My first experience will give you a flavour of what it was like, and what it would have been like if war had broken out.

The exercises were run on a two-shift system, each shift running from eight o'clock to eight o'clock. My first shift began at 0800 hours and, as parking at Proto was almost non-existent, we were obliged to travel to and fro by bus, an hour's journey in each direction. This necessitated my catching the transport at the gate of the *parco* at 0630 hours, not my favourite time of day. Dawn was casting a faint rosy glow over the countryside as the bus arrived, on time, and we set off along Domitian's road towards Rome. We crossed the River Volturno and headed towards Mondragone but, just before reaching this town, we left the main road and with mountains on our left headed inland. The road became narrower, skirting the 2,500-foot Monte Massico, the highest point on the ridge within which lay our destination. We passed through the sad-looking villages of Falciano del Massico and Casanova before finally turning into the mountains, joining a rural track and bumping our way upward. On our right was a creeper-covered cliff; on our left a chasm with cars parked dangerously close to the edge. These belonged to the unfortunate few whose lot it was to work at the war-HQ full-time.

Somewhat sleepily we disembarked and made our way through the security fence, our passes given a desultory glance by the *carabinieri* on duty. An apocryphal tale told of one officer, having forgotten his identity card, waving a piece of toast at the guard and being ushered through! Once through security we entered a seemingly endless tunnel heading into the heart of the mountain. Illumination was faint and footfalls and muted conversations echoed around the bare, damp walls as we moved deeper and deeper into the earth – more like a band of miners than military personnel. After ten minutes or so we came to the work, domestic and accommodation spaces. These were laid out as a series of two-storey tunnels leading off at right angles to the approach tunnel. Submariners must have been in their element in the cramped, artificially lit rooms, unadorned except for numerous pipes and electric fittings. In addition, the residual odour of countless years of unwashed humanity and the all-pervading hum of the air-conditioning system must have felt like home-from-home to those whose careers took them below the sea. Believe it or not, even some non-naval personnel revelled in the atmosphere, chief among them being our old friend, General Parodi Dandini, who stayed happily within the HQ complex for the entire exercise.

The MARAIRMED office was located adjacent to that of the submariners of the Commander Allied Submarine Forces Mediterranean, COMSUBMED, and was identical to the many other operational cells within the complex. As I entered I noticed that the various display boards – all chinagraph and plastic models –

still reflected the end game of the previous exercise held there almost one year ago. I later learnt that, at the announcement of the end of the exercise – ENDEX in NATO parlance – everyone rushed out to catch the first bus back to civilisation; there was no desire to tidy up the operations boards. This brought to mind a visit I had paid to the caves of Gibraltar. Hidden deep in that famous Rock I found status boards that still held information from the last days of WWII.

Cocooned in our unreal world we fought, what was to us, a real war. The changing situation was passed to us through the medium of message traffic from the participating forces, an endless stream of paper containing, amongst other things, all the information we needed to plot the progress of ships and submarines, friend and foe alike. This information allowed us to place our maritime patrol aircraft most effectively. Highlight of the watch was involvement in one of the twice-daily operations briefings. Preparation for this event occupied us for much of the watch period and involved interpreting the intelligence inputs we received and determining the best future use of the assets under our control.

The briefing was held in the Blue Surface Operations Room, larger than ours but with the same low-tech display boards. There were, however, Wrens to do the plotting – a considerable visual improvement on our RAF corporals and ITAF warrant officers. The senior maritime patrol aircraft representative joined the naval hierarchy on a 'bridge' overlooking the operations floor while the MPA Duty Officer presented the relevant portion of the briefing. NATO briefings were – and probably still are – very formal and formulaic: weather, oceanography, intelligence on Orange surface and sub-surface units, Blue surface operations, Blue sub-surface operations, Blue MPA operations and, finally, an overall assessment as to how we were doing.

The fun part, however, came after the main briefing when the Duty Admiral consulted his team of advisers as to the future deployment of maritime forces; often a lively discussion ensued, although we aviators almost always came out unscathed as naval officers rarely understood the nuances of MPA operations. The most entertaining of these admirals was Admiral Kecici of the Turkish Navy. He invariably worked himself up into a frenzy, raising his voice to gale force levels and waving a metal pointer like an Ottoman pirate of old. He was great value. Whatever decisions were reached at our briefing were communicated to the C-in-C at his own briefing, held in another part of the complex. The format there followed the familiar sequence, but with land and air force elements included. Prominent at all these briefings was our old friend, General Parodi Dandini, who lived, worked and breathed the exercise from beginning to end.

As you may have imagined, the work was generally tedious, boredom being rarely alleviated by any excitement. Occasionally there would be a power-cut which, entombed as we were under millions of tons of rock, could be somewhat traumatic. Barring this type of adrenalin-promoting incident, the tedium was alleviated at regular intervals by meals taken in the all-ranks mess, a rather soulless room redolent of a prison canteen. The food was standard US-military: good for Americans but viewed with mixed feelings by other NATO diners. For the British, it was a change; for the Turks and Greeks, a free meal (thus always welcome); for the Italians, such a gastronomic disaster that most of their meals ended up in the waste bin. For those whose duties were less demanding, there was a small cinema. It never failed to surprise me that it was always packed, Italians forming the greater part of the audience. For most people, though, it would be true to say that time did not fly. Occasionally, some wit with time on his hands would produce an authentic-looking document, purportedly from World War II, left by the original German occupants of the tunnels. One example was an instruction from the Chief of Staff, 5th Panzer Division, to his representative in the underground headquarters:

File No. Abwer 206

From: COS 5th Panzer Division   To: Col   S   Pumpernickel

*   Date:].6.43*

1. I view with concern the awful waste of Aryan energy and time in the march to and from the wonderful underground HQ to the billets.

2. It seems to me we should need the bicycles, some]00 in number to be stationed 50 in no. at each end of the tunnel.

3. As the German soldier wears his rifle swuing to the rite across his back and as I expect normal marks of respect with the right hand it is obvious in a curved tunnel and with the right hand to beavailble to shudt rats we must ape the British and drive on the left. Although this is a setback for the civilised world as we know it I believe it acceptable in the circumstances. The FUHRER would approve I think.

4. Bicycles are to be peddled on the balls (Note: This does not translate well. Ed) It wuill of course be necessary to provide tandems for Senior Officers and above, who may steer from the front but may not pedal. Pedals will thus be removed from the front propulsion system. Batmen may be used for chauffer dirties with pistulem mounted.

HEIL HILDA

Gen von Raving

(Translated from original held in the Vatican by Father Tio Pepe)

The oncoming shift was always greeted joyously, heralding as it did escape from the troglodyte existence of the previous 12 hours. For the lucky few, departure followed immediately on the arrival of their relief; for others there was a handover to conduct. The implication of this staggered departure was significant. The first buses departed for home about 20 minutes after the arrival of the oncoming shift; subsequent departures depended on the bus being full, and this could involve an additional 30-minute wait. For those on a two-watch system – 12 hours on, 12 hours off – any delay cut into the already short time between shifts, the total journey time to and from the site being around three hours. I was unlucky; I always had to do a handover. Like most others, I walked more quickly out of the mountain than I did into it, not that it did me much good: 'Sod's law' operated on my shift – no matter when I emerged into the fresh air, a bus had just departed and I had to wait for the next one to fill up.

Day after day, shift after shift, the exercise progressed. For those of us inside the mountain, little changed except the movement of ship markers on the display boards indicating the progress of the exercise. Eventually, though, the final day arrived but although the day was known, the time was not. So an air of eager anticipation reigned as we awaited the official ENDEX message and permission to depart. When this came there was no careful storing of magnetic board markers, no erasing of the final patrol areas and intelligence information, no tidying of desks nor work spaces; everyone made a more or less undignified dash for the escape tunnel and the earliest bus out of the site back to the sunshine and normality for another year.

Not long after I left Naples Proto was deemed to be in a dangerous condition, as it had been for years, and was closed – for good.

13

UNDERGROUND AGAIN

At the time I had thought that the descent near the Stoves of Nero would be the ultimate in subterranean adventure. But it was not! Several months later my son and I were to visit the ancient Roman residential spa of Baia, a resort where Roman writers said that *'men who possessed half a province elsewhere, contended here for a single acre'*. The site was in a ruinous state but sufficient remained to testify to the veracity of this statement.

The resort occupies a series of terraces overlooking the Bay of Baia – and, unfortunately, rusting hulks and an untidy shipyard – with bathing suites, ornate fountains, rich residential suites, shaded porticoes, intimate recreation areas and a variety of shops all linked by impressive marble staircases. On the bottom terrace is a grand, open-air swimming pool with a number of mosaic-decorated niches opening into the sides. Despite the ravages of time and weather, traces of decoration bear witness to the original opulence of the complex: floor, wall and ceiling mosaics; frescoed walls; intricate stucco work; and rich, coloured marble from across the empire merely hint at the conspicuous wealth which was once here displayed. However, the most imposing extant features are three enormous domed buildings, known as 'temples' but which are, in fact, thermal baths. The most complete is known as the 'Temple of Mercury', a large circular hall covered by a cupola with inset windows and a circular hole in the centre. The structure has many similarities with the Pantheon in Rome but may be earlier in date. It does have one major difference, though; unlike the Pantheon it houses a warm water pool fed from deep inside the still-active volcanic hillside. Next to this impressive Roman survival is a wonder of nature: a fig tree that grows upside down from the roof of another thermal building!

On the day in question my son and I explored every nook and cranny of the site, which, as always in those days, was otherwise deserted. We eventually reached the farthest corner of the site where our progress was temporarily halted by a rickety wooden barrier. Remembering my encounter with the local youths at Cuma I ignored the implied bar to entry and we both climbed over and found ourselves in what originally would have been a porticoed courtyard – something like the cloister of a monastery, but on a smaller scale. At the far side were the ruins of a building of different construction to the rest of the site; with its large stone blocks it was more Greek than Roman. Investigating more closely, we discovered that there was a narrow, overgrown stone-lined trench about six-feet deep running from the foundations of the building to the hill forming the backdrop to the site. We carefully lowered ourselves down. As we moved towards the far end of the trench we could see that it was curtained by a profusion of vegetation, an exotic green curtain that hid what, if anything, lay behind. We moved the greenery to one side – and revealed the entrance to a tunnel about six feet in height and less than two feet wide. Bathed in bright sunlight as we were this opening looked ominously black, uninviting and smelt of – well, antiquity is the best description I can give. As luck would have it, I did have a torch with me, albeit a rather meagre key-ring affair. Not without a considerable degree of trepidation, we entered; neither of us, we admitted later, would have done this alone!

Once our eyes had got used to a darkness that was but feebly illuminated by the torch we could see that the tunnel was not only well constructed but also was in remarkable condition given its age and despite the regular seismic activity in the area. We noted, too, many lamp niches – far more than would have been necessary merely to illuminate a service tunnel. The darkness was made more threatening by the presence of giant mosquitoes and other strange insects swaying gently from the smooth, curved roof just above our heads. As we moved slowly further into the hillside the darkness grew more intense, almost tangible in fact. Reality was fast becoming myth and our courage almost deserted us, but we persevered. After one hundred metres or so the tunnel, which had been more or less level, suddenly angled steeply down. The roof here was made of roof tiles, angled to form a ridge. The air was becoming hotter and more humid; our breathing was more laboured. Should we turn back?

Having penetrated this far, curiosity overcame common sense; we continued downwards. Another 50 metres or so further on, the tunnel was flooded with dark, steaming water. Was this perhaps the fabled Styx and the end of our adventure? No, it was not! On the right at the water's edge was a small opening. Crouching low, we entered and found a sort of spiral stairway that brought us out over the top of the flooded tunnel which we could see below through a hole in the floor. Just ahead, the tunnel split and, at the junction, we could see a small aedicule carved into the back wall. Nervously I edged towards the junction and cautiously peered around the corner. A seemingly huge winged creature flew at me – and I let out a cry. Behind me my son straightened involuntarily, banging his head on the roof as his six-foot-two frame was constrained by the six-foot tunnel! In fact, the creature was only a bat, given added stature and presence by the highly charged atmosphere of this ancient place. Having overcome this shock and with our heartbeats back to normal we continued our investigation. To the right the tunnel ran for only a few yards before being completely blocked with soil; to the left the tunnel extended quite a way before it, too, was blocked, but only to within a couple of feet of the roof. We could go no further on this occasion and, not without some relief, we retraced our steps – my son refusing to take up the rear. In the fading illumination of the torch we travelled out rather faster than we went in. Fresh air and sunlight were never more appreciated.

But the tunnel exerted a strange attraction and I returned on several occasions. On one I was pleased to repay Michael Karris, my guide to the Stoves of Nero, with a visit to a place he had not discovered. This time Michael had with him a young student from Rome whose anxious expression as we stood at the entrance was a foretaste of what was to come. Pulling the verdant curtain aside we entered the darkness of the tunnel and headed into the mountain. As daylight faded behind us strange ghostly shadows appeared, dancing on the walls and roof in the light of our torches as if leading us into the Underworld. Suddenly the young lady gave a scream and would have collapsed had Michael not caught her. We had to more or less carry her out of the tunnel and on reaching the outside world it was clear that she had suffered an extreme case of claustrophobia. We did not go back in.

Despite this rather unnerving experience I was determined to learn more of this fascinating underground complex. In particular I thought it would be interesting to explore the partially blocked tunnel I'd seen previously. So, on one Saturday morning, my friend Dick Barnum and I, equipped with torches, overalls and dust masks entered the complex, excitement battling trepidation for ascendancy. Having climbed the steps to the area above the flooded tunnel we donned overalls and masks and started to crawl, single file, along the narrow confines of the tunnel, soft earth beneath us and solid rock a mere two feet above. It was extremely claustrophobic. After about 20 yards of very slow and dusty progress we came across a junction, one arm of the tunnel branching off to the left, the other carrying straight on. We chose the latter. A few yards further on the tunnel was blocked, but in the left wall was a hole, big enough to crawl through, leading to yet another tunnel at a lower level. I calculated that, although I could go headfirst into this tunnel, the fact that its floor was a good six feet lower down would preclude a return. Not wishing to spend the rest of my days in the underworld, I decided that the time had come to retrace our steps. Dick was of the same opinion; besides which we were both feeling the effects of claustrophobia and the somewhat oppressive atmosphere of what clearly had been some sort of sanctuary to the deities of the Underworld.

As on my first visit return to fresh air and sunshine was never more welcome. I never went back into the complex. However, a little later I mentioned our adventure to the site's head custodian. He was horrified, rattling on about the dangers of tunnel collapse, lack of oxygen and poisonous insects, not to mention the violation of a sacred site. I reassured him that I would not enter the underworld again, whereupon he told me that I was not the first explorer of the complex. That honour was due to a Dr Robert Paget, author of the fascinating book *In the Footsteps of Orpheus*. Dr Paget was a British engineer who retired to Baia in 1960. Using the ancient writers as a guide he became convinced that somewhere in the region was to be found the Entrance to the Underworld, once entered by Orpheus on his poignant mission to recover his wife, Eurydice. Orpheus charmed the grim ferryman, Charon, and the dangerous three-headed watchdog, Cerberus, and was thus able to approach Hades, God of the Underworld. Hades' wife, Persephone, touched by Orpheus' grief persuaded her husband to permit Eurydice to leave. There was, however, one condition: Orpheus must believe that Eurydice was following him and not look back. Needless to say, this being Greek mythology, the anxious Orpheus could not resist looking back – and saw Eurydice slip away from him forever.

After investigating scores of possible holes, Paget, accompanied by his American friend, Keith Jones, happened on to the tunnel system of Baia. They quickly became convinced that this was indeed the entrance they sought and in 1962 they began what turned out to be a comprehensive survey of the complex that Paget named 'The Oracle of the Dead'. The flooded tunnel became the River Styx and in 1965 a US Army colonel, David Lewis, and his son Warren, used scuba gear to explore underwater. There they found two arched tunnels from which very hot water was issuing. Following his mythological instincts Paget named these the Rivers Acheron and Phlegethon. For anyone interested in

Greek mythology, I can thoroughly recommend Paget's book. Sadly, public admission to the complex is, and always has been, forbidden.

As an interesting follow-on, in 2002 Robert Temple wrote *Netherworld: Discovering the Oracle of the Dead and Ancient Techniques of Foretelling the Future*. In the book he describes his excitement at the entrance to the Oracle of the Dead, 'the first person to step foot into the mysterious depths since Paget over forty years ago.' Little did he know! However, unlike me, Temple did have official permission to enter.

But the Oracle of the Dead was not Baia's only secret. On a barely accessible terrace high above the partially excavated site lay a rotting wooden box almost invisible in its cloak of dense vegetation. An American friend had discovered it and wanted to show me its contents. 'You'll be amazed,' he said.

The next day we went to the site and having checked there was no-one around we scrambled up the steep hillside pushing our way through undergrowth that seemed intent on blocking our progress. Eventually we made it and, pushing aside the veil of green, I looked into the box. I gasped – for inside was a larger than life-sized rust-stained marble statue of a naked man. He wore a cloak (*chlamys*) over his left shoulder and a strange conical hat (*pilos*); attached to his right leg was the head of a horse. What was more I recognised him; he was one of the *dioscuri*, either Castor or Pollux. I knew this because I had seen his identical twin in the Naples Archaeological Museum.

It seemed fitting that our twin should join his brother, but how to do this given the inaccessibility of the location? Here the United States Navy came to the rescue. You'll recall that the admiral for whom I worked had three hats, including one that involved control of US naval aircraft in the theatre. Among these was a squadron of heavy lift helicopters. My friend Admiral Hacker had left Naples and had been replaced by Admiral Ort and fortunately he was all in favour of rescuing Castor (or Pollux) from the obscurity of his hidden and inappropriate resting place.

Organising the helicopter lift was not a problem but the authorities wanted it to be flown clear of habitation. Thus the statue was taken to the nearby Aragonese castle of Baia. So far so good; Castor, or Pollux, could be reunited with his brother by road. Simple? No, this was southern Italy. The local authority in which Baia was located insisted that the statue, having been found in the area, should stay in the area, a position disputed by the Naples Museum. To cut a long story short the dispute was finally settled, though after I had left Italy, and the statue is now displayed with his brother in the Naples Archaeological Museum. However, nowhere is the above story recorded.

14

REAL EXERCISES – LIVEXES

I've already talked about CPXs, war games that took us into the unwelcome mountain fastness of Proto. In contrast, exercises involving real units, LIVEXES, were more fun; as I mentioned above in these we knew where Orange units were while in the CPXs we did not. Our job in a LIVEX was to engineer as many interactions between our MPA and the Orange surface and sub-surface units. And, another plus, we operated out of our own offices so no tedious commuting nor living the life of a troglodyte! The basic tasking we of MARAIRMED undertook was similar to that of the CPXs, the difference being that real aircraft were involved. The most capable of our assigned units were the US Navy's P3 Orion aircraft, based on detachment from the USA at Sigonella in Sicily. These were sometimes joined by the similarly equipped Nimrods of the RAF. The Italians operated the less capable Atlantique while the Turkish Navy had to make do with the antiquated S2, a former USN carrier-borne patrol aircraft. For the duration of the exercise in question all these aircraft came under our operational control; in other words we decided when, where and what they would do.

As in the CPXs we worked 12-hour shifts sending and receiving messages, plotting enemy report contacts on our manual plot and dealing with any problems that arose: aircraft unserviceabilities, changes to patrol areas or tasking, and so on. Time generally started to drag after midnight if nothing much was happening and on one occasion this provided an interesting glimpse of Italian life. An Italian Navy NCO of COMSUBMED asked if we, the officers on duty, were hungry. Having replied that we were he asked if sandwiches would be welcome and what fillings we would prefer. We gave him the information but as it was about 1.30am we were puzzled as we knew there were no eating places open anywhere in our area. He then telephoned his mother who lived in Naples and put in an order for sandwiches. Half an hour later he asked the SUBMED duty officer if he could go out for 20 minutes to meet his mother half way between our building and her home. He was given permission and 20 minutes later he returned with a large box of freshly made sandwiches with a variety of fillings. Would this have happened in the UK? I think not.

For many of these exercises I was fortunate enough to accompany some of the aircraft to a deployment base in Turkey, either for the duration of the exercise or to help plan a forthcoming detachment. My main role was to ensure that the visitors did not undermine the rather sensitive NATO position on Greek and Turkish issues. This was easier said than done.

My first experience was on a Nimrod captained by my friend from Cranwell days, Wing Commander Dave Baugh, to the Turkish Air Force base of Antalya. I was picked up at Naples Capodichino Airport and we flew an uneventful transit to the south coast of Turkey. Our arrival at Antalya was uneventful and after only an hour or so looking round the facilities on offer our friendly hosts took us to a splendid restaurant overlooking the Mediterranean where we spent a very pleasant few hours. All seemed to bode well for a successful Nimrod detachment; that is, until I raised the question of flight plans. 'Not necessary,' said the Turkish operations officer. I replied that it was CMAM policy that flight plans be filed for exercise missions. Wing Commander Baugh, who was also the squadron's commanding officer, confirmed that his aircraft would expect to file flight plans. Despite the Turkish officers declaring that there would not be a problem, I thought otherwise. My fears were realised after our take-off from Antalya. Although the Nimrod navigator had filed a flight plan giving our routing and timings for the return flight to Naples, Turkish air traffic control handed us over to a Turkish radar station on the divided island of Cyprus close by. When we called Athens control for onward transit they had not received any flight plan, nor were they pleased that we had been talking to an 'illegal' control unit. Needless to say, the Nimrod detachment never took place; but I had enjoyed a splendid lunch in Antalya.

On another occasion I was required to accompany a USN P-3C crew to Dalaman to carry out a site survey in preparation for a forthcoming exercise. The flight from Naples was uneventful and we were met at Dalaman by a Turkish Air Force officer, Colonel Macit, immaculate in a tailored and pressed flying suit and white silk scarf. He had been assigned as the liaison officer for the survey and for the upcoming detachment and he quickly and efficiently showed us round the base, pointing out the aircraft dispersal area, hangarage, technical and aircrew accommodation, air traffic control, communications facilities and so on. However, the colonel spoke only a few words of English, his most common expression being 'No problem', and as we did not speak Turkish a lot of sign language was used in the hope that all would be arranged as necessary and with 'no problem'.

The facilities available certainly seemed adequate and the people we met, some of whom did speak English, were friendly and appeared keen to help. One outstanding problem, though, was that of domestic accommodation for a detachment total of some 40 personnel. The nearest hotel was in Marmaris, an hour or so away by road, and not a good road at that. This would probably have been unacceptable, but here Colonel Macit proved his worth. After some discussion with the manager of a paper mill located just outside the base, he indicated that the entire detachment could be accommodated in the mill for the princely sum of $5 a night. Although not quite up to Holiday Inn or Marriott standards, the rooms were basic but comfortable and the food we ate for lunch, though we had little idea of what it was – apart from the salad – was tasty and the preparation area clean. In short it looked like an ideal place to stay and also had the advantage of keeping the aircrew from the fleshpots of Marmaris. In Dalaman itself there was nothing, except the mosque; mass tourism had yet to reach this part of Turkey.

By early afternoon our survey was complete and we were taken by bus to Marmaris and installed in the Hotel Marti. En route, though, we stopped at a traditional roadside café with wooden tables and chairs scattered around a shaded courtyard with water channels flowing through, adding a peaceful tinkling sound to an already tranquil atmosphere. Colonel Macit treated us all to a glass of *ayran*, a typical Turkish drink of yoghurt and water. It has quite a distinctive taste and I was embarrassed when some of the Americans spat it out with expressions of distaste. I suppose that, having been reared on burgers and coke, their taste buds had been conditioned. I wondered how they would fare on Turkish food back at the paper mill.

The rooms in the Marti Hotel were very much 5-star standard, as was the food and the extensive facilities that included swimming pools, a private beach and a spa. Servicemen and women don't always have to slum it! Marmaris itself had clearly left its origins as a small fishing village behind and was already a major tourist resort, but not yet an overcrowded one. But I had a particular destination in mind and needed to convince the P3 captain that he should stick to his original departure day, which was not the next day but the one after. Being American, and believing the survey complete, he was all for racing back to Italy. I told him that NATO did not rush things and besides which Colonel Macit had booked us in to the hotel for two nights; it would be discourteous to book out early. Furthermore, we still had to complete the formalities for use of the paper mill. He saw the sense of this and gave up his plan to leave early. In return I told him that I would arrange a trip to the Carian archaeological site of Kounos, a place I had read about but never visited.

The next day our good friend, Colonel Macit, arranged a minibus to take us to the charming village of Dalyan. Now it is a tourist destination, advertised in many of our leading tour company brochures; then it was just a traditional fishing village on the River Mugla. The most noticeable building in the village was the white-painted mosque and the most conspicuous feature the river itself. Although the village was typically Turkish, the cliffs opposite gave a clue as to the antiquity of human habitation in the area. Carved into the cliff-face were a number of elaborate tombs, their massive façades reminding me of Greek temples, a row of columns with a carved pediment above, though they were not entirely Classical in style. I had read that the style was in fact Lycian and dated to the 4th century BC. However, the builders of the tombs and their occupants were not Lycian but Carian; it was in this region that the borders of the kingdoms of Lycia and Caria met. Unfortunately the tombs were not accessible but I knew that behind the grand façades were only small chambers cut into the rock and, of course, these would have been robbed centuries ago. Anyway, our destination today was Kounos.

The only way to reach Kounos was by river so we hired, ridiculously cheaply, one of the colourful fishing boats tied up to the village quay. We set off on the crystal clear waters of the river with the high, tomb-pierced cliffs rising up on our right in contrast to the lush green, tree-covered plain on our left. As we travelled downstream through this dramatic and beautiful scenery towards Kounos we came across large nets set across parts of the river; these, our boatman-cum-fisherman told us, were the source of income for the villagers of Dalyan, the name of which simply means 'fishery'. In ancient times, too, the wealth of nearby Kounos was based on the fishing industry as well as the export of salt and figs. At the time of our visit an income from tourism was still in the future.

A mile or so downstream we came to a wooden landing stage at the edge of a reed bed. We climbed out and made our way along a wooden walkway through the reeds. The ancient writers described the citizens of Kounos as being in poor health and having a greenish complexion. Given our surroundings I suspected that they suffered from malaria, a curse of this part of Europe until recently.

A few minutes' walk brought us to the site of the ancient city itself. Like many sites in Turkey there was not much to inform visitors of what the ruins were. However, the view across the lake and marsh that was once the city's harbour to the blue waters of the Mediterranean and of the surrounding mountains, all under the bluest of blue skies, was in itself well worth the visit. The site was extensive and only partially excavated but some of the buildings were familiar from other places I had visited: a grand theatre, carved out of the hillside in the Greek style; a Roman baths suite; a Byzantine basilica; an agora or forum. On the walled acropolis, high above the main city, was a complex of buildings including the foundations of a temple. After a couple of hours or so my American friends were becoming restless but at least they now knew the correct sequence of Carian – Hellenistic – Roman cultures, something that was beyond them when we had first set foot in Kounos. Regretfully I led the way back to our boat, its owner still patiently awaiting our return, and we enjoyed a pleasant and relaxing cruise back to Dalyan. Here we found a modest bar and enjoyed a cold drink – not *ayran* this time!

On the following day we returned to Dalaman and completed the paperwork for the forthcoming detachment's stay at the paper mill. We said farewell to the helpful Colonel Macit and flew back to Naples.

Some weeks later I boarded another P3 Orion at Naples Capodichino Airport, this time accompanied by one of my subordinates, Lieutenant Commander Resai Calyan of the Turkish Navy. We were to act as NATO liaison officers for the P3 detachment at Dalaman. After landing at Dalaman we taxied to the aircraft dispersal where the familiar figure of Colonel Macit was waiting. Arrival at a foreign base is always a trifle fraught: foreign officials on the ground are not sure whether they should board the aircraft; the crew are not sure whether they should disembark. A standoff usually results. On this occasion I broke the impasse by climbing down the aircraft steps whereupon Colonel Macit saluted smartly – then promptly stepped forward and kissed me on both cheeks! This I was used to, having worked with Turkish officers for some months, but the P3 crew looked as if they would rather stay on board the aircraft. I convinced them that they would not be subjected to the same informal welcome and they finally joined me on the ground. Formalities were quickly completed and we made our way to the paper mill via the base operations room that was to be central to the forthcoming exercise flights. Already on base was a Turkish Navy S2 detachment, also staying at the paper mill. These aircrew were great guys, very friendly and all able to speak English.

You might wonder what use was a NATO liaison officer on these detachments. You may recall that Colonel Macit spoke little English, his usual response to any query being 'No problem'. I quickly learned to watch his face and, after a while, I was able to translate these two words as: 'I don't understand you', or 'There is a problem but I'm not going to admit it', or, occasionally, 'There is not a problem'. However, the main role of a liaison officer was to deal with any NATO-type problems that arose. As soon as the first P3 flight was scheduled, such a problem did arise. The Turkish air traffic authorities would not accept flight plans! The NATO policy for the exercise was that flight plans should be filed with the appropriate authority and this I passed on to the American detachment commander. Eventually, after several flights had been cancelled, a compromise was reached, helped by the fact that the P3s were, for the exercise, under the operational control of Commander Maritime Air Forces Mediterranean. As I mentioned earlier, this officer was also the *national* commander of the P3s and could, therefore, be pragmatic in his approach. The compromise saw the P3 crews hand a flight plan to the Turkish air traffic control personnel who would accept it gracefully, and put it in the bin when the Americans had left. The P3 crew would then refile their flight plan with the Greek airspace controllers when airborne. The Greeks, as usual having elected not to participate in the exercise, complained, but the system, while not exactly conforming to NATO policy, did work.

Another problem concerned the Turkish Navy detachment. The aircrews were keen to fly in support of the US Carrier Battle Group that was operating in the eastern Mediterranean; the Battle Group was the main Blue, i.e. 'friendly', formation in the exercise and the S2s would help protect it from Orange submarines, the 'baddies'. Unfortunately, the Americans did not want the S2s, presumably considering the protection that these aircraft could provide was too limited. This was true, but the whole point of a NATO exercise was to give all those units assigned by nations as much training as possible; it was not a real war. Eventually, after I'd made many telephone calls and sent a stack of messages, the Americans relented and the S2 crews did fly a number of missions.

Before we reached this state of affairs I often visited the Turkish detachment and, on a few occasions was invited to play backgammon, I think the most popular game in Turkey. However, it was soon pointed out to me, very politely, that I was too slow. Watching the rapid move of the counters, without any apparent thought, following the throw of the dice I realised that my carefully considered approach to each move was probably incredibly irritating! After that observation I just watched.

My colleague, Resai, was also very helpful. When not dealing with professional problems we walked around the village of Dalaman. Resai was very religious and often asked if he might go and pray in the local mosque. Before going he always managed to find me a place to sit and drink – soft drinks only, of course – with some of the locals. Unfortunately none of them spoke English but, on his return, Resai would answer their questions about why this foreign officer was in Dalaman, why the American aircraft were flying from the nearby airfield and why we were staying at the paper mill. They seemed quite content with the answers and were certainly very friendly.

The same applied to the workers at the paper mill. They soon accepted our presence among them and, through Resai, I was able to hold conversations with some of them. I learnt that many came from far away and, although paid a pittance by our standards, they considered themselves well off. There was a shop at the mill where they could buy basic commodities – tea, sugar, tobacco etc. – at subsidised prices. When at leisure they sat in the open courtyard under the trees and played backgammon, cards, watched TV, drank tea from small tulip-shaped glasses and smoked the ubiquitous *nargile*, that we call *hookah*, or smoked foul-smelling cigarettes. Meal times were very popular and the food, which was very tasty, was also very cheap; thanks to Resai I even learnt what I was eating. As I noted above, there was not much to do in Dalaman so, on days off duty, Colonel Macit arranged a bus to take crews into Marmaris. I even managed a second trip to Kounos. The Americans all seemed keen to buy Turkish carpets and Marmaris proved to be a happy hunting ground for them and I'm sure that, across the United States, there must be scores of carpets that owe their present position to this NATO exercise. I was sad to leave after our two weeks at the mill but I felt that I had learnt much about the country, something that, as a mere tourist, I would have missed.

On another occasion I attended a Post Exercise Discussion, or PXD, in Ankara. On this occasion I was accompanied by my friend, Lieutenant Commander Serhan Sevim. We first flew down to Sigonella in Sicily where we spent the night before boarding a USN executive-style jet very early the next morning. Poor Serhan had picked up a stomach bug and, as we sat at the end of the runway awaiting clearance to take off, he asked, in a rather plaintive voice: 'Are there any rest room facilities on this aircraft?' There were not; but fortunately he survived the flight, though not without a certain degree of discomfort.

The PXD was a standard event following any of the exercises

and was done to analyse the various events that had taken place in order to learn any lessons. Of course, the exercises were precisely scripted so they were not subjected to the 'fog of war' that would no doubt have arisen had we been involved in a real war. Nevertheless, they were always interesting and on this occasion we assembled in a large theatre to hear how the exercise had gone.

During the breaks between presentations a team of Turkish Navy sailors handed out small glasses of strong, sweet *cay*, tea. By now I had learnt to hold the glass by the rim as *cay* is always served boiling hot. At one of these breaks the sailor handing me a glass dropped it. Immediately one of the Turkish officers berated him in no uncertain terms. I told the officer that no harm had been done, and he calmed down and moved away. The hapless sailor then thanked me – in perfect American spoken with a strong New York accent. He said that without my intervention he would have been in real trouble. When I asked how he spoke 'English' so well he told me that in 'real life' he lived in New York, where he was the manager of a small hotel, and that he was currently doing his National Service in the Turkish Navy. He said that Turkey could be a bureaucratic nightmare but one thing it could always do was to find those who were eligible for conscription, no matter where in the world they might be living.

The PXD over, Serhan took me to a street of, seemingly, a thousand restaurants. Here, he said, men (no women) would come at the end of a working day, drink raki and eat white cheese. This we did and added just about all the parts of a sheep that I wouldn't touch at home and which included the lungs and brain, but fortunately not the eyes. Clearly Serhan's stomach had recovered. Before we ordered our food a small altercation arose. The waiter, having glanced at Serhan, ignored him and asked me, in fractured English, what I wanted. At this Serhan blew up and told the waiter in no uncertain terms that, while I was English, he was Turkish and the waiter should, therefore, address him. The men at the nearby tables nodded their agreement. I felt sorry for the waiter. This small incident should perhaps have forewarned us that the evening might not go as smoothly as we might have wished. Anyway, our unusual but enjoyable meal over, we went to the US Officers' Club where we were to stay the night. Or so I thought. I had a room, but Serhan did not. In fact I had a VIP suite with three bedrooms opening off a central lounge area but there were no other rooms available. It did not seem to present a problem as I only needed one bedroom of the three. However, the manager told me that it was not permitted to have a junior officer staying with a senior. After a heated discussion, which included my request to speak to the Commander-in-Chief Allied Forces Southern Europe (a bit over the top this, but he was our ultimate boss in Naples), the manager relented but asked me to sign a form indicating that Serhan was staying at my request.

The next morning we went to the airport to catch our flight back to Naples. Here another altercation arose. As we were on NATO business we were travelling on NATO Travel Orders. I had no problem going through passport control, but Serhan was held up. Although I was outside the building I could hear raised voices, Serhan's raised more than others. Eventually he emerged, red in the face and muttering, presumably Turkish oaths, under his breath. When he had calmed down he told me that the official on duty had tried to charge him for leaving the country. Apparently this charge was levied on all Turkish nationals to provide funds for housing the poor. Serhan's position was that he was, on this occasion, not a Turkish national leaving the country but a NATO officer on duty. This was finally accepted but not before Serhan had threatened the official concerned, probably with death.

15

NAPLES – THE NEW CITY

Having been well and truly warned off Naples before even leaving the UK I was somewhat reluctant to face the potential dangers to my person so vividly foretold by the Italian family at my farewell dinner. However, I found it impossible to ignore what was, after all, once the capital city of an independent kingdom, a city that was now on my doorstep. Before venturing into the unknown, though, I thought it would be a good idea to learn a little of Naples' history and determine what of interest there was to be seen. And what a complicated and fascinating story I discovered.

According to the Greeks Naples was built on the spot where the siren, Parthenope, was washed ashore after being rejected by the hero Odysseus. More factual archaeological evidence indicates that the city began life as a Greek colony, probably founded by settlers from nearby Cumae following the decisive naval victory over the Etruscans in 474 BC. They named their city after the siren and, thanks to its favourable position on the Bay of Naples, it quickly expanded to such an extent that a new city, *nea polis*, was soon built adjacent to it.

A peaceful future, though, was interrupted by the expansion of Rome whose troops had, in the 4th century BC, moved into Campania and embarked on a war against the Samnites. Naples initially resisted but soon realized that there was more to be gained by surrendering to this new power. As a reward Naples was granted a favourable treaty and, despite now being under Roman control, in language and customs it remained a predominantly Greek city. Unlike most southern Italian cities it did not support Hannibal during the Second Punic War of 218 to 216 BC and was besieged by the Carthaginians for its temerity. In the Social War of 91-88 BC Naples backed Sulla against his rival,

Mario, a decision that led to the sacking of the city. However, it soon recovered and as the *Pax Romana* came into effect Naples prospered once more and was graced with a plethora of Roman public and private buildings.

But all good things come to an end and as elsewhere in their empire Roman authority, at least in the west, gradually weakened. In the 6th century Naples became part of the Byzantine Empire based in distant Constantinople. In fact, it managed to retain much of its independence through to the 8th century when it became an autonomous duchy. It continued its traditional way of life, largely avoiding entanglements with invading Goths and Lombards, until finally falling to the new strongmen of Europe, the Normans, in 1139 when it was absorbed into the Kingdom of Sicily. Norman rule was short-lived as in 1194 the German, Henry VI, son-in-law of the Norman king Roger II, took the throne. This dynasty, called Swabian or Hohenstaufen, ended when Charles I of Anjou, son of King Louis VIII of France, was crowned King of Naples and Sicily in 1266. Then, to consolidate his hold on the crown Charles had the last surviving Hohenstaufen heir, the 16-year old Conradin, beheaded in Naples. Charles ruled his kingdom from Naples, which turned out to be just as well for in 1282 a revolt in Sicily, known to us as the Sicilian Vespers, lost him control of the island and 3,000 Frenchmen their lives. Naples, now the capital of the Angevin kingdom, prospered anew – or at least the aristocracy did – and many spectacular castles, monasteries and churches were built.

Angevin rule ended in 1442 when Alfonso V of Aragon gained the throne, though not without having to defeat a rival with perhaps a better claim – Rene, the son of King Louis II of Naples. Alfonso's main achievement was to reunite the thrones of Naples and Sicily but this reunion did not survive his death in 1458.

In 1503 Naples ceased to be an independent kingdom and was made a colony of Spain. Under the ruling viceroys the city quickly expanded to become the largest in Italy. Not everyone was happy, though, and the imposition of ever-harsher taxation finally resulted in a serious revolt led by a Neapolitan fisherman, Masaniello. The insurrection was partially successful in that the Viceroy acceded to many of the people's demands; however, as an example of how fickle people can be, Masaniello was assassinated by the same people who had previously followed him.

As I quickly learnt, the 18th century was, politically, a complex one for Naples though not necessarily for the citizens who toiled on paying taxes to whoever ruled. Covering this period very briefly, the 1713 Treaty of Utrecht ceded Sicily to the Duke of Savoy while in the following year the Treaty of Rastatt handed the former Spanish territories of Naples, Milan and Sardinia to Austria Then, in 1720, the Austrian king Charles VI, Holy Roman Emperor – you'll probably remember the HRE from school days (it wasn't holy, it wasn't Roman and it wasn't an empire!) – and the Duke of Savoy swapped Sicily for Sardinia. Once again Naples and Sicily were united as the Kingdom of the Two Sicilies. Austrian rule was, though, relatively short-lived as in 1734 the young Charles I of Parma, eldest son of King Philip V of Spain, captured Naples and was crowned king the following year. To add a level of confusion he ruled as Charles VII of Naples and Charles V of Sicily. Thus began the Bourbon period, an era that saw the construction of spectacular buildings such as the Royal Palace, the Palace of Capodimonte, the San Carlo Opera House and the Albergo dei Poveri. Naples became a 'must see' part of the Grand Tour, a city of magnificence – albeit one with a majority, impoverished underclass.

The Bourbons continued their extravagant reign until the arrival of Giuseppe Garibaldi in 1860. After landing in Sicily with a rag-tag army, 'The Thousand', under the watchful eye of Royal Navy warships, he proceeded to defeat the Bourbon army before crossing to the mainland and driving the Bourbon forces out of the kingdom. Later that year he met King Victor Emmanuel II of Sardinia at Teano where he handed over control of the now leaderless Kingdom of Naples. On 17th March 1861 Victor Emmanuel became King of Italy, united for the first time since the 6th century. Following the precedent set by Charles I, V and VII, he did not renumber himself, so the first king of Italy was Victor Emmanuel II.

Following reunification Naples slipped into a serious decline. The densely packed slum areas coupled with a lack of clean drinking water and an inadequate sewerage system led to several outbreaks of cholera; one in 1884 killed more than 14,000 people. And despite the government clearing the slums and improving the sewerage system the city suffered another serious outbreak in 1911.

Under the later Fascist regime a number of public works were constructed: some good, like the Mostra delle Terre d'Oltremare; some bad like the Ilva steelworks we've already encountered just outside the city at Bagnoli, an immense industrial site built on the most beautiful bay in the area.

The Second World War had a devastating effect on Naples. It was the most heavily bombed city in Italy and suffered extensive damage as the Germans retreated under a 'scorched earth' policy; for the unfortunate Neapolitans, starvation was a constant threat. Again Norman Lewis' account of this period in *Naples '44* brings home the real hardships suffered by the people. It took a long time before the city returned to anything approaching normality despite aid from the central government. From 1950 to 1984 large sums of money were poured into the Naples area under the *Cassa per il Mezzogiorno* project. Sadly, the improvements made did not reflect the financial support provided as much of the money was siphoned off by the *Camorra*. The most visible sign of this are the large-scale illegally-built apartment blocks sited in the most unsuitable of locations; the tentacles of the *Camorra* did, and still do, reach into all aspects of Neapolitan life.

Having researched the fascinating history of Naples, one thing struck me above all: the Neapolitans themselves had, since their

Greek foundation, lived under the rule of foreigners. This, as I was to learn, moulded their approach to life and especially their attitude to authority. However, I now felt ready to venture forth into the maelstrom of what my American friends called 'Downtown Naples'.

A first foray into Naples is always traumatic, unless choosing a Sunday afternoon between 2 and 4pm when the city is deserted. As with most cities it was not designed with the motorcar in mind so today it attempts, only partially successfully, to absorb about three times as many vehicles as it can reasonably hope to accommodate. The result is almost permanent chaos and driving there requires nerves of steel, an overt disregard for other road users and a studied indifference to scratches, scrapes and bumps. With these factors in mind I decided, wisely you might think, that my initial trip into Naples would be by train. Fortunately Naples' answer to London Transport's Metropolitan Line, the *Metropolitana*, had its suburban terminus in nearby Pozzuoli. From there it was only about 30 minutes into the centre of Naples. The journey was no more comfortable than on London's Metropolitan Line, but it was far cheaper.

On this first visit I wanted to see the remains of Naples' Greek and Roman origins; the obvious first stop, therefore, was the National Archaeological Museum. This is, without doubt, one of the world's foremost museums of the Classical world containing, as it does, thousands of artefacts – sculpture, mosaics, frescoes, and jewellery as well as valuable and mundane household and everyday items – from the buried sites of Herculaneum, Pompeii, Boscoreale and Stabiae.

The grand building itself started life as a 16th century cavalry barracks, modernised in the 17th century to house Naples University. After the discovery of Herculaneum and then Pompeii the Bourbon King of Naples, Ferdinand IV, decided to found a museum to house the many works of art that were being uncovered. His Royal Bourbon Museum was subsequently opened in 1816 and became the National Archaeological Museum after Italy's reunification in 1861.

My initial half-day in the museum was sufficient only to gain an overall view of the treasures on offer; however, it was but the first of many visits over the next several years.

Coming out of the museum I was faced with a two-way torrent of traffic along the wide, one-way main road in front of the building. And to reach the historic centre of the city I had to cross over! There were traffic lights at the junction with the main road that ran alongside the museum, but not all the traffic stopped when the lights turned red and there was no warning as to when the lights changed to green; besides which, much of the traffic was on the move before the lights changed anyway. I decided to watch the locals as they all seemed to make the crossing without incident. The first lesson was to cross anywhere except at the traffic lights. The second was to step out into the road without making eye contact with any driver. The third was to walk confidently across the road, ideally holding up a rolled newspaper. Believe it or not, it worked!

My next destination was to a place where I could see what remained of the city's Greek walls. This was but a short walk down the Via Santa Maria di Costantinopoli, passing the 16th century Baroque church after which the road is named. Legend has it that, during an outbreak of the plague in 1527, an elderly woman saw a vision of the Virgin Mary who pleaded for a church to be built on the site where her image stood on a wall. The image was identified, the plague was banished and the church was duly built. (Naples is awash with similar stories!) The road was also interesting in that it housed small workshops, many occupying a single barely-lit cave-like room, involved in the restoration of works of art, mainly furniture and paintings. Much of the work was being carried out on the pavement, the workshops themselves full to overflowing with tools of the restorers' trade and objects awaiting attention. In between the workshops were a few *tavola calda* bars, ideal places for a quick snack lunch either standing at the bar – *al banco* – or sitting at a table by the roadside. I remembered that sitting down doubled the price of any food or drink; I opted to lunch *al banco*.

The Greek walls I was seeking were another 300 or so metres down the road in the Piazza Vincenzo Bellini, named after the Italian opera composer. His statue stands on an imposing plinth in the centre of the piazza, which is enclosed by impressive 18th century four-storey *palazzi* with shops at ground floor level and apartments above. Trees give an air of the countryside and a number of cafés nestle in their shade. In one of these I was able to drink a glass of local wine from the slopes of Vesuvius and look down on the excavated Greek walls constructed of large rectangular blocks of stone and now several feet below the modern street level. It was fascinating to sit in the present among the grand buildings of what was once the capital of an independent kingdom and see below me the very origins of the Greco-Roman city. It was this link with the past that impressed me rather than the short stretch of relatively ordinary walls in their rubbish-strewn fenced pit.

Continuing down the road I came to the beginning of the original street grid plan of Greco-Roman Neapolis, here the Via San Sebastiano. The buildings, 4- or 5-storeys high, pressed in on either side of this very narrow street, paved in large blocks of black volcanic stone, squeezing together the many people, cars and motor scooters. To the Americans this was Music Alley, named for the many shops selling musical instruments. Others displayed handbags, shoes, clothes, groceries and everyday items. All were small, independent retailers – no department stores, chain stores nor multi-national businesses here! People expertly sidestepped the steady stream, fortunately one-way, of cars and motor scooters, occasionally taking refuge in one of the many bars. Multi-coloured washing hanging from upper floor balconies added an air of gaiety to what was a very vibrant and lively scene.

At the end of Via San Sebastiano the street became the Via Santa Chiara after crossing the Via Benedetto Croce (a very religious part of Naples, this) otherwise known as *Spaccanapoli*, 'Naples Splitter', so called because it cuts through the heart of the ancient historical centre of the city. Originally this was the *decumanus inferiore*, one of three main east-west streets of the Greco-Roman city of Neapolis; it was, and still is, linked to the *decumanus magggiore* (now the Via dei Tribunali) and the *decumanus superiore* (now the Via Anticaglia and Via della Sapienza) by a number of lesser north-south *cardini*. This system of *decumani* and *cardini* gave Neapolis its grid plan layout copied many centuries later by the Americans.

Walking the length of *Spaccanapoli* I counted eight churches, only two of which were open; ten palaces, all seemingly converted into apartments; and a strange statue of a reclining deity that I later learnt represented the River Nile. I also found the *cardo* called Christmas Alley by the Americans as its many shops were almost exclusively given over to the production and sale of Christmas decorations and the structures and figures for the Neapolitan speciality of *presepe* – nativity scenes in which you are as likely to find a pizzeria as you are the Holy Family.

Everywhere was crowded, the people being rather more animated than would be found in a British city; in fact, every conversation appeared to be a heated argument accompanied by much gesturing. I was soon to learn that this was quite normal behaviour in this part of Italy. The men mostly appeared villainous and, given that Naples had a reputation for being the pickpocket capital of Italy if not Europe, I felt somewhat concerned even though the level of actual violence was low. I remembered some advice I had been given before leaving the UK: don't act like a bewildered tourist and blend in as much as possible; don't show off conspicuous wealth; take only sufficient money for your immediate needs; keep any valuables out of site. Ticking these off mentally, I reckoned it would be impossible to blend in as everyone else was shorter, darker and clearly Neapolitan. In contrast I was clearly a northern European and as a Royal Air Force officer did not own any wealth, conspicuous or otherwise; however, my 50,000 lire, although appearing to be a small fortune, was worth only about £25 and was firmly in my front pocket and my wallet was back in my accommodation. I concluded, therefore, that I had done as much as possible and the loss of my 50,000 lire was probably the worst that could happen. In fact, I was to learn that Neapolitans, whether appearing villainous or otherwise, were very kind-hearted and hospitable people.

Another unusual thing that fascinated me was the shouted cries of roving vendors pushing small carts on which were foodstuffs such as fruit, vegetables and bread. Often in response a basket on a rope would be lowered from an upper washing-strewn balcony and goods would be placed in the basket, which would then be hauled back up and returned with a fistful of lire. Clearly the converted palaces were not equipped with lifts.

Having reached the Via dei Tribunali I decided it was time to meet Naples' most famous citizen, San Gennaro, the city's patron saint. He was Bishop of Benevento and you'll recall he was martyred in Pozzuoli around AD 305. I knew that his bones and vials of his blood were housed in the Cathedral of Santa Maria Assunta, a short walk away so off I set. Soon I was standing in front of its impressive gleaming white neo-Gothic façade, 'neo' because it was reconstructed in the 19th century although the church itself was completed in the early 14th century.

On entering I was struck by the length of the nave over which stretched a magnificent gilded coffered ceiling. Aisles on each side were separated from the nave by eight tall Gothic arches. I walked up to the chancel, an apsidal Baroque creation in which stood the High Altar with its shiny white marble sculpture of Mary, her eyes focused on heaven, surrounded by a riot of angels and putti. But I was here to meet Gennaro, not Mary, so I retraced my steps and found the entrance to the saint's chapel in the south aisle. Going through the gilded gates I was faced with the most elaborate Baroque chapel I'd ever seen: all marble; silver statues, sacred vessels and candlesticks; colourful frescoes; religious paintings and a dome with gold-framed paintings. Taking centre-stage was the saint himself, a life-sized bronze statue in an elaborate niche at the rear of the marble altar. Slightly lesser niches housed bronzes of Saints Peter and Paul while Gennaro put in a second appearance in the form of a gold and silver reliquary bust complete with mitre and stole. There was no sign of the vials and I learnt later that they were kept locked in a safe. For the people of Naples the blood is of extreme importance. Normally it is in a solid state but three times a year the Archbishop of Naples reveals it to local and regional dignitaries and thousands of citizens – and tourists – who throng the cathedral in the hope that it will liquefy and thus bring good fortune to the city. The atmosphere is highly charged and many people become ever more hysterical as they await the miracle to occur. Fortunately for Naples it generally does. There is a scientific explanation but not one you should discuss with fervent Neapolitans. The substance in the vials may be thixotropic, a mixture of salts that change from solid to liquid when shaken or stirred. Or, of course, the substance may be San Gennaro's blood.

So overawed was I by the Baroque ostentation that I almost missed the crypt in which San Gennaro's remains lie buried. Descending the steps I found myself in a beautiful space decorated in High Renaissance style, elaborate but not over-the-top Baroque. It had a polychrome marble floor divided into three by eight marble columns with intricate capital while around the walls were carved niches sheltering plain stone tomb chests. And taking pride of place was the life-sized kneeling figure of Cardinal Carafa, who built the chapel in 1497, facing the final resting place of the saint. I was sure he'd approve. What was certain though was the importance San Gennaro was to the people of Naples. As an example, in 1987 Napoli won the Serie A league title for the first time. Celebrations were truly epic and houses, cars and even people were painted the team's colour of blue while across the streets of Naples huge banners were erected picturing on one side the figure of the saint and on the other the face of – Maradona, the star of the team.

Returning to the nave I crossed to the north aisle where there was an entrance to the original 6th century Christian basilica dedicated to Santa Restituta, a lady I was to meet later on the island of Ischia. Entering the church it was clear that probably only the many ancient columns remained of the original church; the decoration was what I would call 'subdued Baroque'. However, through a doorway in the east side of the apse was the oldest baptistery in Europe, dating from the 5th century. In the centre was a shallow stone pool for baptism and in the dome overhead some superb Byzantine-style mosaics: a gold chi-rho set in a starry sky at the apex and finely detailed biblical and pastoral scenes around the inner surface.

I was fascinated by this journey back through time but I hadn't finished, for under the floor of this church were remains from Greek and Roman times, some floors, mosaics and walls. These were interesting but there was one more place where I could see the ancient city as it was originally. To do this I had to find the Basilica of San Lorenzo Maggiore, not difficult to do given the convenient grid pattern of the ancient city. The basilica itself was very interesting, having been built as a convent church in the 13th century for the Franciscans. However, my aim was not medieval Naples on this occasion; I was more interested in what lay beneath the church, which had been built on the site of the Roman *macellum*, the market. Sadly the excavations, although they had been in progress for more than ten years, were not open to the public. (That did not happen until 1992.) However, one of the excavators showed me part of what had been uncovered to date. I had to climb down about 20 feet or so to reach the excavated level and there I stood on the original Roman road surface. In front of me, partially excavated were brick arches, looking as if they had just been built, while on one side were unmistakable frontages of Roman shops. It was a real thrill to find myself right in the Roman marketplace, a part of Naples more than two thousand years older than the streets I had just been walking. There was clearly much more to be uncovered but on this occasion I would have to be content with this brief glimpse into the past.

My mission successfully completed I made my way back to Pozzuoli where my car, remarkably I thought, was exactly where I had left it. Over the next three years I was to revisit Naples many times to see the castles, churches, palaces, and innumerable works of art with which this once capital city, in the 1980s one of decaying grandeur, was endowed.

16

BACK TO SCHOOL

As I've shown, the military organisation of NATO during the Cold War was both extensive and complex. As its structure was invariably discussed in abbreviations and acronyms, there was an attendant problem that no-one outside the Alliance had much of an idea of how it functioned. For those of us newly posted to a NATO position there was, however, a solution to be found at the NATO School, splendidly located in the attractive Bavarian village of Oberammergau, famous for its Passion Play.

The play was first performed in 1634, the result of a vow made by the villagers to act out the Passion of Christ every ten years if only they were spared the effects of the bubonic plague sweeping the region. They were; they did; and they still do! The school lies just outside the main part of the village in the Hotzendorf Kaserne, a German barracks built in 1935. During the Second World War the site was occupied by the Messerschmitt Company, which carried out rocket engine development in a complex of tunnels and caves dug into the mountain behind the barracks. The site was taken over by soldiers of the US Army as they advanced through southern Germany in 1945. In the post-war years several US Army training units occupied the Kaserne, including the Special Weapons School. Then, in 1953, the then SACEUR directed that this school was to teach two courses on strategy and conventional and nuclear weapon development to allied officers and senior civilians. In 1972 the unit became the NATO Weapons Systems School and three years later it was granted a NATO charter to become the NATO School (SHAPE). One of the school's 'bread and butter' courses was, and presumably still is, the NATO Orientation Course, a week's immersion in the complexities of NATO's command structure and its Transition to War procedures, which I discussed above.

A few weeks after arriving in Naples I was nominated for one of the courses. Having worked in a joint national/NATO headquarters back in the UK I was fairly familiar with the intricacies of the Alliance – but who would pass up an all-expenses-paid week in one of Bavaria's most attractive villages? Furthermore, being NATO, it was generally accepted that wives would accompany their husbands (no 'partners' in those days!); indeed, a separate – and, dare I say it – more interesting programme was arranged for spouses.

So one Saturday Monica and I took to the A1 *autostrada*, European route E45, and headed north for the first leg of our one thousand-kilometre journey. We planned to stop the first night at the Hotel Motelagip at Modena, just over half way to Oberammergau. Unlike British motorways the A1 was not especially busy, apart from the *Grande Raccordo Anulare*, the ring road around Rome, which brought back memories of the M25. The other difference was that we had to pay to use the *autostrada*. Motorway driving is generally somewhat monotonous, and this part of the journey was no great exception. However, it was interesting to see the varied scenery, ranging from the flat Campanian plain at first to the more mountainous region of the northern Apennines with its countless tunnels. We also had the chance to admire the impressive Abbey of Monte Cassino, poised majestically almost two thousand feet above the plain. Further north we passed the ancient Etruscan city of Orvieto, perched snugly on a hilltop like many Tuscan towns, its magnificent 14th century cathedral silhouetted against the deep blue western sky. After about five hours we arrived at the hotel, conveniently positioned right on the *autostrada*. The receptionist even found a member of staff to open our car after I had managed to lock it with the keys inside. He did this so expertly it crossed my mind that, perhaps, this was a skill known to all Italians.

After a splendid meal in the self-service restaurant, a good night's sleep and a reasonable (for Italy) breakfast we were ready for the second leg of our journey. Just beyond the hotel we turned north onto the A22 towards Austria. As on the previous day the first few miles were across a plain, this time of the River Po. The scenery was reminiscent of northern France. Ahead we could see the impressively high barrier of the Dolomites and the Alps, a barrier we would penetrate by way of the Brenner Pass. After we had skirted Verona we began to climb, following the Adige River.

Soon we were really in the mountains as we passed Trento, then Bolzano. We noticed that the architecture here was more Alpine than Italian, not surprising really as this region, South Tyrol, was part of Austria until 1919. In fact we found, on stopping for fuel (half price with our NATO coupons) and a coffee, that the people spoke German. Also, we noticed that the towns and villages were named in both Italian and German, for example: Bolzano/Bozen; Vipiteno/Sterzing.

Continuing onwards and upwards the road became ever more hemmed in by the mountains. Every so often an impregnable looking, and clearly still occupied, castle loomed above us, guardian of this important route. Finally, at a height of 4,495 feet, we reached the border where Italian and Austrian officials quickly completed formalities, just a quick glance at our passports. Still on the E45, but now on the Austrian A13, we passed the frozen Brennersee and continued towards Innsbruck, now travelling downhill. As we neared the city we were amazed by the *Europabrücke*, which carried the six-lane *autobahn* on slender concrete pillars 623 feet above the River Sill. It is an engineering masterpiece but was incredibly difficult and dangerous to build, so much so that 20 workers and three of its engineers lost their lives during construction.

Descending towards Innsbruck we passed close to the Bergisel ski jump and then turned westwards along the Inntal autobahn around the city before turning towards Seefeld. Just beyond the small village of Zirl we were faced with perhaps the steepest gradient with which I have ever been faced, my confidence not helped by the number of gravel emergency run-off traps on the downhill side of the road. Fortunately the ascent was uneventful, largely because we did not have to face any runaway vehicles hurtling downhill. Thereafter the road ran through pleasant alpine scenery past the ski resort of Seefeld and on to the next border crossing, into Germany, at Schamitz. Again, formalities were minimal and we continued through wooded countryside and the town of Mittenwald, famous for the manufacture of violins, and on to Garmisch-Partenkirchen. Garmisch and Partenkirchen were originally separate villages either side of the River Partnach but were forced, by Hitler, to unite in time for the 1936 Winter Olympics. It remains united, a neat and pleasant town with many alpine-style buildings decorated with colourful frescoes. Just to the south lies the impressive Zugspitze, at nearly 10,000 feet Germany's highest mountain. Leaving Garmisch-Partenkirchen behind (avoid referring to the town as 'Garmisch' – it really upsets the residents of Partenkirchen!) we continued on the main road to Oberau where we branched off for another steep climb to Ettal with its famous monastery and, finally, after a four and a half hour drive, to Oberammergau itself.

The town, nestling at the foot of the Alps by the River Ammer, is chocolate-box pretty, many of its alpine-style houses adorned with colourful frescoes, known as *Lüftlmalerei*, depicting religious scenes, fairy tales or fascinating *trompe l'oeil* architectural detail. Strangely, the only ugly structure is the Passionspielhaus, the Passion Play Theatre, a sombre but functional building in which the famous Passion Play is performed every ten years; its interior resembles a massive hangar with a stage at one end actually open to the sky. Towering above the town is the 5,500 foot Laberberg with its cable car for those who wish to view the town from on high or to chance their arm – or leg – on the black ski run from its summit. On the other side of the Ammer Valley stands the impressive and craggy cone of the 4,400 foot high Kofel, the subject of many postcards.

We had chosen to stay at a bed-and-breakfast establishment run by Frau and Herr Kuschmierz, Wilhelm and Martha, whom we'd met on our first visit to Oberammergau when I'd completed a Nuclear Weapons course in my previous job. Actually it was Martha who ran the business, her guests being almost exclusively NATO officers. She was a big woman with a jolly face and a very friendly personality. Wilhelm was a compact, rather taciturn man who, unlike his wife, spoke no English but invariably wanted to talk about the world's political situation, something of a trial given that my German was not extensive. Martha and Wilhelm were not Bavarian but Prussians from Königsberg and had a remarkable tale to tell of how they came to be in Oberammergau.

Towards the end of the Second World War Wilhelm had been in the German Army fighting in the Italian campaign as the Germans retreated northwards. At the end of the war, thankful to have survived, he began working for the Americans in Garmisch-Partenkirchen. Martha had remained in Königsberg with their young son. Then, with the Russians advancing on the city, she joined the terrified population in attempting to flee by the only safe route – the sea. In fact Admiral Doenitz had implemented Operation Hannibal in January 1945 to evacuate both military and civilian personnel from what was then East Prussia. The evacuation was largely successful in that over one million made it to safety. However, Martha and her son were extremely lucky to miss, by just a few people, places on the passenger ship, *Wilhelm Gustloff*; this was torpedoed by a Russian submarine shortly after sailing and over 7,000 passengers died. Fortunately Martha was able to board a small freighter that sailed as the city, or what was left of it, fell to the Russians. She landed in Denmark where she spent many months while she sought information on Wilhelm: was he still alive and, if so, where was he? She eventually learnt that he was in Garmisch-Partenkirchen so she travelled the length of Germany to join him. They could not return home, of course, because Königsberg had become Kaliningrad and was part of Russia. So, they settled in Oberammergau.

Staying with Martha and Wilhelm was always great fun – we returned on many occasions – once we had survived Martha's welcome feast, that is. A key element of this was a glass of *'Gesundheitschnapps'*, Martha's speciality cure for all ills consisting of schnapps in which a whole bulb of crushed garlic had been steeped for several weeks. Drinking a glass of this was mandatory for all new arrivals and it was accompanied by numerous slices of home-made cakes and many cups of coffee – whether you wanted them or not.

Having settled in to our accommodation it was time to check-in at the nearby NATO Club where both Monica and I were given details of our respective week's programmes: a series of lectures for me; a number of outings for Monica.

Apart from the lectures, which proved to be interesting if not exactly exciting, there was plenty of time to meet fellow student officers from all NATO nations. The school coffee bar was a great informal meeting place and there was a more formal cocktail party on the first evening held in the well-appointed NATO Club. In addition, Wednesday afternoon was set aside for an outing into the nearby countryside for all of us, husbands and wives (I should add that, in the 1980s, female students were exceedingly rare and 'partners' had not been invented). Our trip was to the Palace of Linderhof, built by the Bavarian king, Ludwig II, patron of Wagner.

King Ludwig ruled from 1864 to 1886 when he was deposed on the grounds of mental illness. In fact, Ludwig was more eccentric than mad. He was only 19 when he succeeded his father and he quickly became popular with the Bavarian people, though not with his ministers as he took little interest in affairs of state and, whenever he could, avoided any formal function. In his early 20s Ludwig became engaged to Duchess Sophie, the sister of his childhood friend, the Austrian Empress Elizabeth. However, he cancelled the engagement after a few months and spent the rest of his life a rather lonely and reclusive bachelor, spending much of his time and money on the construction of a number of castles. In fact although the German word *Schloss* translates as 'castle' most of Ludwig's buildings would more properly be called 'palaces'. He was greatly taken with the works of Wagner, whom he met on a number of occasions, and evidence of this can be seen in the decoration of these 'castles'.

Sadly, Ludwig's behaviour led to a self-seeking group of courtiers and ministers having him declared insane so that they could depose him and install his uncle, Prince Luitpold, in his place. Ludwig was then placed under 'house arrest' in Schloss Berg, a castle on the shores of the Starnbergsee south of Munich. There followed a real murder mystery that has not been solved to this day!

One storm-threatened afternoon shortly after his confinement Ludwig asked one of the doctors who had declared him insane to accompany him on a walk in the castle grounds. They never returned. As night fell, a search party set out, their search not helped by the storm-force winds and heavy rain. Later that night the bodies of both men were found in the Starnbergsee lying in the shallows. Ludwig's death was recorded as suicide by drowning but, as he was a strong swimmer, this is unlikely. Furthermore, there were clear signs that his companion had been strangled. Could Ludwig have sought revenge for his unjust and cruel treatment and lost his own life in a fierce struggle? We'll never know. A simple cross now rests in the lake marking the spot where Ludwig's body was discovered.

But, to return to Schloss Linderhof. The palace is the smallest of the three built by Ludwig and the only one to be completed in his lifetime. It has a very flamboyant rococo façade overlooking a large ornamental lake with a gilt fountain in the centre, while to the rear of the building is a marble cascade with a Neptune fountain at the foot. The interior is very ornate, although we found the overall atmosphere surprisingly intimate. Strangely only four of the rooms appeared to have any real purpose. Of particular interest was the dining room. When Ludwig dined, always alone, the dining table was raised from the floor below laden with food and drink, with four place settings. Our guide told us that Ludwig liked to converse with people such as Louis XIV or Marie Antoinette, imagining that they were his guests. Mad or eccentric? In the grounds we found Wagnerian references in the artificial Venus Grotto designed to reflect Wagner's opera *Tannhäuser*. Within this remarkable cavern Ludwig liked to be rowed on its lake in a golden boat shaped like a swan while the grotto was bathed in light of changing colours. It must have been an extraordinary experience but, poignantly, apart from his oarsmen, Ludwig was always alone.

On later visits to the NATO School I was able to visit Ludwig's other 'castles', Herrenchiemsee and Neuschwanstein. Herrenchiemsee was intended to be a copy of Louis XIV's Palace of Versailles and, as you might have guessed, was built on Herren Island in the Chiemsee, Germany's largest lake, close to the Austrian border and Salzburg. Although the castle was never finished, the part that was built was both impressive in size and extravagantly decorated; for example, the one hundred yard long Hall of Mirrors, a riot of glass and gold, is longer than Louis' original. Given the level of decorative opulence, it is little wonder that Ludwig ran out of money.

Schloss Neuschwanstein, 'New Stone Swan Castle', is a tremendously impressive landmark that actually looks like a castle, and a familiar one at that as Walt Disney used it as the inspiration for the Sleeping Beauty castles we see on every visit to Disneyworld or to a Disney film. Like Herrenchiemsee, this castle was not finished in Ludwig's lifetime despite building work ongoing for more than 20 years. Had it been completed it would have had over 200 rooms; as it is, only about 15 or so were finished, the largest, known as the Hall of the Singers, being expansively decorated with themes from Wagner's *Lohengrin* and *Parsifal*.

Speaking of later visits one in particular stands out in my memory. We had decided to visit Venice on our way back to Naples and, not wishing to leave our car in the multi-storey car park just outside Venice, we had chosen to stay on the mainland in a small hotel in Mestre with secure – we thought – parking. The town is unattractive, modern and busy but a bus service connects it to Venice across the two and a half mile long *Ponte della Libertà*. The hotel was clean and comfortable and we enjoyed excellent seafood pasta and a bottle of local prosecco before retiring for the night. The next morning we made our way to the bus stop for our trip across the lagoon secure in the knowledge that our car was safely behind the locked gates of the hotel garden. We'd been to Venice before so we avoided the touristy places and wandered around the side streets, climbing aboard one of the *vaporetti* whenever we felt tired.

Several hours later back at the hotel we enjoyed another splendid meal; this time the highlight was *risotto nero* the black colour coming from cuttlefish ink. It's fair to say it tasted better than it looked. An early night was called for after our energetic day and we were both asleep as soon as our heads hit the pillow.

In the early hours I was awakened by my wife shaking me and telling me that something was going on somewhere in the hotel. I assumed it was just noisy visitors arriving back late and told her to go to sleep. Wives, of course, are always more curious than husbands so she had to go and see what was happening.

'THE HOTEL IS ON FIRE!' she shouted a moment or two later. That energised me. I leapt out of bed and ran to the door. Looking down the corridor I could see flames shooting up past the window at the end – but they were outside not inside. I ran to the window and looked out. To my horror I saw that the flames were coming from our car but as I watched I almost felt the explosive whoosh as the adjacent vehicle also went up in flames. Now there was an even more impressive column of fire and the window started to melt. Stopping only to grab a dressing gown, and my camera, I fled downstairs and out into the road. Despite the hour a goodly crowd soon gathered, probably alerted by the always-dramatic noise of an arriving fire engine. The crew quickly and efficiently started to tackle the blaze; sadly this involved smashing the car windows and sticking a hose through to fill the vehicles with foam. I took a couple of photographs – for insurance purposes – and watched dejectedly as our best car quickly became a burnt-out wreck. When the last embers had been extinguished one of the firemen came over and told me: *'Questo incendio è stato avviato deliberatamente!'* So, the fire had been started deliberately. But who would want to set fire to a three-year-old Renault 20 in the locked car park of a hotel?

The reason was not too difficult to deduce. The Americans had just bombed Libya, an unpopular action among many Italians especially the young and our car had AFI number plates. These signified that the owner was a member of Allied Forces Italy but it was a common misconception that the letters stood for *American* Forces Italy. Annoyingly the arsonists had failed to notice the small Union Jack I'd stuck on the plates. I took a couple of photographs and we went back to bed for the second part of the night.

I was convinced the owner of the hotel would want us to leave the following morning especially as the other torched car was his wife's brand new mini. But no! At breakfast he asked how we were feeling and told us he'd arranged a special private lunch. He also said he'd help us book train tickets for our return to Naples. He winced when he mentioned Naples and explained that he never took bookings from Neapolitans. He had done once and the family, having booked a double room, arrived with five people and when they departed so did all the fittings from their room, including the TV. The story reminded us of the warnings we'd received back in the UK before we left for Italy.

Before we could make any travel arrangements a couple of *carabinieri* officers arrived to interview us. Having explained our reason for being in Mestre I told them that I was a NATO officer serving in the Allied Forces HQ in Naples. This seemed to cause some concern for they then asked us to accompany them to their HQ to make a formal written statement. There followed an interesting ride in their smart Alfa Romeo with blue lights flashing and siren wailing. Not strictly necessary, I thought, but fun. A few minutes later we pulled over and one of the officers climbed out and went into a tobacconist's – to buy cigarettes, I guessed. Wrong! This was to obtain the official form required for our statement. Five minutes fun driving later we arrived at the HQ and completed the formalities. As NATO was indirectly involved the Italian authorities were clearly treating the matter seriously. We had to ask for a lift back to the hotel though.

Before going into the hotel I went to look at the car. It was a sorry sight as burnt-out cars always are. But to my surprise the associated legal documents required to be kept in the car had survived the conflagration; they were behind the glare shield, scorched but still legible. I pocketed these and also unscrewed the number plates, evidence for a subsequent insurance claim.

As promised the owner had arranged lunch with him and his wife, and very good it was too. Half way through I received a telephone call from ACI. I assumed this was the *Automobile Club d'Italia* of which I was a member and which might arrange to collect my ruined vehicle. However, the questions seemed a little suspicious to me: 'Were you followed?' 'Did you mention NATO to anyone?' So I asked the questioner to confirm my assumption. 'No sir. This is Allied Counter Intelligence,' came the reply. The outcome was that they would arrange to have my car taken from the hotel to the nearby US/NATO base of Vicenza. One problem solved.

After lunch we went to Metre railway station where I was able to purchase tickets for our return trip. Back at the hotel I telephoned my friend Dick Barnum of underground Baia fame and he agreed to meet us on our arrival in Naples.

The following day we took the train and seven hours later we were in Naples. On the drive home Dick told us that the story of our incident had preceded us – except that it told how our car had been found burnt-out at the side of the *autostrada* with us nowhere to be found! He also told us of his involvement with the fallout from the American bombing of Libya. The following are Dick's own words:

'It was a delightful spring day in April 1986. Having once visited Milan Cathedral without family, and being duly impressed, I wanted to share that experience with my wife, Lynda, and my mother, on our drive back to Naples, Italy after having attended a NATO conference at Mons, Belgium. This was after I had received a speeding ticket on the German Autobahn the previous day.

As we were driving into town, late in the morning, with the windows rolled down, we encountered some traffic which slowed our advance.

"Oh," I exclaimed. "It looks like we're moving along right next to a parade."

"Roll the windows up," Lynda said.

"Why? It's really nice outside."

"Roll the windows up now," Lynda said more forcefully.

About that time I noticed a car next to us which had two painted cardboard missiles attached to the roof and there was music playing. I also noticed some individuals carrying pro-Libya and anti-American signs. This was about a day or two after the United States had launched an airstrike against Libya and we were in the middle of a demonstration. I quickly turned off that road and, not to deny my wife and mother the opportunity to see the Cathedral, I proceeded to the Duomo and parked on a side street. Somewhat begrudgingly, we toured the Duomo and crossed the street to Galleria Vittorio Emanuele II, a shopping mall, to get a cappuccino. As we came out of the Galleria, the protest march was proceeding down the street between us and the Duomo and where I had parked the car. There were lots of groups represented in this march, with flags and signs. We had groups which were 'pro-Libya', 'anti-American', 'anti-NATO', 'Italian Communist Party', and others, all represented.

We were just standing there along with a number of Italian families and businessmen. When I noticed a break between groups approaching, I took my mom's hand and said, "We're going now." Mom and I made it across, but Lynda hesitated, so now Mom and I were on one side of the protest march and Lynda was on the other side, looking displeased. As the next break in the action approached, Lynda positioned herself next to an Italian family with children who were also preparing to cross. When they started across, Lynda moved out, ready to take one of the Italian family's little girl's hand with the thought that, if the marchers attempted to grab her, that little girl was coming too.

As soon as we were clear of the protest, Lynda wanted to know why I had abandoned her. There was a chill in the air as we walked back to the car, despite the day being warm and sunny. Lynda still periodically mentions that day when talking with friends about our time in Italy.'

So two NATO officers and families were inadvertently caught up in a military action, which had nothing to do with NATO *per se*. None of us would forget our experience in a hurry. There was, however, a happy ending: thanks to my recovery of the car's number plates and scorched documents I received a generous insurance pay-out. In this I was helped by a bizarre photograph in the local Mestre press of me taking a photograph of my burnt-out car with the caption, *'Police special branch photographer gathers evidence into arson attack on NATO officer's car.'*

17

HILO TOURS

While most of the British service personnel were delighted to find themselves in southern Italy the same could not be said of the Americans. In terms of their appreciation of Italy they fell into one of two categories: they either hated it and could not wait to return Stateside, or they wanted to see and learn as much about the country as they could. My wife and I were fortunate to fall in with a group of the latter: the US medical and dental officers' wives. My wife was the first to venture out on one of their trips – to Paestum – and she returned full of praise both for the Greco-Roman site itself and their guide, Professor Michael Karris, with whom I later had the underground adventures. So we decided to join the group, which I was happy to see included husbands, for a weekend trip to Gubbio, an ancient town in the north of Umbria. The main attraction of the weekend was to be the annual crossbow festival in which the crossbowmen, arbalesters, of Gubbio take on those of Sansepolcro, yet another ancient town just over the border to the north in Tuscany. It is said that this town was founded around AD 1000 by two pilgrims who brought with them from the Holy Land a stone from the Church of the Holy Sepulchre, hence the name, San Sepolcro. Perhaps its most famous son was the Renaissance artist Piero della Francesca whose masterpiece *The Resurrection* is in the town's civic museum. But I digress.

We set off by coach at an ungodly hour of the Saturday morning – our leader, Michael Karris, 20 Americans and we two Brits – and arrived in Gubbio in time for an early lunch taken in a dark but cosy bar steeped in the ambiance of the Middle Ages. Lunch over, we began to explore the town. Gubbio is set on the steep slope of Mount Ingino and its narrow, winding streets are bordered by attractive *palazzi* and more modest, but no less attractive, town houses, their pale honeyed stone providing a backdrop for the brilliant colours of spring flowers in the many window boxes and growing wild in garden walls. In the centre of the town is the Piazza Grande built over four enormous barrel vaults, necessary to provide a level, terraced surface on the steep slope. At one end of this grand square stands the imposing 14th century Palace of the Consuls with its crenelations and slim bell tower; opposite is the somewhat less impressive Palazzo del Podesta, now the town hall. We looked towards the top of the mountain over a stately Renaissance brick terrace to see a number of other impressive pale stone buildings with the dark green, pine-clad slope of Mount Ingino beyond. In the opposite direction we could see over the lower town and far across the Umbrian countryside.

Our first stop was the Roman theatre, now much ruined but evidence that the Romans were once here in this ancient town. In fact Gubbio was an early ally of Rome and, indeed, flourished under later Roman hegemony. Our next stop, a short distance away, recorded that not all occupiers had been so welcome: the Mausoleum of the Forty Martyrs houses the remains of 40 Gubbio citizens executed by the Germans in 1944.

Heading back uphill, at Michael's usual brisk pace, we visited the Municipal Museum, housed fittingly in the Palace of the Consuls. Of special interest were the unique bronze plaques known as the Eugubian Tablets. Dating from the 3rd century BC to the 1st century AD, they are written in the Umbrian alphabet and record religious acts and rituals performed by a group of priests of the god Jupiter. Their importance, apart from shedding light on the Umbrian language, is that they give a rare insight into early Roman religion. But, no time to loiter as Michael led us ever upward to the Ducal Palace, an impressive and elegant Renaissance architectural gem, built by Duke Federico da Montefeltro of Urbino who became patron and protector of Gubbio in the 15th century. You would probably recognise him from his portrait, either the original, which is now in the Uffizi Gallery in Florence, or one of the many copies. He is shown in profile with a haughty expression, hooked nose, bright red hat (like a railway buffer!) and scarlet coat. The ladies of our party expressed sympathy for his wife, Battista Sforza, when we were informed that Federico married her when he was 35 and she 13; she bore him seven daughters before dying at the age of 28 giving birth to a son.

One of Gubbio's major events is the *Corsa dei Ceri*, the Race of the Candles, held on May 15th, the eve of St Ubaldo's feast day. St Ubaldo is the patron saint of Gubbio and the *ceri* are three enormously heavy wooden platforms on which are placed the statues of St Ubaldo, St Giorgio and St Antonio Abate. Teams of men – presumably strong men – parade the *ceri* through the streets crowded for the occasion with the entire population before embarking on a madcap race up the steep, winding road out of the town to the Basilica of St Ubaldo high up the mountainside.

We would not see the race but we would be able to visit the basilica. However, even Michael balked at following the tortuous route of the race on foot and we were pleased to learn that there was a cable car that would whisk us effortlessly to our goal. This was, quite naturally, greeted with relief – until, that is, we reached the cable car station. The 'cable car' was more like a birdcage with the top half removed; the 'cars' were on a continuously moving loop. On the ground under the track of the cable two circles were painted, about five yards apart. To board one of these cages you had to stand on the first of the circles, look over your shoulder and step smartly into the cage as it arrived. The person on the second circle then did the same. Fortunately we all embarked without major incident and enjoyed the ascent with its spectacular views over Gubbio and the Umbrian countryside. All went well – until we realized that disembarking from a moving cage was going to be somewhat more of a challenge than embarking! Fortunately there were a couple of guys at the top ready to assist; this being

Italy, the younger and prettier the female passenger, the more assistance they received. The men, of course, were left to their own devices. Anyway, we all survived the experience and followed Michael to the 13th century basilica. Inside we were able to admire the *ceri* and wondered how ordinary men could lift them, never mind race with them up the mountain. They looked something like two-stage rockets and must have been at least 15 feet tall. On a more macabre note we were able to meet St Ubaldo himself, perfectly preserved above the High Altar where he has lain since his death in 1160.

Sightseeing over for the day, we decided to walk back down to the town to our hotel, a comfortable two star conversion of a Renaissance home – small bedrooms, grand public rooms, and painted ceilings with mischievous-looking *putti* looking down on us with apparent amusement. For dinner, though, we assembled at the splendid Taverna del Lupo, a member of the *Unione Ristorante Buon Ricordo*. Apart from fine food this chain offers the bonus of a complimentary hand-painted ceramic plate, each with its own design reflecting its provenance. While enjoying the restaurant's speciality, *coniglio all tavernierci*, we discussed what would be a suitable name for the type of tour we were enjoying. After much debate we decided on 'HiLo Tours' – tours that were high in energy (required to keep up with Michael) and low in cost (sticking to 2* establishments – rare for Americans). This tour of Gubbio, therefore, was the first HiLo Tour, but it was not to be the last.

The next day we enjoyed a leisurely but basic Italian breakfast of coffee and *cornetti* before hitting the town, as our American friends put it. The crossbow competition was not due to start until after lunch, so we had time to look at a few of the many churches, all dating back to the Middle Ages and each with interesting paintings. My favourite was a short distance outside the town: the small church of Santa Maria della Vittorina, so called to commemorate a 9th century battle in which the citizens of Gubbio defeated a band of raiders, Saracens from a far off land. The church's exterior is simple but, inside, the decoration, although damaged, is simply breathtaking; the walls of the single nave are alive with colourful frescoes under an elaborately painted and gilded, vaulted ceiling.

Three centuries later St Francisco here remonstrated with a large wolf that had taken to dining on Gubbio's citizens and managed to convince the animal to change its ways. Thereafter the people of Gubbio ensured the wolf never went hungry and after its death built the church of Saint Francis of the Peace on the site of this miracle. During restoration work in 1872 the ancient skeleton of a large wolf was discovered under a slab just outside the church and reburied inside.

After our rapid and remarkably extensive tour of Gubbio's religious heritage we just had time for a snack lunch before taking up position in the stands that had been erected in the Piazza Grande. The town had taken on a festive air, the multi-coloured floral displays being challenged by huge, colourful heraldic banners flying from every vantage point. Soon the square was packed: sombre old women in black, dignified old men in their ancient suits, excited younger families in the more colourful dress of modern fashion, lively children in their Sunday best, even babes-in-arms dressed for the occasion. The mood was one of mounting excitement and anticipation.

High above the square the bells of the Palace of the Consuls began to ring, the bell ringers standing in the tower alongside the massive bells and using their legs and arms to swing them. Soon, above the noise of the bells, we heard the deep, rhythmic beat of drums interspersed with the strident call of trumpets. Faint at first, a mere backdrop to the strident and somewhat disorderly peal of the bells, the rhythmic, military sound grew ever louder until we were able to see a procession, led by the band, approaching along the Via XX Settembre. Behind the band was a group of men carrying brightly coloured flags and they were followed by a large number of what we assumed were citizens of Gubbio. What made the scene so memorable was that one and all were dressed in elaborate Renaissance costume; not for the first time did we see how easy it was for the modern Italian to slip back into the persona of a Renaissance man – or woman. For us, it was as if we had been transported back in time, a more colourful and stately time.

The procession moved into the square where the men with the flags took centre stage; these were the *sbandieratori* who proceeded to put on a display of 'flag-waving', a term that seriously underrates this ancient art. These displays date from at least the 14th century and involve the large, brightly coloured heraldic banners being waved in intricate patterns, thrown high into the air (and caught again) and thrown from one *sbandieratoro* to another. Here in Gubbio we were treated to a spectacular demonstration of great skill, rich in historical overtones, against a backdrop of medieval architecture and a late May sky of the deepest blue.

Of course, the *sbandieratori* were but the prelude to the competition itself. The home team – 14 I think – of both young and old men were dressed in medieval costumes of purple and black and were all members of the *Società Balestrieri di Gubbio*. Their opponents from Sansepolcro were similarly garbed but their colours were yellow and black. The crossbows used were more like artillery pieces than personal weapons; the arbalester sat on a bench behind the bow, which was supported on a stand, rested the butt on his shoulder and took aim at a small, round target 36 metres away at the far end of the square. Unusually, this was not a team competition as such; the winner was the crossbowman whose bolt, a wooden shaft with an iron head and fletch of turkey feathers, was closest to the centre of the target. The accuracy was amazing; all bolts hit the target and many of them were within a whisker of the dead centre. Finally, though, the winner was announced: an arbalester from Gubbio. Apart from the honour of winning, for himself and for Gubbio, the victor received a valuable *palio*, a beautifully worked banner, before setting off in triumph in the retiring procession. We felt privileged to have been part of this magnificent and emotionally charged event, one in which past and present seemed to have coincided.

The medieval atmosphere remained as daylight faded. The streets, still thronged with people dressed for a different age, were illuminated, not by the harsh electric light of the 20th century, but by living torches whose flickering, softer light cast dancing shadows on the walls of the narrow streets and added to the feeling that we were back in a more colourful and exciting era. By this time we had explored the town thoroughly and even managed to absorb its timeless atmosphere. But there was one thing left to do: become *matti di Gubbio*, 'madmen of Gubbio'. To do this we made our way to the medieval Palazzo del Bargello, headquarters of the *Società Balestrieri*; there, in front of the palace, was a fine fountain, *la fontana dei matti*. A little self-consciously we each ran three times around the fountain, applauded by some passing locals, sprinkled some of its water on our faces and, behold, we were now baptised as *matti di Gubbio*, a suitable ending to an excellent and informative weekend, the first HiLo tour. Happily, there were to be more: Rome, the *Via Appia Antica*, the *trulli* houses of Alberobello, the Norman castles of Puglia and Sicily being the most memorable.

18

THE BRITISH WAY OF LIFE

Now, what do you think British families miss when serving overseas? Probably many things, though I doubt these would include the weather. But surely the English village fete must figure prominently among them. Here in Naples we were lucky in that the British military community, ably assisted by members of the city's Anglican Christ Church congregation, recreated the traditional atmosphere and activities in the crater of an extinct (it was hoped) volcano. The venue was, in fact, no other than the US Rest and Recreation Centre at Carney Park. Every 4th of July part of this complex was turned over to the celebration of this American holiday, an event that, among many other things, required the erection of food, games and craft stalls. And this is where the British community, lacking any comparable facility, moved in. For a nominal charge the US authorities rented the area and the stalls the weekend before their own festivities for what was called the Brit Fete. And, importantly, this came with a guarantee of good weather, something that cannot be said of fetes in Britain. Nominally the purpose of the fete was to raise funds for Christ Church, but the proceeds were in fact split between several charities.

As with all such tri-service ventures a committee, usually of pressed men (and women) was formed immediately after the preceding fete, chaired in turn by each of the three services. The committee's activity, painfully slow for several months, accelerated as the great day loomed closer and became a hectic rush in the final few days before the event. By tradition each department took on one of the stalls or activities: the Brits of MARAIRMED were assigned the Ploughman's Lunches stall. Italian cuisine is not, of course, noted for its ploughman's lunches so the major ingredients of Cheddar cheese, Branston pickle and pickled onions had to be acquired – at rip-off prices – from the NAAFI in Germany. Italian bread, on the other hand, was more than adequate and we negotiated an excellent deal with a local baker. The makings having been organised we could concentrate on preparing our stall, an activity that began on the Friday afternoon with negotiation for a well-positioned pitch. Then we had to erect the stall – reminiscent of building flat-packed Ikea furniture – before decorating it with posters kindly provided by the English Tourist Board and pictures of suitably pastoral scenes. Now we were ready for the big day, the last Saturday in June.

Final preparation began early on Saturday morning, the chaos of Friday afternoon having been transformed into an orderly assembly of brightly decorated stalls, games and activities areas forming a double row around three sides of a central arena. Even before the official start time of ten o'clock, the sun had cleared the rim of the crater and the temperature was hitting the high 80s. Just outside the entrance to the site Stan, the Peugeot dealer, had arranged some of his latest models, shiny now but soon to be coated in a thick layer of dust. At the entrance sat the Grand Draw ticket seller, strategically placed to catch all those arriving, while in a commanding position at the side of the arena stood a stage; here the Senior British Officer and the Vicar of Christ Church, the Reverend Brian Swinnerton, who shared my love of speedway and who remained a friend until his death recently in the UK and whose family are still friends, would declare the fete open.

Later, the excellent US Sixth Fleet band would perform. Beyond the entrance stood the stalls: barbecue, cold drinks, cream teas, Pimms, ploughman's lunches, champagne and strawberries, books, bottles, bric-a-brac, and a 'British products' display. The beer tent and sitting-out area occupied a central position while a fish and chip van, always hugely popular with visitors, was placed at one end where the enormous queues would not interfere with any other activity. Interspersed were the various games: 'splat-the-rat', darts, smash the plates, target football, lucky dip and soon to be star attractions, the 'Yard of Ale' and 'Dunk the Celebrity'. This latter was particularly popular among the celebrities – mainly senior officers and service and civilian bosses – as a drop into a barrel of cold water was a most refreshing relief from the ever higher temperatures in the crater as the day wore on. Promptly, at ten o'clock, the fete was declared officially open, though a number of visitors had been munching, drinking and purchasing 'bargains' for some time.

Back at my stall the first customers had arrived. These were mainly ex-pat Brits and Italian civilians who knew what a ploughman's lunch was. Later would come the Americans to peer at the Branston pickle and pickled onions suspiciously before asking what a ploughman's lunch was and even, on occasion, what was a 'pluffhman'!

Gradually the site filled: Brits in country fete dress, local Italians in their Sunday best, NATO and US personnel and their families in a variety of colourful casual fashions. Elegant Italian ladies in dramatic summer dresses and expensive shoes queued with US Marines in baggy shorts, horrendous shirts, sneakers and Number One haircuts; British officers in lightweight suits and Panama hats served strawberries and cream to overweight American matrons in voluminous iridescent shorts and tent-like blouses. Children of all nationalities ran about everywhere, lucky ones clutching prizes won at one of the busy stalls. At the ploughman's lunches stall the entire work force became immersed in frantic production-line activity: cheese and bread were cut and placed on paper plates and dollops of pickle and pickled onions added. The beer tent became ever busier as the day wore on and the temperature rose, the crater trapping everyone in a cauldron of hot and dusty air. The noise level, aided now by the splendid Sixth Fleet Band, grew steadily in proportion to the amount of alcohol consumed. The 'Yard of Ale' and 'Dunk a Celebrity' had become particular noise centres. At the 'Yard of Ale' the US

Marines were confident of victory, as they were every year, although they never won, and gave much vocal encouragement to every participant, marine or not. At this particular time a nun was in the lead; the eventual winner turned out to be the wife of one of the Brit soldiers based in Naples, a rather impressive tattooed lady who looked, and sounded, as though she had had some considerable experience in downing quantities of ale. Human nature being what it is, everyone enjoys seeing people deposited into deep, cold water, especially if it is their boss! So the 'Dunk a Celebrity' activity attracted another large and vocal crowd.

Also extremely popular were the 'Splat-a-Grams' and 'Kiss-a-Grams'. For a fee anyone could order one of these for a friend or loved one. The 'Splat-a-Gram' entitled the recipient to have a custard-pie equivalent 'splatted' in his or her face, the result being recorded on a Polaroid camera. 'The Kiss-a-Gram' was, really, a men-only affair, although nowadays this would not necessarily be the case. The recipient in this case was kissed by the youngest of the Wrens who was dressed in rather fetching and scanty underwear, the moment again being recorded for posterity. Note: HM armed forces were not so politically correct in those days!

At intervals the general activity was interrupted by arena displays: the Brit School pupils performed gymnastics, the Martial Arts Club members demonstrated methods of killing each other, and Royal Navy, Royal Air Force and Army personnel exercised their brawn in a tug of war competition.

The finale was the Grand Draw with prizes ranging from a new car to a weekend on Capri. I should add at this point that, although I attended many Brit Fetes and bought many tickets, I never won a thing! This event over, the crowd started to drift away and we of the ploughman's lunches stall intercepted them at the exit and attempted to sell them our remaining loaves of bread. For some reason we (I) never did get the bread order right!

Although the setting was very alien and the majority of the participants not British, the fete successfully transported a piece of English tradition to southern Italy; everyone enjoyed themselves and Christ Church, as well as a number of charities, benefited financially. For those of us who manned the stalls, however, we were glad the day was over. Not that this was the end of our efforts. On Sunday morning we returned to clear the site in preparation for the Americans' 4th of July celebrations and, amid the stalls and ghosts of another successful Brit Fete, participated in a service of Holy Communion.

Perhaps I should also mention that Carney Park was also the setting for the quintessentially British seven-a-side cricket competition. The pitch was of matting on a concrete base and surrounded as it was by the tree-clad inner walls of the crater it was a far cry from the usual cricket venues. The standard of play was mixed; some had never played before but others had played at club level in the UK; George Gale's fast bowling would have earned him a place in any team and I was always grateful that we were on the same side. The matches always drew a large crowd of Americans who were clearly puzzled at, what to them, was a totally incomprehensible game. On one occasion the surrounding hillsides caught fire and burning embers started falling on the field of play. The spectators ran for cover but we continued as the match was an important one. Batsmen occasionally walked down the pitch in a professional manner, not to pat down bumps in the pitch but to extinguish fiery pieces of vegetation. We finished the match and had an account of our exploits published in the American's local newspaper. Mad Brits? I don't think so, merely an example of British determination in the face of adversity on a foreign shore.

The second big event of the social calendar was the Bazaar, organised by the Allied Officers' Wives Club and held each October to raise money for charity. The British contributions were a typical pub, complete with genuine beer and buxom bar maids, and a stall selling a variety of British produce. The stall was always popular with our NATO allies who eagerly purchased such gourmet items as marmalade, marmite and HP sauce. But it was the pub that was the star of the bazaar, always crowded, noisy and full of laughter. To add to the authenticity, the British wives made countless cottage pies, which, for a short time on the base, outsold pasta dishes! Needless to say, the Brit Pub, aided by a lively Dutch Auction run by an enthusiastic George Gale, was always very successful financially and thus helped a number of worthwhile local causes.

Many of these causes helped disadvantaged people in the Naples area among whom was a number of aged ladies who lived in a run-down building, a one-time hotel, in the oldest part of Naples. Once a month my wife or one of the other Allied officers' wives collected a van-load of basic foodstuffs – flour, sugar, pasta, cooking oil and the like – at the NATO base and went into Naples. Fortunately, given the chaotic driving in the city and the extreme narrowness of the streets in the old part, the base administration provided a driver inured to the perils of such a venture. First stop was a convent where the foodstuffs were offloaded. This was always a somewhat fraught operation as the van blocked the narrow street and to its usual noisome bustle was added the symphony of car horns and raised voices. Not to be intimidated my wife soon adjusted to this un-British behaviour and could hurl back abuse with the best of them while helping offload the consignment. It was then divided: part left at the convent for further distribution and part bagged up and taken to the ladies in question, a procedure organised by a wonderful good-hearted Neapolitan, Signora Paola Peppe.

The final destination had, it has to be said, seen better days. Although there were many rooms, only the dozen or so occupied by the ladies were in use. These were located on the second of three floors and opened off a dismal corridor, its paint peeling and its uncarpeted floor holed. The atmosphere was one of neglect and abandonment. However, as one often finds in Naples, a decrepit exterior belies the cleanliness and neatness of the interior. So it was with the ladies' rooms; each had made herself a home and brought with her mementoes of a former, and no doubt happier, life. The ladies themselves, all Italian except for one German, were charming and very grateful for the monthly supply of basic goods. Seeing their faces made all the hard work that went into organising and running the bazaar very much worthwhile.

NATO may be a political and military alliance but, in Naples, it showed a humanitarian side as well.

19

ALL AT SEA

Not long after my arrival in Naples George introduced me to the NATO Naples Yacht Club. This was based at the NAVSOUTH Headquarters at Nisida and was largely run by British personnel, although the membership also included Americans and Italians. Apart from bring a good place to learn to sail it was an excellent social centre. George had already booked me on a week's sailing course to take place each afternoon, NATO being on the summer working hours of 0730 to 1330. As an aside, these hours were traditional for Mediterranean nations and, of course, for the British overseas. The Americans could not, however, understand how anyone would wish to miss a whole afternoon's work and the senior US commanders attempted annually to consign summer hours to the dustbin of history. Fortunately, the Italian, Greek and Turkish commanders were vociferous in their support of the status quo; the British were neutral, not wishing to admit that we were less keen than the Americans, but I'm sure that we all kept our fingers crossed. Eventually the Americans succeeded – but, happily, not while I was working in NATO.

Anyway, back to the course. We used the Bosun dinghy, an aged but sturdy boat, a number of which as I mentioned above had been shipped across from Malta after Mr Dom Mintoff had summarily banished NATO from the island. Coincidentally I was captain of the Shackleton aircraft that conducted a fly-past of the departing Italian admiral, Commander Allied Naval Forces Southern Europe (COMNAVSOUTH) as he left Malta on board the ITS *Andrea Doria* on 20th October 1970. The course was good fun, the highlight being the test at the end of the week which included a 'man overboard' incident and a capsize drill. The latter always collected a number of spectators, all shouting advice, mostly conflicting, as to how best to right the dinghy. Course completed, we were given a certificate and, from thereon, we were let loose to learn 'on the job' as it were. I have to say, though, that there were some very experienced and competent club members who were more than willing to share their expertise.

We sailed in the Bay of Bagnoli, bounded by the island of Nisida to the south and the port of Pozzuoli to the north. About half way along the eastern side of the bay were the docks of the Italsida steel mill, the arrivals and departures of enormous supply ships adding an additional challenge to we inexperienced sailors.

From time to time the club arranged regattas, usually for two-man crews but sometimes with single-handed races. It was during one of these latter events that the wife of the British Admiral's secretary, a newly qualified sailor – let's call her D – made a name for herself. It was a windy day, a brisk north westerly stirring up the normally placid waters of the bay. All boats, except hers, were safely back alongside. Then, in came D, mainsail and jib tight in the stiff breeze, in a dead straight line for the quayside. And it was in this rig that she collided with the wall, bits of her dinghy as well as from a couple of others that she hit flying off in all directions. Having bounced off the solid stone jetty and still travelling fast she bore down on the yachts moored in the marina, hit a number of them, and finally came to rest alongside an expensive looking motor yacht. Our safety boat retrieved her and the Club Commodore, speaking rather patiently I thought, asked D what she thought she had been doing.

'That was what I did on the course,' she said. 'Approach from the mouth of the harbour and come starboard alongside. That's right, isn't it?'

The commodore winced slightly before asking, 'What about the wind direction? You are supposed to come alongside heading in to wind and using just the jib.'

'Oh!' said D, 'Nobody ever said anything about that.'

What could he say?

I must say that I was not without fault and my inexperience showed at times. The physical presence of Nisida Island added an extra dimension to racing as the wind around the rock was anything but predictable. This led to boats being rather more scattered than would be the case if the wind were steady. On one occasion I was heading at right angles to the majority of the fleet. In particular one boat, captained by an elderly and experienced Italian lady with a young, and pretty, Italian girl as crew appeared ahead on a near collision course. She had right of way but I estimated that we would pass just astern. We did – but managed to shear off her rudder in the process leaving her boat wallowing in a lively sea.

On another occasion I managed to ram the admiral on the starting line, pushing him back from first to last as the race got underway. He was quite good about it; and anyway, I was not in the Royal Navy so my career prospects, such as they were, remained unaffected. Indeed, shortly after this incident I was able to obtain a coxswain's certificate for his motor launch – one of the advantages of working closely with the Royal Navy. The launch had seen service on board one of our last 'proper' aircraft carriers and was ideal for family outings to the islands in the Bay of Naples. On one occasion, having booked the boat for an afternoon trip to Procida with friends, I was disappointed to be outranked and gazumped by a Royal Navy captain. I have to admit it was with some satisfaction that I learnt the next day that the boat's single engine had failed dramatically halfway to Capri and the captain had to accept a tow back to Nisida.

Two American members of the NNYC became particular friends: Don and Alice Larson. Don was a counsellor at the US High School, located next to the Naval Support Activity where I worked; Alice was a teacher at the American School at Pinetamare a few miles up the coast. Don and Alice owned a splendid 35-foot yacht and were kind enough to invite us on board on a number of occasions. In conversation on one I asked Don about the mysterious island of Ventotene, mysterious because it only appeared on the horizon on rare occasions; for most of the time it seemed not to exist at all and I hadn't met anyone who'd ever been there. Don suggested that we go and look for it one weekend; the upcoming Labour Day weekend seemed perfect.

One Friday afternoon in September a few weeks later we set off from Nisida westwards towards Capo Miseno, the northern extremity of the Bay of Naples, and thence to Ischia's little sister island of Procida where we moored for the night. Sleeping proved a challenge as our 'cabin', entered through the toilet compartment in the bow, had little headroom while its V-shape was not really designed for two adults to sleep stretched out. However, after much wriggling we eventually adapted to our new arrangements though sleeping was somewhat fitful.

The next morning, after an excellent cappuccino and pastry on shore, we set sail and, leaving Ischia to port, headed out into the Tyrrhenian Sea. To start with the sea was calm and a gentle westerly breeze helped us on our way. The silence of the morning, broken only by the sound of the hull cutting through the water, was quite soporific as we sat back in comfort and enjoyed the majestic sight of Monte Epomeo, the highest of Ischia's seven volcanoes, slowly receding in our wake. Soon, however, the breeze died away and a mist enveloped us, the faint sunlight filtering through it giving an eerie glow to the scene. The sails and rigging took on a ghostly air as if they were props in a B-movie. We seemed to be isolated in a strange new world. The sails were no longer of any use so down they came and we fired up the diesel engine. We had some 25 miles to go and, with limited visibility and without radar, we needed to take it slowly, our progress now accompanied by the steady throb of the engine.

After four hours or so the mist began to clear and we had our first glimpse of land, not Ventotene but the smaller island of Santo Stefano. Shortly afterwards Ventotene itself appeared lying directly across our path and we turned a few degrees to starboard and headed towards the east end of the island where a white lighthouse marked the entrance to Ventotene's Roman harbour, still very much in use after more than two thousand years. As we entered we could see that nearly all the structures on the quayside, mostly arched openings cut into the tufa rock face, were clearly Roman, and were being put to good use as small bars or storage areas. We Med-moored, stern to the jetty, among a line of colourful fishing boats and disembarked to take a look around the island.

In Roman times the island was called Pandataria and it became a favoured place among emperors for the banishment of recalcitrant, mostly female, family members. Among these unfortunates were Augustus' daughter, Julia the Elder, banished for excessive adultery; Tiberius' grandniece, Agrippina the Elder, exiled by Tiberius and who died there of starvation; Agrippina's youngest daughter, Julia-Livia, who was exiled twice, once by her brother, Caligula, for attempting to depose him, and once by her uncle, Claudius. She, too, died of starvation. Finally, Nero banished his first wife, Claudia-Octavia, to the island before having her executed. Evidently being a Roman emperor's wife had its disadvantages. The small harbour in which we were moored was where these ladies disembarked for their lonely and short life in exile.

As if to welcome our arrival, the sun had banished the mist and revealed the island to us. We walked along the narrow quay overlooked by a pink and white painted apartment block, past piles of fishing tackle and up through the attractive small town of pink, yellow and ochre rectangular buildings and into the small square, Piazza Castello, overlooked by the impressive 18th century municipal building. The island is less than two miles in length and barely half a mile wide so it didn't take us long to walk around it. We were impressed by the number of water channels and associated cisterns cut into the bedrock. Most impressive were the so-called *carcerati* (prisoners) massive water cisterns constructed by the Romans and used to house prisoners who were sent to the island in the 1700s to build the present village. We also found the remains of the enormous villa once the summer palace of Augustus and no doubt the residence-in-exile of his promiscuous daughter.

As on the island of Capri, there are no natural springs so, unsurprisingly, there was not much greenery and the grandest scenery was confined to a series of seascapes and views of the nearby island of Santo Stefano. On it we could see a rather grand edifice glowing faintly pink in the afternoon sunshine and resolved to visit the next day. For now we decided that it was time to seek out a suitable eating-place as evening was almost upon us. Our return route took us past the modern harbour – a necessary evil – where the ferries from mainland Formia and the island of Ponza dock. Tourists, rather than exiles, now come to Ventotene. The much smaller and atmospheric Roman harbour lay just beyond and, after freshening up, we made our way along the quay to a small restaurant. The speciality was swordfish. Alas, none had been caught for a couple of days and so that was off. There was lentil soup, however, lentils being a local crop. My mind wandered back to the time of Imperial Rome when the disgraced, exiled ladies perhaps sat at this very spot sipping a watery lentil soup every day of their remaining lives. I decided to give the lentil soup a miss.

The next morning, after a much better night's sleep, we were awakened by the harsh-sounding voices of fishermen preparing for a day at sea. Perhaps they might even catch a swordfish! Just above our heads in the bunk was a small hatch. By sitting up we could survey the world with our eyes at deck level. Crewmembers on the yachts either side of us wished us *'Buon Giorno'* apparently quite used to addressing disembodied heads. The novelty of this new view of the world eventually wore off and, after rather cramped ablutions, we joined Don and Alice aft in the open cockpit for a morning coffee and discussed the day's proposed adventure. Our plan decided, we enjoyed a modest breakfast at the nearby bar, boarded the yacht and sailed across the two-kilometre strait to the small, circular and rocky island of Santo Stefano. The day promised to be warm, the sun now quite high in a cloudless blue sky, and the sea, an almost unbelievable blue, appeared calm as we anchored just offshore opposite an area where there was a narrow break in the jagged, volcanic cliffs. However, when we transferred to the yacht's dinghy we found that there was a tricky swell running, which made landing at the island's sole, tiny quay quite a challenge. In fact we had to jump ashore one at a time, rather inelegantly as it happened, when the dinghy crested a wave. Apart from a couple of grazed knees and a fair amount of stress, we managed the transition from sea to land successfully. We pulled the dinghy ashore and began our adventure.

Santo Stefano is small, only about 500 metres in diameter, and is dominated by the magnificent prison built by the Bourbon King of Naples, Ferdinand IV, in 1797. The prison remained in use until 1965 when the last remaining prisoners and their warders must have just walked away leaving everything as it was. This was our destination.

After our rather graceless arrival on the island we climbed an overgrown path to the highest point on the island and soon came to the prison, a most unexpected and imposing building. The frontage consisted of a massive rectangular block, in which was set the entrance. Two large wings extended on either side. Behind this was a horseshoe shaped structure on several levels each decorated by neat rows of window openings. In front of the prison, just outside the walls, was a large accommodation block, presumably the quarters of the prison guards. These were still in a reasonably good condition and none was locked. In one of the lower rooms I came across an old magazine with a faded photograph of a very young Sophia Loren, the colours overlapping somewhat in the manner of the newspaper colour photos of that era. There were even some items of cutlery, and furniture – beds, cupboards, tables and the like – probably insufficiently valuable to warrant the trouble and expense of removing. We all felt the atmosphere within the block to be rather melancholic; no doubt it would be more so inside the prison, always assuming we could enter.

The approach to the main entrance was along a paved pathway with a raised and overgrown garden, mainly of bushes, on either side. The rectangular entrance-block was still impressive despite the peeling plaster and faded ochre paintwork. Barred windows guarded a rather unimposing doorway with a celebratory marble inscription set in the wall over it. Above, three large windows centred on the doorway, their glass long gone, stared down the approach path while, on either side, empty doorways at first floor level opened onto small balconies. Two enormous drum towers, one on each side, completed this monumental, but not overwhelming, entranceway. Somewhat to our surprise the door was open; there was not even a notice, polite or otherwise, telling us to KEEP OUT. And so we entered.

The entrance block was built around a courtyard. Passageways led to what were clearly a workshop and a dining facility. As the prison was designed to hold 600 prisoners, these were very spacious and even retained some of their equipment. Although the plaster was peeling from the walls and there was a layer of dust over everything, the overall condition was remarkably good and the atmosphere not at all oppressive. After wandering around these rather grand halls, and some of the nearby rooms, we moved out into the heart of the prison.

We entered a big horseshoe-shaped courtyard, bordered by three levels of cells behind open arcading, the two bottom levels with elongated arched openings, the upper level with rectangular openings between widely spaced, plain pillars. Set a few yards into the courtyard was a low, circular wall surrounding a centrally positioned square tower. This wall was divided into two separate semi-circles by two diametrically opposed, walled passageways that led from the outside of the courtyard to the tower. The tower itself had large, arched openings in each side and a cupola-type roof armed with four spotlights. A flight of steps led up to its floor level, which was the same height as the top of the encircling wall. From within there was an unobstructed view of all the cell doors. Compared to a modern prison the overall effect was rather pleasing and was enhanced by the red and ochre painted plasterwork on the walls. There was an opening in the floor of the space enclosed by the circular wall that gave access to a massive cistern. As at Ventotene, there are no natural springs on the island.

Climbing some stairs we came onto one of the vaulted corridors that led around the inside of the horseshoe-shaped cellblock. Despite the openings in the wall to our left, the corridor was gloomy and strewn with debris. There was a cell every few yards behind a rusting, steel door outlined in the peeling and fading ochre-painted wall by a white stone frame. Each door had a substantial lock and a rectangular spy hole at head height while most had a further, heavily barred opening above the door.

The cells themselves, of which we counted over 90, were quite small and were without a view, the window being well above head height. One or two, perhaps those of favoured prisoners, had walls painted with patterns rather than in the usual monochrome. One of the cells (we could not identify it positively) was specially constructed for Gaetano Bresci, the Italian anarchist who assassinated Umberto I, the King of Italy, in 1900. He was sentenced to life imprisonment, the first seven years of which were to be in solitary confinement. In fact he served only ten months as he was found hanged in his three by three metre cell despite being chained by his legs to the wall. It is quite likely, therefore, that he was murdered. Many prominent anti-fascists were imprisoned here during the reign of Mussolini, including Sandro Pertini who went on to become President of Italy from 1978 to 1985. Another, Altiero Spinelli, here wrote the *Ventotene*

Manifesto that promoted the idea of a federal Europe after the end of World War II.

For each of us, standing in a cell, feeling the walls closing in and imagining being incarcerated here for life, brought on a deeply sombre mood. Even in what was probably the exercise area this mood remained despite the blue sky and the fading but still handsome architecture; to a captive song bird a gilded cage is still a prison. We were not disappointed to conclude our visit and make our way back to the landing stage where the brilliant sunshine, the azure sea and our means of escape awaited. It had been an interesting day, a window on relatively recent, troubled Italian history.

Our sombre mood was banished by a lively evening at a *ristorante* back on Ventotene. The food was simple, but tasty, and the local wine quite drinkable. No swordfish though! After another good night's sleep – we were obviously becoming used to the nautical life – we set sail on our return voyage. This time the weather was fair and it was not long before the island of Ischia came into view, at first but indistinctly in the late summer haze. Strangely, when we looked behind, Ventotene and Santo Stafano had disappeared, once more cloaked in mystery.

20

LIGHTHOUSE OF THE MEDITERRANEAN

You may recall that I had served in Malta flying the venerable Shackleton maritime patrol aircraft. During that time I often flew around the volcanic island of Stromboli, one of the seven Aeolian Islands situated between Sicily and the Italian mainland. Stromboli was always an impressive sight, a near perfect cone smoking by day and spitting out fire by night. Not for nothing is it named 'The Lighthouse of the Mediterranean'. I promised myself that, one day, I would set foot on the island. Now, living in southern Italy, I realized that there was at last an opportunity to do just that.

Of course, the only way to visit the island is by sea and, as luck would have it, there was a ferry service from Naples to the largest of the Aeolian Islands, Lipari, which called in at Stromboli. However, this being Naples, buying ferry tickets proved to be less than straightforward. The ferry departed Naples in the evening so my wife and I drove down to the port in the relatively light traffic of the mid-afternoon ('relatively light' for Naples, that is – anywhere in the UK the same traffic would be regarded as 'heavy'). There we found that ferry tickets were not sold at the port but at the Shipping Agent's office located somewhere in the back streets of the city – and it didn't open until 4.30 pm, or thereabouts, just as the traffic was building up to its frenetic rush-hour or so chaos.

After stopping for a surprisingly good cappuccino at the port's less than salubrious cafeteria, we drove out into the maelstrom of Naples to find the Agent's office. In fact it was not too distant and we arrived outside just before 4.30. In the Naples of the mid-1980s parking was not a problem: you just stopped the car wherever was convenient (for you!) got out to conduct whatever business was required, then climbed back and drove off – no yellow lines, nor any other sort of lines, no signs giving parking restrictions and no traffic wardens. Although in theory you could be fined for causing an obstruction, the sheer volume of traffic caused its own constant obstructions so your contribution would not even be noticed. So, our purchase was quickly made and, feeling confident that we had not stopped the roar of Neapolitan traffic, we drove back to the port, parked the car, and returned to the cafeteria to await the arrival of the ferry.

The ferry arrived as night was falling, the Bay of Naples lighting up and taking on a more romantic air. Once aboard we made our way to our cabin, a somewhat spartan cubicle in the style of such ferries. However, since our journey was relatively short, albeit over most of the night, it would suffice. An evening meal was simple, but enjoyable – *spaghetti alle vongole* – and was helped down by a local wine from Vesuvius. Then we went on deck to observe the second most interesting aspect of a ferry trip: the departure. With skill born, no doubt, of long practice the captain eased the ship from the quay and headed out into the bay. Behind us the city began to display its night-time character, coming alive with lights, its daytime poverty veiled for a few hours. To the left the Royal Palace and the Castel Nuovo stood proud close to the waterfront, while the Certosa di San Martino and the Castel San Elmo loomed over the city.

Once we cleared the main breakwater we could see the bulk of the Castel dell'Ovo rising from the sea, the tiny fishing community of Santa Lucia nestling in its shadow. According to legend, the Roman poet Virgil placed an egg in the foundations of the castle to support it, hence the name: the Egg Castle. As we headed south and out into Homer's wine dark sea we could appreciate the enormous extent of Naples and its adjacent towns, once separate but now subsumed into an almost continuous band of light. Ahead of us the bulk of Capri was outlined against the horizon, decorated by the lights of Capri town and Anacapri; to our left the lights of

Portici, Ercolano, Torre Annunziata and Castellammare di Stabia directed our gaze towards the Sorrento Peninsular while in the background Vesuvius, quiescent now since 1944, loomed high above them all, lights part way up its slopes testimony to the optimism of folk who are content to live on perhaps the world's most dangerous volcano. To our right we could see the lights of Posillipo, where Admiral Nelson carried on his affair with Lady Hamilton, and beyond them Capo Miseno, once the headquarters of the Roman Fleet whose admiral was Pliny the Elder, who as we saw was doomed to lose his life in the eruption of Vesuvius in AD 79. Further still we could make out the small, low-lying island of Procida and its much larger and taller neighbour, Ischia. Now the Sorrento Peninsular passed on our port side, the coastal towns backed by the dark mass of the Latteri Mountains, dotted here and there with points of light. Then came Sorrento itself, proudly standing high above its port, its tourist-driven affluence illustrated by its illuminated grand hotels. Finally exclusive Capri passed to starboard and we were in the open sea.

Gradually the land-locked lights receded and we retired to our cabin for a few hours' sleep. Some five hours later, in the early hours of the morning, the alarm clock roused us from all too short a sleep and, after the briefest of ablutions, we made our way on deck. Ahead lay the dark cone of Stromboli. As we watched a shower of glowing material shot into the night sky like a giant firework display. This was repeated as we came ever closer but, to our relief, the ship kept away from the falling fire-bombs, and headed to the east of the island. Even though dawn was still several hours away the quayside at the tiny port of Scari was crowded. Clearly the arrival of the ferry was a significant event. As we reversed – or went astern, I should say – onto the jetty we just hoped that, among the crowd, there would be someone from the hotel in which we were booked for three nights. We needn't have worried; a man holding a board inscribed with our name stood by one of those ubiquitous three-wheeler vehicles that are part motorcycle and part car that we called 'elephant trucks'. Our suitcases were quickly placed in the back, we hopped aboard and set off through the deserted and strangely dark lanes of Stromboli, the loud noise of the labouring engine echoing around the closely-packed houses and disturbing the tranquillity of the sleeping village. Barely five minutes later we arrived at our hotel where we hoped we'd be able to enjoy a few more hours' sleep.

Rosy-fingered dawn had long departed when we finally came to. We enjoyed a light breakfast – excellent coffee and freshly baked rolls – on the hotel terrace. The view was stunning. Between the beach of black sand and us lay a cascade of white, single-storey houses reflecting the bright sunlight, their whiteness slashed here and there with the brilliant colours of bougainvillea. Gone was the wine dark sea of the previous evening; in its place was a shimmering expanse of the deepest blue, patterned by countless wavelets that twinkled as they caught the sun's rays. Some way off the coast a large rock topped with a small lighthouse rose sheer from the water. This was Strombolicchio, little Stromboli. Behind us the bulk of the volcano loomed over all, not surprisingly as the island itself is nothing more than the top of a volcano.

Breakfast over we decided to explore the village of Stromboli. In fact, despite its small size, there are several districts of Stromboli: Scari, where we landed, Ficogrande and Piscita. As we had seen from the hotel, the architecture was generally rectangular with white the predominant colour. We strolled to the highest point where we came upon the very impressive church of San Vincenzo. Its baroque façade was painted a pale yellow with contrasting grey engaged pilasters and was surmounted by a steeply angled pediment. This impressive feature was decorated with grey stucco work: a trumpet lying at an angle over an open book, the whole resting over and between an elegant garland. To the right was a handsome tower in matching colours carrying a peal of bells that could be seen through arched openings. The church faced onto a terraced square from which there were marvellous views, the sea on one side and the ubiquitous backdrop of the smoking volcano on the other. The interior of the church was light and splendidly baroque, lots of different coloured marble arranged in geometric patterns on the floor of the nave and two side aisles, striated marble panels on the walls and pillars. The 'everyday' altar lay beneath a beautifully decorated dome resting on complex columns. Beyond, at the end of the apsidal chancel, was an extraordinarily ornate high altar reaching high into the space of the chancel and framing the gold-clad figure of St Vincent himself. The whole effect was of an unexpected prosperity on such a small island, testimony to the fact that, although the population of Stromboli was now only some 500, many years ago it was several thousand strong.

Having admired the church we continued our exploration. There were no real streets in the village, only narrow lanes; hence the use of 'elephant trucks', the waspish buzz of which were a constant background noise all morning. A little further along the top lane we found a second church dedicated to San Bartolo. Its façade was almost identical to that of San Vincenzo, except that the colour scheme was pink and white, and the tower was on the left. The church was not open but the area around seemed less prosperous than that around San Vincenzo with several houses deserted.

We found no more architectural gems, but we did come across a red-painted house on which was fixed a plaque telling us that this was where Roberto Rossellini stayed while he directed the 1950 film *Stromboli terra di Dio* which starred Ingrid Bergman. She played the part of Karin, a displaced Lithuanian who escapes internment by marrying an Italian prisoner of war. He is a fisherman from Stromboli and in due course they move back to the island. However, the main interest in the film seems to have been the famous affair between Ingrid and Roberto, who were in fact both married to other people at the time. Ingrid became pregnant and they had a son, Roberto, who was born in February 1950. This caused a great scandal in the USA and Ingrid was declared a *persona non grata*. Nevertheless, after she was divorced from her first husband she married Rossellini and they had twin daughters, Isabella and Ingrid, in 1952. Sadly, as with many characters in the entertainment industry, their marriage broke up in 1957.

Having exhausted the possibilities of Stromboli village we retired for lunch in a pleasant *ristorante* with the now familiar and relaxing sea view on one side, the threatening bulk of the volcano on the other. It was as if we were in a rather magical painting. The owner asked us if we'd visited the village of Ginostra on the other side of the island. As we hadn't he suggested we take a boat trip as the footpath was no longer useable. We thanked him and resolved to do this in the afternoon.

It was not difficult to find a boat in Scari to take us around the island. We joined a few other visitors and set sail on our circumnavigation of Stromboli. In daylight we could see that the lower slopes of the volcano were quite verdant, the greenery stretching perhaps two thirds of the way to the summit. Above lay the burnt cinders, the more usual landscape of an active volcano. We could also see that the village of Stromboli was on the least steep part of the island, in fact the only part on which a substantial settlement could exist. Along the south-east and south-west coasts the slope plunged steeply down into the sea. Finally we came to Ginostra, a scattered collection of dwellings with the narrow finger of a jetty pushing out into the sea. Here we disembarked and wandered through what was a largely deserted settlement. According to the boatman most of the inhabitants had emigrated to Australia in the 1950s along with many other islanders. Now only a couple of dozen still live in Ginostra – and there's no electricity!

Back on board we continued past the western tip of the island and soon arrived opposite a horseshoe shaped depression in the side of the volcano, the Sciara del Fuoco, the Stream of Fire, caused by a succession of collapses on this side of the cone. Although there was no lava flowing at the time we did see some red-hot rocks tumble down the slope and hit the water with a great splash and a fountain of steam; and we could clearly make out the tracks of several flows that had reached the sea. The volcano was smoking and occasionally spitting out debris. In fact this type of continual eruption, in which small explosions occur at intervals expelling incandescent volcanic bombs, is termed a Strombolian Eruption.

Although normally moderate these eruptions can, on occasions, be much more energetic. In 1930 one such event here killed several people and destroyed many houses. We were not too sorry to leave this particular part of the island and continue to Strombolicchio. This lies just over a mile from the shore and rises dramatically, almost vertically, to a height of 140 feet. On top, surrounded by jagged pinnacles, is a small, white painted lighthouse. This rock, of grey volcanic basalt, is actually what is left of the plug in the core of the original volcano. We could see a flight of steps cut into the rock – apparently there are 220 – but we were not allowed to land. The water was a beautiful iridescent blue and incredibly clear. We watched a group of divers and were amazed that we could continue to see them under the water no matter how deep they dived. We were disappointed that we had not brought our swimming gear with us so we missed what would have been a special experience.

Our circumnavigation completed we returned to the hotel for a welcome drink, a shower, another drink and an excellent meal of grilled local fish, *patate fritte* (not vulgar chips, you'll note), *insalata mista* and a bottle of Sicilian, *Bianco D'Alcamo* wine. For dessert we had a wonderful selection of ice creams and *biscotti* accompanied by the sweet local wine, *malvasia*. And to end, and ensure a good night's sleep, a chilled glass of *limoncello*. Seldom had 'Never at the Office' felt so good.

Of course, the main draw of Stromboli was the volcano, by which I mean the actual volcanic crater. So we decided the next day that we would climb the 3,034 feet and view the crater at close quarters. To conserve energy for the assault on the north face, for that is the way up, we spent most of the day on the beach. Unlike the golden sands of the UK the sand on Stromboli is black and so becomes extremely hot, making the short journey from towel to sea quite a challenge, with much hopping from one foot to the other. I noticed that the locals all wore flip-flops that they left at the water's edge. Once reached, though, the sea was beautifully warm.

An ascent of the volcano was only permitted with a guide so that evening, as the light began to fade, we joined a small group of like-minded explorers, and a black dog, on the seafront. Much to my embarrassment the guide sent me back to the hotel for a long-sleeved shirt to wear over my short-sleeved version. As the temperature was around 85 degrees I could not immediately see the need for this but our guide assured me that, at midnight at the crater some 3,000 feet above the sea, I would welcome the extra layer. Needless to say, he was quite right! Anyway, having fetched my shirt I had to run to catch up with the group who were heading along the lane towards the start of the climb. So much for my earlier attempt to conserve energy! After a mile or so the lane ended and the narrow track began. We took up a single file and began to climb. At first it was relatively easy going, the track winding through the undergrowth and remaining paved underfoot. As night fell, though, the climb became steeper and we had only the light of a half moon and torches to ensure we stayed on the track. Above us the sky glowed intermittently red as the volcano kept up its characteristic, mild, eruptions. I couldn't help thinking that sometimes it forgot itself and killed people.

After a further mile or so the paved path ended and we stopped for a breather. From this point we had a good view of the Sciara del Fuoco, its smoke and steam clearly visible in the pale moonlight. Then it was time to move on. Soon the path became even steeper and entered a narrow gully, probably the result of water erosion. By now the temperature had fallen but we were kept warm by the sheer activity of climbing. Once through the last of the greenery – broom, I think – we came out onto the rock and finally ash, less steep but hard work as we slipped one step back for every two forward. Finally, about three hours after leaving the village meeting point, we reached the summit and stood as close to the main crater as the guide thought safe. Closer to the edge were a number of photographers, buried into the ash with just their heads and cameras visible. Like them we waited for the outpouring of incandescent material. And waited. And waited. And began to feel cold.

At last a glow appeared in the mouth of the crater. The guide told us to take a deep breath and hold it. This we did as a wave of hot gases overwhelmed us; but the glowing material remained within the volcano. This sequence was repeated three or four times in the next hour so, although we certainly smelt the eruptions, we were not to be amazed by a spectacular firework display. Somewhat disappointed we made our way down the quick way, the Rina Grande ash slope. This was fun but almost certainly more hazardous than our ascent as we took great strides down a steep slope in a thick layer of fine ash. Soon we were black from head to foot, sweating from the exertion of the descent. Only the dog was unchanged; it just shook off the ash and trotted off into the night. We thanked the guide and expressed our admiration that his dog had managed the whole seven-hour tour only to be told that it was not his dog; he had no idea where the dog had come from as it certainly didn't belong to any of the tourists. The mystery of the dog unsolved we made our way through the unlit lanes back to the hotel and a long shower.

We left Stromboli, somewhat sadly, the next day and sailed back to Naples. I had kept a promise, albeit one to myself, and I had not been disappointed.

21

AN ITALIAN INTERLUDE

It is perhaps not generally appreciated that Italy is a mountainous country, a characteristic that provided us with some alternatives to the seaside activities around Naples. For example, in just under two hours we could be on the ski slopes of the Abruzzi Mountains. The towns and villages of this region have a completely different atmosphere from that of Naples with alpine-like architecture, designed to cope with the snow of the relatively harsh winters, and having numerous shops selling everything you might need for mountain activities.

The ski resorts of Roccaraso and Rivisondoli, although very small in comparison with those of the Alps and Dolomites, provide ample scope for a weekend's skiing and the British community took full advantage of their facilities through a series of all-ranks skiing weekends. Of note, these were the only occasions on which I'd ever had to use snow chains; putting them on and taking them off was a real challenge and the locals ran a lucrative business doing this chore for a not insubstantial fee. It was well worth the money though. The ski weekends were always great fun even if the weather, like that in Scotland, could in no time turn surprisingly arctic with biting winds that froze ears and noses accompanied by low cloud that reduced visibility to the tips of one's skis. On a jollier note it was fun to watch coachloads of Neapolitans enjoying their first experience of snow, rolling about and pelting each other with snowballs. More sophisticated Roman youths, dressed in the latest expensive ski wear, skied the pistes with panache, only stopping to collect dry gloves, hats and other accessories from Mamma, dressed in furs and standing patiently at the foot of the lifts.

But we at MARAIRMED enjoyed quite a different mountain

activity: an international *bocce* tournament in the remote and picturesque village of Atina. This came about courtesy of our Admin Officer, Lieutenant John Christman USN, a P-3 aviator who'd had the good sense to marry a girl from the village, who'd been at university in the States. Her family ran a restaurant in Atina, at the rear of which were a number of *bocce* courts. *Bocce*, a very popular game in Italy, is like the French *petanque*, in which players aim to throw their *bocce*, small metal balls, to land as close as possible to the *boccino* or 'jack'. Most of us drove up from Naples to Atina, but not Captain Pedisich and his wife – they cycled the 70-odd miles, the last 15 uphill!

The setting was really dramatic with high mountains encircling the village. Our programme began with a few aperitifs followed by a superb, traditional Italian lunch – the sort of meal that has so many courses that you think it will never end. We sat down at a long table set under the cooling shade of a massive, ancient vine, poured glasses of chilled *prosecco*, and began to eat. To start, *antipasta* with olives, *provolone* cheese, slices of *salami* and small balls of *mozzarella* (the soft cheese made from the milk of the water buffalo of nearby Campania) accompanied by local bread and home-made wine; then the *pasta* course followed by grilled chicken and roast potatoes. As if this were not sufficient, there followed the *dolce*, sweet, calorie-packed pastries and, to end, an essential to aid the digestion, a bitter-tasting *digestivo* reminiscent of an ancient cough medicine. Needless to say, this feast took us well into the afternoon; fortunately, the game doesn't require a great deal of physical activity – well, not of the running variety anyway.

Finally the serious business of the tournament began. The standard of play might not have been of the highest, but the level of competitiveness helped make up for any lack of skill; we certainly made as much noise as any group of local players. As the steel balls (*bocce* is the plural of *boccia* the Italian for 'ball') were thrown with great enthusiasm, if not a matching expertise, down the 30 yards of the court any that landed close to the jack, or displaced an opponent, were greeted with a yell of delight. The noise even attracted a number of locals; or the attraction might have been the banner: MARAIRMED ANNUAL INTERNATIONAL BOCCE TOURNAMENT. Actually, although we had American, British, Greek and Turkish players, the only Italian player was the Admin Officer's wife. No doubt the locals went home secure in the knowledge that there was no international threat to their sport, at least not from NATO.

The last *boccia* was thrown as the shadows lengthened and we were all bathed in a warm glow as the sun sank towards the nearby peaks. The Commanding Officer was declared the winner (he always won!); we all said we had let him win but, in fact, he was the star of the game, perhaps unsurprisingly as he cycled out each Sunday to Bacoli, a town north of Naples, and played with the locals there.

After a farewell drink we said goodbye to our splendid hosts and thanked our Admin Officer for his wise choice of bride. Then it was time to leave the tranquillity of the mountains for the urban chaos of the Naples area, already looking forward to the next tournament.

22

IN THE SHADOW OF VESUVIUS

For those with an interest in the ancient world the area around Naples is a veritable goldmine of sites. The most famous of these is undoubtedly Pompeii, the Roman city smothered by the volcanic eruption of Vesuvius on 24th August AD 79. (This date has recently been challenged based on a charcoal inscription including the date 17th October of that year and the fact that wine fermenting jars were sealed, an activity that took place in October.) Needless to say I visited Pompeii many times during my stay in Naples and got to know the town extremely well. It is an amazing experience to travel back in time to the 1st century AD: to walk the streets, go into the private houses, experience the grandeur of the public buildings and, through their physical remains, pictures and tombs, even meet some of the inhabitants of this long-dead city. Viewed across the *forum*, beyond the Temple of Jupiter, Juno and Minerva, Vesuvius looms still, its shadow a reminder that it is only slumbering and will, one day – perhaps very soon – burst once more into fiery, violent life. Yet paradoxically Vesuvius did less harm to Pompeii than the ravages of nature and, above all, the millions of visitors who have been given access since the city was uncovered.

Pompeii was rediscovered in 1748 after planned excavations, under the auspices of the Spanish King of Naples, Charles Bourbon, in the area known as *La Citta* where many Roman artefacts had been found. In fact the site was not identified as Pompeii until an inscription was found in 1763. Work continued throughout the 18th and 19th centuries, albeit unscientifically at first, and was largely concluded in the mid-20th century by which time some two thirds of the city had been uncovered. For the first time in history a complete Romanised ('-ised' because Pompeii was centuries old before the Romans arrived in this part of Italy) town was revealed: the basilica, baths, markets, temples, theatres, amphitheatre, shops, bars, private houses of both rich and poor, even a brothel were laid open to our inquisitive gaze.

You can walk round the defensive town wall, admire the decorative architecture, enjoy the ubiquitous and colourful wall frescoes and floor mosaics, read the amusing and sometimes scurrilous graffiti, and perhaps learn something new from the erotic images painted on the walls of the brothel. And in the National Archaeological Museum of Naples you can see thousands of artefacts rescued from the site: marble and bronze statuary, sophisticated jewellery, a whole variety of household goods and everyday items both mundane and exotic. On a more macabre note you can even observe some of the inhabitants, frozen at the exact moment of their death. This poignant window on the past is thanks to Giuseppe Fiorelli, the Director of Excavations at Pompeii in the late 19th century. He devised the technique of injecting plaster into voids in the volcanic ash caused by the presence of bodies, and indeed other organic material, that gradually rotted away leaving perfect moulds around their skeletal remains. The contorted bodily positions and the expressions of horror still discernible on the faces of these long-dead people brings home, as perhaps nothing else on the site can, the sheer horror of those events on that terrifying night in August AD 79 (or perhaps in October!)

The ash that covered Pompeii has allowed us to examine the town in almost indecent detail. However, there is a downside. While everything remained buried the absence of air and moisture preserved most objects, including the most fragile such as wall frescoes and even wooden writing tablets. However, exposure to the atmosphere has allowed weathering, erosion, growth of vegetation, exposure to sunlight and water damage to take their toll. In addition, excessively rapid and poor methods of excavation, inferior reconstruction techniques and materials, and inadequate protection have led to significant deterioration. We, too, have not helped. While we cannot be blamed for the massive earthquake of 1980, which caused major structural damage across the site, the influx of millions of tourists has imposed too great a strain on what is essentially a fragile environment. And, I should add, we must not forget the politics surrounding the administration of the site, a study of which leads us to the inescapable conclusion that Pompeii has been badly let down by the Italian state.

On visiting in 1984 I was shocked to see how these various issues had affected Pompeii since my first visit 15 years previously. Many buildings were no longer open to the public, many roads were blocked off, scaffolding was supporting walls in several areas and, most troubling of all, several frescoes had all but disappeared. And I did not wish to know that, '*Giulio ama Anna apr 1978*', a message crudely carved into the beautifully painted wall of a *triclinium* of a house in a well-to-do part of the town. However it did demonstrate that people haven't changed much over the centuries. For example here are AD 79 *graffiti* from a more modest house in a side street, '*Figulus diligit Idaia*' and from the same house, '*de Atimetus gravida me fecit*' (Atimetus got me pregnant). There's even the equivalent of the saucy advertisements of the type found in London telephone boxes; this one is carved above a bench just outside the Marine Gate, '*If anyone sits here, let him read this first of all: if anyone wants a fuck, he should look for Attice; she costs 4 sestertii.*'

But back to Pompeii's recent deterioration. Things improved in 1984 when Professor Baldassare Conticello became the Superintendent of Pompeii. He immediately began a programme of restoration and later organised a fascinating exhibition 'Rediscovering Pompeii' which toured Europe and North America. However, I learnt from him that there were two underlying factors that undermined his best efforts: too little money and too much politics!

Although Pompeii is the most famous Vesuvian site it was not the first to be discovered; this honour goes to Herculaneum, a smaller and more preserved town nine miles north west of Pompeii. It was discovered accidentally in 1709 when a workman digging a well brought to the surface pieces of finely worked marble. Further digging revealed the stage of a theatre on which was an inscription naming the town as Herculaneum. Excavation by means of tunnelling with the aim of recovering works of art and valuables – treasure hunting, we might say – began in 1738 and continued until 1748 when attention turned to Pompeii, a site that was much easier to dig. The reason for this was that Pompeii, being five miles downwind of Vesuvius, was directly under the volcanic ash cloud and was gradually smothered under an ever-thickening blanket of light volcanic material. This is easy to dig. Herculaneum, on the other hand, although closer to Vesuvius, was not under the ash cloud that rained such destruction on Pompeii.

However, just after midnight on 24th August AD 79 the weight of material in the eruptive column caused it to collapse on itself. This resulted in a pyroclastic surge of superheated gas and ash at a temperature of around 500 degrees centigrade that raced down the mountain's slopes at more than 100 miles an hour. Seconds later it hit Herculaneum, killing everybody still in the town; at a temperature of some 500 degrees centigrade flesh vaporised, blood boiled and skulls exploded, death coming in less than a second. Hard on the heels of the surge came a pyroclastic flow of heavier volcanic material, though not lava, sealing these unfortunate folk in a macabre jumble of skeletons like a Renaissance tableau of hell. Five more of these devastating events overwhelmed Herculaneum before the volcano's energy had been exhausted, leaving the town entombed in a 65-foot airtight layer of material with the consistency of rock. This is extremely difficult to dig.

Proper excavation of Herculaneum, slow and painstaking, did not commence until the middle of the 19th century, not helped by the myriad tunnels dug by the Bourbons two hundred years earlier nor by the fact that the modern town of Ercolano, formerly Resina, sat right on top of the ancient site. Remarkably though, many of the structures uncovered were more or less intact up to roof level. This was the result of the buildings being filled from the bottom up. Furthermore, the intense heat of the first pyroclastic surge carbonized organic material and thus preserved such things as wooden beams, window frames, furniture, foodstuffs and even papyrus scrolls. That so much was preserved for us to admire is due largely to the efforts of the famous Italian archaeologist we met at Cuma, Amedeo Maiuri, who worked extensively in the Campania region from 1924 to 1961 and was responsible for the excavation and conservation of Herculaneum from 1927 onwards.

But there is more to Herculaneum than the shell of a city; the people are still there. And, thanks to Doctor Sara Bisel, a physical anthropologist and classical archaeologist, I was able to learn a great deal about some of them at least. Their story began on the night of the eruption. Many terrified inhabitants made their way towards the seashore, perhaps in the forlorn hope of escaping the volcano's wrath by sea or, more likely, to seek shelter in one of the boat chambers fronting the beach. Tragically they were unaware that their assumed place of safety was to become their tomb. Sometime after midnight these people, clinging to each other in fear – young and old, rich and poor, free and slave – were overwhelmed by the pyroclastic surge. Death was instantaneous and the following pyroclastic flows sealed them in their makeshift tombs. And there they lay for more than nineteen hundred years.

In 1981, during work to drain the original beach area, now trapped between the town wall and 65 feet of solidified volcanic material, workmen uncovered several skeletons of people who had been hurled down from the town wall some 30 feet above by the force of the pyroclastic surge. Further investigation led to the opening of six of the boat chambers and the discovery of 55 skeletons: 30 males, 13 females and 12 children frozen in grotesque attitudes at the moment of death. This was an especially important discovery as before this few Roman skeletons had been available for study as the Romans generally cremated their dead.

Sara, who was working in Greece at the time, was called in and commenced the first in-depth study of such a group. Over the next few years she was able to examine 139 skeletons: 51 were male, 49 female and 39 children, whose sex is difficult to identify. By using a combination of physical and chemical examination she was able to build a picture of this representative population. She was able to determine the sex, age, height and general health together with details of nutrition and lifestyle. According to Sara the average height of the men was five feet six inches and the women just over five feet; nutrition was generally good with evidence of much seafood in the diet; and, in the absence of sugar in ancient world, the condition of their teeth was fine, although some showed evidence of periodontal disease

Since the early 1980s more boat chambers have been excavated, each one revealing a poignant tableau of the people of Herculaneum, united in fear as never in normal life, life extinguished by a force they could have never imagined nor understood. Studying these sad remains and, through Sara, learning more about them as individuals, I was able to appreciate much more fully the true horror of Vesuvius' eruption, an appreciation I never felt when walking the streets of the town.

Sadly Sara was not able to complete her work as she was taken seriously ill in the late 1980s. She never recovered and died in 1996. However, her pioneering work at Herculaneum made a significant contribution to the science of paleodemography in general and to knowledge of Herculaneum's population in particular. There is, however, a sad postscript to the story of Herculaneum's people. Even during Sara's study the forces of Italian chauvinism were at work. Despite the best efforts of the Director of Excavations at Herculaneum, Giuseppe Maggi, who foresaw the dangers of excluding foreign experts, the chauvinists carried the day. Maggi was sacked and study of the skeletons was handed over to Italian 'experts'. The remaining skeletons were left in situ as a tourist attraction, though tourists were rarely given access, and they gradually disintegrated and disappeared under a layer of vegetation.

The problems I highlighted at Pompeii were, with the exception of visitor numbers (Pompeii has always had the lion's share of tourists) even more severe at Herculaneum. Because of Pompeii's fame Herculaneum had been treated like a poor relation and had been sadly neglected since the retirement of Amedeo Maiuri in 1961. As a result the decay was so severe that, at the time I left Naples in 1987, there was a strong possibility that the site would, in just a few years, have to be closed to the public.

Post Script. In 2000, thanks largely to the efforts of Professor Andrew Wallace-Hadrill, Director of the British School at Rome, the Herculaneum Conservation Project was set up by David W. Packard of the philanthropic Packard Humanities Institute. The initial aim was to support the local archaeological authority and to this end a memorandum of understanding was signed in 2001. In 2004 the British School at Rome joined the project and Professor Wallace-Hadrill was appointed director with a scientific committee of Italian and international experts in a wide range of archaeological and conservation disciplines. Given earlier chauvinistic attitudes of the Italian state, this grouping was nothing short of miraculous. Happily the project has already made great strides in arresting the decay of the site and has, in addition, made some exciting new discoveries.

Pompeii and Herculaneum are undoubtedly the best-known sites in the immediate area of Vesuvius, but they are by no means the only ones. In fact more than one hundred have been unearthed, mostly by 19th century landowners seeking valuable items – 'treasure hunting' we would call it today. Most of these were subsequently reburied, their existence usually attested only by sparse written notes or a few artefacts. However, several have been re-excavated more scientifically and, thanks mainly to my great friend Mattia Buondonno who worked for the Director of Pompeii, I was able to visit most, if not all, of them. Most of the time we had them to ourselves as they are off both the beaten track and the regular tourist route; as a result I was better able to study the detail of the buildings and, more particularly, to absorb their atmosphere, without the constant interruption of tourist groups.

Mattia told me that there were a number of villas open to the public on the site of ancient Stabiae, another victim of the eruption, which were first discovered in the 18th century. However, their riches plundered, they were reburied and were not to see the light of day again until the 1950s. By the time I arrived in Naples three of these villas had been properly excavated and I was keen to explore this area and perhaps even see the villa in which Pliny the Elder stayed just before he died in the eruption of AD 79. So, one afternoon in late autumn my wife and I took on the now familiar challenge of the *Tangenziale* and the notorious A3 past Ercolano and Pompei and descended into the hell that was Castellammare di Stabia, the modern(ish) town on the site of ancient Stabiae.

If we had expected signposts, we were to be disappointed. The roads were narrow, choked with traffic and people and devoid of anything that might have directed us to an archaeological site. However, I guessed that the villas would have to be above the modern town – no Roman in his right mind would ignore the magnificent views to be had from the ridge that extended above the town, itself overshadowed by the bulk of Monte Faito. Eventually, through a process of trial and error down ever-narrower rubbish-strewn lanes, and not a few private drives, we found a rusting sign indicating the locality of the Villa San Marco.

We parked the car on a piece of waste ground, paid a modest

entrance fee and entered – the sole visitors to the site. I guessed that the custodian was grateful for someone to talk to as he accompanied us through the impressive entrance porch into a fine *atrium*. From him we learnt that the villa was one of six discovered by the Bourbons but that only three had been excavated and that its name came from a nearby 18th century chapel. Having remarked that this villa was one of the largest in Campania, he proceeded to show us round a whole variety of rooms: private apartments, bedrooms, an elegant baths complex of cold room – *frigidarium*; warm room – *tepidarium*; and hot room – *caldarium*; colonnaded courtyards – one with a large pool – and a monumental *nymphaeum* and summer dining room – *triclinium* – which would have enjoyed splendid views over the sea. The present view, regrettably, was over the packed rooftops of the modern town, the sea, which once lapped the narrow beach at the foot of the cliff now being much further away. We admired the remains of the sophisticated frescoes and mosaics but the custodian told us that the best pieces of art were no longer in situ but had been moved to the National Archaeological Museum in Naples. In fact we had already spent many hours in the museum and had found, among many other items, art works from all of the Stabian villas.

Having taken our leave of the enthusiastic custodian, and rewarded his enthusiasm with a reasonable tip, we followed his directions to the villa I knew from pictures of its frescoes, most of which were also in the Archaeological Museum – the Villa Arianna, named from the fine fresco showing Dionysus rescuing Ariadne from the island of Naxos. My favourite fresco was, and still is, the graceful personification of Spring: against a green background a young woman in flowing white and yellow robes moves away from the viewer, holding in her arms a basket of flowers. She reaches out with her right hand to lightly touch a delicately-rendered bush, spring flowers instantly blooming on its fragile branches. Having admired her in the museum I wanted to see from where she had come. In fact her villa was not far away and, this time, not only were we the only visitors, we were left to our own devices.

This villa, too, was immense and had not been fully excavated. We were able to explore the entrance peristyle, the main *atrium*, numerous private apartments and bedrooms, sea-view rooms, including a grand garden *triclinium*, and a small part of what was clearly an enormous peristyle or garden. We were also able to study quite a lot of the wall decoration, although I knew that the best of it was in Naples. We also came across what I thought was a rather unusual feature: a series of tunnels that appeared to connect the main body of the house with the seashore, originally some 50 metres below. Unfortunately we were not able to explore these but it reminded me that I wanted to relive the last hours of Pliny the Elder; this seemed the ideal place to do this. I had brought with me a copy of Pliny the Younger's letter to Tacitus in which he describes in detail the events of Vesuvius' eruption and how it led to the death of his uncle, Pliny the Elder.

The elder Pliny was the *praefectus* of the Roman fleet based at Misenum on the other side of the Bay of Naples. On observing the eruption, and receiving a plea for help from one of his friends, Rectina, who lived at the foot of Vesuvius, Pliny set sail on an ill-fated rescue mission. While my wife wandered around this impressive home I sat down on a broken column and looked across the bay. To my right the malevolent cone of Vesuvius was darkly shrouded while, overhead, threatening storm clouds scudded across a dark and forbidding sky while the wind, blowing hard from the north west as it had on the day of Pliny's rescue mission, whipped up the sea into a series of massive white-capped waves. Unfortunately I could not see the surf pounding the beach below me; my immediate view was of the red-tiled roofs of close-packed apartment blocks. Nevertheless, the atmosphere was not, I thought, totally unlike the situation on that fateful day in AD 79. I opened my book and began to read. I soon became completely absorbed as though I, too, were part of the tragedy unfolding before me.

Having ordered several warships to sail Pliny boarded one and set course across the Bay of Naples towards Vesuvius. As the fleet grew closer it came under an increasingly dense fall of burning debris and hot volcanic ash. Eventually the way was blocked as volcanic material near the shore had rendered the water too shallow to continue. Rather than return to base Pliny decided to sail on to Stabiae where his friend Pomponianus lived. On arrival Pliny found that Pomponianus had prepared to escape by sea but the wind that had favoured Pliny was preventing him from leaving. Wishing to reassure his friend Pliny asked to take a bath after which he dined before retiring for a nap. While he slept peacefully the situation outside was fast deteriorating as the eruption became more violent. Earth tremors were shaking the house, darkness deeper than night had fallen and the villa's courtyard was rapidly filling with ash and lapilli threatening to trap Pliny in his bedroom. He was awakened and it was decided that it would be safer to leave the house. This they did, tying pillows on their heads to protect them from falling debris, and went down to the beach in the hope that conditions would be favourable for sailing. They were not. Pliny lay on a sheet and asked for water to drink. Some time later the approach of flames and a strong smell of sulphur caused the group to flee. Pliny was helped by two slaves but suddenly he collapsed. He was found two days later, uninjured and looking peaceful in death.

Reading the account I could picture in fine detail those events so vividly described by Pliny's nephew and I wondered whether this was the very villa belonging to Pomponianus and whether the drama had been played out exactly where I was sitting. So absorbed was I that I completely forgot that, in the 20th century, these sites had an official closing time and it was a rather irate custodian who brought me back to the present and hustled us out of the site.

The Stabian villas were clearly residential, seaside properties belonging to the great and the good. However, more typical of rural villas were the three that Mattia took me to see being excavated at Terzigno on the south-east slope of Vesuvius. These *villae rusticae*, unimaginatively named Villas 1, 2 and 6 (I don't know what happened to 3, 4 and 5!) had a relatively small residential quarter but a much larger area for the production of wine: a *torcularium*, where the grapes were pressed, and rows of large earthenware jars, *dolia*, set in the ground to store the grape juice as it fermented. In Villa 2 five skeletons were found, these people having been overcome by the pyroclastic surge as they attempted to flee. They were no peasants, though; their belongings, strewn about them, included bejewelled gold necklaces, gold bracelets, silver household goods and a purse full of silver *denarii*. In contrast, the remains of people in Villa 6 had no personal effects with them and could, perhaps, have been slave workers.

Another of our outings was but a short distance away, at Boscoreale – the name means 'Royal Wood' and was so named by the Kings of Naples who hunted hereabouts – where three more rustic villas had been excavated. The Villa Pisanella was excavated in the latter part of the 19th century but, sadly for me, it had been reburied on completion of the excavations. Of particular interest, the villa had yielded an astonishing collection of silverware and, although I was not able to see it at the time, later in my career I saw some of it in the Louvre. I remember particularly a silver wine vase decorated around the outside with a number of skeletons engaged in everyday activities. Each was labelled with the name of a philosopher and there was an inscription, as true today as it was then: *'Enjoy life while you have it for tomorrow is uncertain.'*

The latest villa to be unearthed, the Villa Regina, was discovered only in 1977. This was very much a working farm dedicated to the production of wine and was similar to those I had seen at Terzigno. In contrast the third, named traditionally as the

Villa of Publius Fannius Synistor, was a much grander affair, the owner's accommodation taking up most of the building. It was excavated in 1900 and, although I enjoyed visiting the site, I was always saddened that, in keeping with the methods of the day, the truly magnificent wall paintings were stripped off the walls and auctioned off to the highest bidder. The majority ended up in the Metropolitan Museum in New York. In 1991 a museum was opened in this villa, its most striking exhibit a facsimile of the wall paintings.

Having been fortunate to visit many of the villas around Vesuvius I came to realize that this part of Italy, Lucky Campania, must have been quite densely populated with rich villas on the coast and working villas inland taking full advantage of the fertile volcanic soil. I dreamed of finding one myself. Little did I know that, soon, my dream would be realised.

23

THE INTERNATIONAL ARCHAEOLOGICAL SOCIETY

Surrounded by history as we were and with our appetites whetted by our HiLo Tour adventures a number of military personnel and wives decided to form a group of enthusiasts who would study in detail local archaeology and, if possible, add to the sum of knowledge. So was born the International Archaeological Society under its first Chairman, Claudia Allemang, ably supported by her husband, John, a US Navy dentist. Membership was predominantly NATO and US military with a small number of American, British and Italian civilians. We were especially fortunate in having two professional archaeologists on the team: Dr Sara Bisel, the American physical anthropologist we met above; and Dr Paul Arthur, a British lecturer at the University of Salerno.

Having established a constitution we embarked on a programme of lectures and visits. A few of the highlights will give you a flavour of how we were able to take full advantage of our presence in this fascinating part of the world.

Dr Bisel told us of the work she'd been doing at Herculaneum on the skeletons discovered in the boat chambers and explained how they had met their sad end. Not surprisingly her lecture was fascinating but this was surpassed by a visit to her laboratory a little later. This was in the Museum of Herculaneum that was opened in 1974 – and immediately closed (it did not open to the public for another four decades – remember this is Italy!). However, it did make a perfect place for Sara to work on the skeletons. We arrived to find each skeleton – each person – lying in a crate. It was strange to come face-to-face with some of Herculaneum's Roman inhabitants and we were soon amazed as Sara put 'flesh' on their bones. Of particular interest to the military members of our group was the skeleton of a soldier.

Sara told us he was aged about 37, taller than the average at five feet eight and a half inches and was well nourished and muscular. He was identified as a soldier by his sword and belt while on his back he carried a pack of tools – Roman legionaries were required to carry out building work as well as killing barbarians and other enemies of Rome. His upper legs were well developed from horse riding as, without a saddle, he would have had to grip the horse with his thighs. Perhaps he was a cavalryman home on leave with one silver and three gold coins in his purse.

Of more interest to the ladies was a woman wearing two gold rings, gold earrings and gold bracelets in the form of snakes. She, too, was well nourished and slightly above average height at a couple of inches over five feet. One of the Herculaneum elite we might presume. At the other end of the scale was a 14-year-old girl cradling a seven-month-old baby; maybe the older girl was her sister we thought. 'Not so,' said Sara. 'The baby wore jewellery so was likely of the upper class whereas the girl had marks on her arms indicating she had been required to do very heavy work and ridges on her teeth suggesting she had suffered near-starvation at a very early age. I think she was a slave.' Another woman that Sara had named Portia also had a story to tell. Sara said that she didn't like to cast aspersions on a person long dead, but the only skeleton she'd examined that had such tell-tale marks on her pelvic bone was that of a New York prostitute! One by one Sara brought to life in front of our eyes these people who once had lived and worked in the town just outside. A poignant experience indeed.

Dr Paul Arthur delivered a series of lectures on the history of the Roman town of Sinuessa and the surrounding area of northern Campania, once the home of the Aurunci people. Sinuessa is a little known site about 25 miles north-west of Naples on the ancient Via Appia that ran from Rome to Brindisi. The ruins of the town are mainly under the sea and on the beach at Mondragone, a popular holiday resort that lies at the foot of Mount Petrino.

Coincidentally Sinuessa was also a popular holiday resort in Roman times and on our later guided visit Paul pointed out the ruins of a large thermal baths complex. His theory was that the people of Sinuessa abandoned their city once the Roman Empire had crumbled and coastal sites were being raided and moved uphill founding a small and safer settlement. The Longobards, who ruled this part of Italy from the sixth century until the coming of the Normans in the eleventh, built a castle in the ninth century, the ruins of which stand proudly above the modern town. When more peaceful times arrived in the later Middle Ages the people moved back down the mountain to the far more convenient coastal site.

Thanks to my working alongside US national military staff I was able to hitch a ride on the C-in-C's helicopter for a training flight during which I was able to take a series of aerial photographs of the medieval castle and village. These proved useful the following week when a group of us climbed up to the village; the views from on high were amazing, well worth the stiff climb. We spent a very interesting couple of hours rooting around the abandoned houses and the ruined castle trying to imagine what life must have been like high above the plain – safe but hard we concluded.

We had all visited Baia, the one-time top holiday resort for very rich Romans, and knew that much of the original town lay under the sea, a result of the bradyseism that affects this part of the coast. One of our members, Raoul Botello, was a keen amateur diver and he gave a lecture on his underwater adventures along the coast. Following this he led us on a snorkelling tour of the sunken Roman remains. They lay in crystal clear water no more than 20 feet deep and we were able to see the street layout, the walls of domestic and commercial premises and even a grand villa. This had a central *atrium* with rooms, some with geometric black and white mosaics, leading off it. Well-fashioned fallen pillars, parts of marble statues and scatters of high-quality pottery completed the picture of a once urbane town. At a later date our naval members were especially interested in our visit to the sunken site of *Portus Julius*. You'll remember that Agrippa – Marcus Vipsanius Agrippa, to give him his full name – built the port in 37 BC for Octavian's fleet during the civil war against Sextus Pompeius. It was connected to Lake Lucrinus and Lake Avernus by canal and to the port of Cuma by tunnels. However, soon after victories against Sextus and Mark Antony the port began silting up and Octavian, taking on the honorific name of Augustus, moved the fleet to Misenum where a new port was constructed, the fleet being named after the location; the *classis misenensis*. Swimming through the clear waters we were amazed to see the entire layout of the harbour: quays, piers, columns, port facilities and much mosaic decoration. It was thrilling to be at a place from which naval forces departed for battles that changed the course of European history.

Having members from the local Italian community gave us opportunities that were never available to the public. One such opportunity was arranged by Roberto, a retired engineer. This time we would be on dry land, albeit underground: the theatre of Herculaneum. According to the guidebooks, that never let the facts spoil a good story, the theatre was found by chance in 1709 by a farmer digging a well. Remember, Herculaneum was filled by a pyroclastic surge and flows that hardened into a rock-like consistency and completely submerged the town. Digging through this material was hard work but eventually at a depth of 60 feet the farmer hit an even harder surface; it turned out to be the stage of Herculaneum's theatre. He brought up some pieces of rare marble that quickly came to the attention of a nearby landowner, Prince d'Elbeuf, an officer in the Austrian Army (Austria ruling the Kingdom of Naples at the time) who was building a villa close by. He purchased the farmer's land and immediately ordered more tunnelling to see if there was anything more of value. There was, especially fine statues of marble and bronze. Austrian rule did not last long, however, and from 1738 under the Bourbon King Charles VII (who in 1759 became Charles III of Spain – European history is a trifle complicated around this time!) more systematic and state-sponsored looting was carried out by a Spanish military engineer, Joaquin de Alcubierre. Fortunately some of these remarkable statues can now be seen in the Archaeological Museum of Naples and in museums elsewhere in Europe.

To our surprise we found that the modern entrance to the theatre was on one of Ercolano's busy main streets. As we closed the door on the modern world we swapped the hustle and bustle of the lively 20th century town for the relative quiet and tranquillity of the 19th century entrance hall. With an official custodian in the lead we went cautiously down the dimly lit 18th century stone steps into the damp and claustrophobic atmosphere of the theatre itself. As our eyes adjusted to the darkness we saw that we were on the upper curved seating area, the *summa cavea*, which disappeared into blackness on either side of us. We could see little else for only part of the structure had been tunnelled out of the solid casing. However, at least we could stand upright, unlike the original tunnellers of old.

Walking to our left we came to a passageway that led down through the rows of seats, though most were still buried, to the marble floored *orchestra*, the clear area in front of the stage. On reaching it we found two flights of steps that led up to the stage. Now we could turn and face the audience and try to imagine what a full house would have looked like. For a fleeting moment I thought I could see rows of anonymous happy faces and hear laughter – Roman plays were rather saucy unlike the seriousness of Greek tragedies. But the sensation was ephemeral; the ghosts of the Herculaneum audience had fled long ago. And who could blame them? Where once they had been surrounded by the sheen of precious marble and shared their experience with wonderful statues they would now have only the sombre uniform grey of the volcanic material and bare walls, the only decoration being the green patina of dampness.

It was interesting to be in the heart of Herculaneum's theatre-land if only for the sight of the amazing network of tunnels. The faces I thought I had glimpsed were anonymous – but there was one individual that I would have recognized, without doubt the most important citizen of the city. His statue once stood close to where we were standing on the stage and the base was still in situ. On it an inscription gave his name:

M. NONIO. M. F. BALBO
PR. PRO. COS
HERCULENSES

(TO MARCUS NONIUS BALBUS, SON OF MARCUS
PRAETOR, PROCONSUL
FROM THE PEOPLE OF HERCULANEUM)

This was the inscription that positively identified the buried site as being Herculaneum. Marcus was not from the city; he was born in Nuceria near Pompeii, a city that was to become famous for the major punch-up in Pompeii's amphitheatre – think Millwall playing away against Leeds United. The fracas in which a number of spectators were killed or wounded led to Nero's banning games in Pompeii for ten years. Marcus left Nuceria for Rome where he became a career soldier and politician being elected to one of the Republic's important magistracies, Tribune of the Plebs, in 32 BC. Later he became a *praetor* and *proconsul* and, having supported Octavian against Mark Antony, was awarded the consulship of Crete and Cyrene. On his return to Italy he moved to Herculaneum where he became the city's main benefactor. He financed building of the walls, the suburban baths where he had a private entrance leading from his villa, and the repair of the basilica. I knew what he looked like as I had seen several statues of him in the Naples museum as well as a fine copy of an equestrian statue in

Herculaneum itself. This stands alongside an altar enumerating his achievements on a terrace overlooking the sea.

A week or so later Roberto took us on another underground adventure, this time to the famous Villa of the Papyri, probably owned by Julius Caesar's father-in-law, Lucius Calpunius Piso. Like the theatre it was discovered by farmers digging a well in what looked like open countryside in 1750; in fact it was just a few hundred yards north west of Herculaneum and completely covered. The modern name derives from the complete library of nearly two thousand papyrus scrolls found within, the only complete library from the Greco-Roman world ever discovered. Fortunately the treasure-seeking Alcubierre had moved to Pompeii in 1748 and the work at Herculaneum fell to the Swiss military engineer, Karl Weber. While by no means an archaeologist as we understand the term today, Weber was much more methodical in his approach; for example he excavated whole rooms instead of driving holes through walls in search of treasures. Under the patronage of Charles VII and his son Ferdinand IV Weber produced detailed plans of the villa, which still form the basis of our investigations today. Without doubt it is one of the most luxurious private villas ever discovered in the Roman world. It stretches more than two hundred yards parallel to and overlooking the sea and was packed with the finest examples of Greco-Roman art: wall paintings, mosaics, bronze and marble statues. A realistic impression of its grandeur can be experienced in the faithful reproduction built by John Paul Getty in Malibu while the original artwork is represented by a collection of more than 80 superb bronze statues housed in the Naples Archaeological Museum.

I had seen Weber's plan, some of the papyri and the famous bronzes in the museum; now I was standing in the middle of a field next to greenhouses filled with gladioli. An engineer, a friend of Roberto, unlocked and lifted a steel cover to reveal an apparently bottomless black hole. One by one we followed our guide warily down a metal ladder set vertically in what was clearly a well shaft. Sixty feet down we reached the first of Weber's tunnels. As in the theatre there was room to walk upright; no crawling for us. Of course, Charles and Ferdinand were not going to show off their remarkable find to the princes and aristocrats of Europe and have them on their knees. We found Weber's plan to be remarkably accurate and we moved slowly through the corridors and rooms and, as VIPs had no doubt done in the 18th century, admired elegant marble columns, beautiful mosaic floors and sophisticated frescoes, though these latter were for the most part only partially complete. It was a rare privilege to follow in the footsteps of rich Romans and 18th century aristocrats; few had trodden these floors for over two hundred years.

Our guide told us that the papyri were of particular interest. The ones that had been deciphered were the work of one man, the Greek Epicurian philosopher Philodemus who was born around 110 BC in Gadara, a town now in Jordan. However, if this were a complete library there should be a Roman section that may include works by such authors as Virgil. This would be a find indeed.

There were other IAS trips to many of the sites in the Naples area and beyond. We were fortunate in that NATO was held in high regard and through the good offices of Italian military personnel and civilian members who had access to the local archaeological authorities we were able to visit places that were not – and are still not – open to the public. And perhaps more importantly we all learned much about the Greco-Roman history of the area in which we were privileged to live and work.

24

THE ASCENT OF VESUVIUS

Of course, having viewed the effects of Vesuvius' eruption in AD 79, it was only a matter of time before I took a closer look at the volcano itself. Although I had made a brief visit during my enforced stay in Naples some 16 years earlier, I had not then paid much attention to the ascent, except to remember that it was by chairlift. Furthermore, bearing in mind that Vesuvius was still considered to be active, I thought it would be wise to learn something more of its history and character before returning to the fabled mountain.

Mount Vesuvius is about five miles to the east of Naples and, at just over 4,000 feet high, stands as a dramatic and somewhat ominous presence overlooking this very densely populated area. The distinctive cone of the volcano is partially encircled by the caldera of Monte Somma, the remains of a much larger volcano that erupted in antiquity. This volcanic complex was formed by the action of the African tectonic plate being forced under the Eurasian plate, a process known as subduction.

Even before the famous eruption of AD 79 Vesuvius had demonstrated the awesome power of nature on a number of occasions. For example, around 1800 BC a massive eruption engulfed a number of Bronze Age villages, their poignant remains being found only recently. Since AD 79 there have been many more eruptions, that of 1631 in which over 3,000 people were killed being the most deadly. Thereafter there were six eruptions in the 18th century, eight in the 19th century and three in the 20th. The last eruption was in 1944, an event that disrupted the Allied war effort; the nearby airfield at Terzigno was blanketed in a thick layer of volcanic material and more that 80 aircraft of the resident United States Army Air Force unit were destroyed. However, none of these later eruptions had the massive, explosive force of that which devastated the area in AD 79. As well as describing the last days of his uncle Pliny the Younger left us a detailed descriptive record of the AD 79 event. Based on his account, the first phase of such an *explosive* eruption, in which a column of pumice and ash is hurled to a height of over 60,000 feet, is named 'Plinian' after his dramatic account. The subsequent collapse of the column, which produces a deadly outflow of pyroclastic material at ground level, is called the 'Peléan Phase' after the eruption of Mount Pelée on Martinique in 1902.

The archaeological evidence suggests that the inhabitants of Pompeii, Herculaneum and other settlements and farms in the area were caught unawares by the eruption. It is probable that they did not know that Vesuvius was a volcano despite the fact that some of the ancient writers of the late 1st century BC – Vitruvius, Diodorus Siculus and Strabo – had mentioned signs of volcanic activity associated with the mountain. What the people of Campania would have known is that the Thracian gladiator, Spartacus, having escaped from the Gladiatorial School at nearby Capua, had sought refuge with a small group of fellow gladiators on the mountain in 73 BC. A Roman army commanded by the Roman general, Gaius Claudius Gaber, was sent to destroy them, eventually setting up camp at the foot of Vesuvius. So confident of success was he that he didn't even bother to build the usual defences around the camp. Mistake! That night Spartacus and his men climbed down the mountain using ropes made from vines, attacked the unprotected camp and defeated the Roman army. Thereafter Spartacus continued to run riot around Italy until he was finally beaten and killed in battle against the Roman general, Crassus, not crucified on the Appian Way, a fate that befell Kirk Douglas in the famous film! While they probably knew this story the people of Pompeii almost certainly saw Vesuvius as a benevolent and fertile mountain, renowned for its wine production. A wall painting from the so-called House of the

Centenary in Pompeii shows Bacchus, dressed in a robe of grapes, standing by a conical mountain that has vineyards on its slopes; underneath is painted the presiding spirit of vineyards, Agathodaemon, represented here as a snake. It is possible that this fresco shows Vesuvius as the Pompeians knew it.

Now knowing a little more about Vesuvius, including the sad fact that the chair lift was no more, and concluding that it was not in imminent danger of erupting, I thought it about time to tackle the ascent. So, one winter's day my wife and I set off, armed with a map of questionable accuracy, along the *Tangenziale*. Keeping Vesuvius ahead of us and by-passing Naples we continued along the ever-busy A3 towards Torre Annunziata where, following our map, we exited the motorway and struck out for the volcano. Thanks largely to the inadequacy of our map there followed a confusing drive through the small but crowded townships of Trecase, Boscotrecase and Boscoreale, each appearing less salubrious than the one before.

We looked in vain for a sign pointing us towards 'Vesuvio' but eventually had to stop and ask, not so easy when you don't speak Italian well and the people look slightly villainous! However, the people we asked were friendly enough and directed us, with many incomprehensible arm movements, onto the Via Cifelli. At first the road through the built up areas was not bad. Soon the buildings were largely left behind and we passed through more open countryside with a surprising number of restaurants alongside the road. A little further on we entered a densely wooded area and, shortly afterwards, the road became more of a track with an increasingly slippery surface of volcanic material. Coming out of the trees, the cone of Vesuvius now towering threateningly ahead of us, we came across a small hut. A man came out and took our entrance fee for the crater. He also repeated, with considerable emphasis I thought, the word *'piano'*. Not having one with us, and not expecting to come across one, we ignored this Italian eccentricity and continued on the final leg of our ascent. The track was now very narrow and steep; more worryingly, the downhill side had crumbled away in many places. I had considerable difficulty in manoeuvring round the hairpin bends, the car sliding dangerously close to the edge. It was then that my wife found the word *piano* in her dictionary: 'slowly' or 'gently'. Now the man's advice made good sense – and I followed it as best I could.

A few hundred yards further on we arrived, with a sense of relief I might add, at a more open, flat area where the track ended – clearly the car park. We were the only ones there. From here a very narrow footpath led steeply up and across the bare volcanic cone that had the appearance of a huge pile of cinders. Underfoot the *lapilli*, small pieces of volcanic material, had a nasty tendency to roll if they were overlying a rocky surface; it was like walking on a bed of ball bearings and the steeper the path, the more we slipped.

After twenty dusty minutes or so, we made it to the top, tired but triumphant. Now it was time to look into the crater, source of such destruction. To be honest, I have to admit that this was a disappointment. Looking down more than 600 feet into the vast hole we could see only faint traces of steam issuing from the walls – no smoke, no bubbling lava, only layers of differently coloured volcanic rock, most evident on the far crater wall some 600 yards away. In fact the crater had not smoked since the 1944 eruption.

One thing did puzzle me though: as I mentioned earlier, ours was the only car in the car park, yet there were quite a few people walking around a path around the rim of the crater. We could work out their nationalities by their dress: Germans in serious walking gear; Italians in clothing that owed more to fashion than practicality; a group of French children identifiable by their Gallic boisterousness. Surely they had not walked all the way up here? This question was answered when we followed the path clockwise around the crater's rim (you can walk round about one third of the crater's circumference). When we reached the end of this particular path we could see that people were ascending on a much grander path than we had found, and at its foot was quite a large car park on which were parked a number of cars and even a tour coach. I learnt later that the main route up Vesuvius began in Ercolano and that the road was metalled, and wide enough for tourist buses to pass each other, right up to the car park. Knowing this, I never again visited Vesuvius by way of the decidedly hazardous 'back door' but drove up the same way as everybody else! Apart from the hairpin bends, and oncoming tourist coaches, I was to find the drive up past illegally built villas and restaurants and through the wooded slope an easy one. From the car park there was a half-mile walk up the final 660 feet to the summit – and the path had a wooden fence on the downhill side, very good for instilling confidence.

But back to our first ascent. Although the view into the crater was not especially impressive, that across the Campanian countryside was. The historic city of Naples and its surrounding towns, now forming one massive conurbation, was spread out below us with the whole sweep of the Bay of Naples beyond, its blue waters criss-crossed with tiny, toy-like ships. In the distance, to the north west, we could see the flat top of Capo Miseno, whence Pliny the Elder sailed on his ill-fated rescue mission and his nephew observed the unfolding tragedy of AD 79. Off Capo Miseno the volcanic island of Ischia and its smaller companion, Procida, lay basking in the winter sunshine.

Closer at hand, and at a slightly lower level, was the jagged rim of the massive Monte Somma crater, dwarfing that of Vesuvius. Below it a broad expanse of dirty white rock seemingly flowing down the mountain was in fact the petrified lava flow of the 1944 eruption. Had this not occurred many visitors would, no doubt, have preferred to ascend by way of the funicular railway, now buried beneath the lava spine but made famous by the 19th century song *Funiculi Funicula* written by Pepino Turco and set to music by Luigi Denza in 1880.

Returning to the other side of the crater, where we had arrived at the summit, we could see the long line of the Lattari Mountains and the whole Sorrento Peninsular with expensive Capri just off its tip. We were lucky on this particular day; of the many subsequent visits I made to Vesuvius, very few were blessed with the same visibility. In summer, especially, conditions were invariably hazy and you would be lucky even to see Naples, something of a disappointment for the many tourists who had trudged up the steep and slippery path, especially those (women mostly) who'd chosen footwear for fashion rather than practicability. At least there were tacky souvenirs on sale by the concrete base of the former chairlift, a reminder that it was a long way back to the main car park.

Having enjoyed our first ascent of this infamous volcano, we made our way on foot and by car – *piano, piano* – to the maelstrom of the overcrowded roads in the shadow of Vesuvius. Not for the last time I wondered what would happen if, or rather when, Vesuvius erupted once more?

25

THE SLEEPING GIANT

Although the people of Pompeii were caught unawares by the eruption of Vesuvius, it is not true that the Romans in general had no knowledge of volcanoes. Their descriptive name for a volcano was *mons igneus*, 'fiery mountain' and on the island of Sicily Mount Etna performed spectacularly from time to time, as was related by the Greek historian, Diodorus Siculus, writing between 60 BC and 30 BC. Well-read Romans would also have been familiar with the works of the Greek philosopher, Empedocles, who, it was said, threw himself into the fiery crater of Etna to prove himself immortal; as the volcano spat out one of his bronze sandals, we can probably assume he was not. In addition, those aboard ships passing between Sicily and Rome would have sighted Stromboli, the active volcanic Aeolian island we saw earlier – 'The Lighthouse of the Mediterranean'. And there was even an accurate description of Vesuvius as a volcano, written by the Greek geographer, Strabo, who was active between 64 BC and AD 25. He wrote: *'Above these places lies Mount Vesuvius, which, save for its summit, has dwellings all round, on farm-lands that are absolutely beautiful. As for the summit, a considerable part of it is flat, but all of it is unfruitful, and looks ash-coloured, and it shows pore-like cavities in masses of rocks that are soot-coloured on the surface, these masses of rock looking as though they had been eaten out by fire; and hence one might infer that in earlier times this district was on fire and had craters of fire, and then, because the fuel gave out, was quenched.'* Vitruvius, too, writing in the 1st century BC, noted that Vesuvius had once *'spouted flames'*.

Had they but recognised it, the people of Pompeii were, in fact, surrounded by signs of Vesuvius' previous eruptions: the main building material of their houses and public buildings was the volcanic tuff, also known as *tufa*. As the year AD 79 approached the mountain gave warning of impending activity through a series of earthquakes. We know about the one of AD 62 or AD 63; in fact, much of Pompeii was still being repaired in AD 79, which suggests that there may well have been more than one such event. It is also likely that sources of water were affected as the magma chamber deep below the earth began to move. But to people with no experience of a volcanic eruption, the signs could not be interpreted and they remained in blissful ignorance until Vesuvius literally blew its top. Those blessed with foresight joined those driven by fear to flee as quickly as possible; those who remained condemned themselves to a few final hours of heightening fear until their lives were snuffed out by suffocation, poisonous fumes or, in the last seconds of Pompeii's existence, the pyroclastic surges and flows that had already sealed the fate of their neighbours in Herculaneum.

That, of course, was a long time ago. Surely, I thought, science in the late 20th century had given us the tools to avoid such a disaster today?

Scientific observation of Vesuvius began in the reign of Ferdinand II, King of the Two Sicilies, who built an observatory on the slopes of Vesuvius in the mid-19th century, the first such institute in the world. Ferdinand obviously had a good eye for siting his building as it miraculously survived the eight eruptions that occurred between 1850 and the last one in 1944, massive streams of lava filling in the two deep valleys either side of the observatory. In 1970 a new observatory was erected while the original building became a museum. Later, after my time in Italy, the main data inputs were directed to an operations centre in Naples.

From one of the volcanologists I learnt that there were around a hundred monitoring stations in and around Vesuvius as well as in the other volcanic region of the Phlegrean Fields on the other side of Naples. These monitored the temperature within the crater, the composition of gases emitted and seismic activity in the area. As I have already mentioned, in the 1980s the whole area was subject to the phenomenon known as 'bradyseism' in which the ground either rise or falls due to movement of the underlying magma chamber. In the region of Pozzuoli we were in a period of uplift, which eventually raised the ground level by 1.8 metres. Associated with this movement were a number of earth tremors, up to 200 a day, which, as I mentioned earlier, caused the whole population of the ancient centre of Pozzuoli to be evacuated.

All these data were monitored on a 24-hour basis and passed in real time to the civil authority responsible for the evacuation plan. Unfortunately, said the volcanologists, despite there being a wealth of data that would help show up any changes in Vesuvius' activity, there was still no reliable method of determining precisely when an eruption was likely to occur, nor was it possible to forecast what type of eruption was likely. The civil authority had based their evacuation plan on the explosive eruption of 1631 in which some 3,000 people were killed. This plan required 600,000 people to be evacuated from the 'Red Zone', an area that extended 2.7 kilometres around Vesuvius. Based on hope rather than fact, the plan required about one month's warning and would be completed in two or three days. I could not comment on the likelihood of receiving a month's warning but, having driven around the Vesuvius area, I could not imagine that a mass movement of local inhabitants could be achieved in three weeks let alone three days.

Occasionally I would ask Italian friends living in the shadow of Vesuvius what they thought of the potential danger from the volcano. Without exception they just shrugged their shoulders and said that they didn't think about it. And indeed, visiting the villages around Vesuvius I saw no signs that anyone has made any preparation to leave, nor was there anything to show that the people considered their homes, businesses and little towns anything but permanent. New businesses were started, new homes were built, modern hotels were constructed and illegal structures appeared ever higher up the slopes of Vesuvius. After all, parents and grandparents who had experienced Vesuvius' last eruption in 1944 said that it wasn't too bad; compared to German occupation it was nothing. However, it is certain that one day Vesuvius will erupt again; whether or not sufficient warning will be given is not so certain. Furthermore, false warnings or warnings given too early may prove just as problematical: more than one false warning will lead to people refusing to move; a warning given too early will see people returning to their homes. What was clear to me in the 1980s was that the task of organising a mass evacuation was definitely a poison chalice. But worse was to come!

Post Script

In 2001 archaeologists surveying a site for a new supermarket at San Paolo Bel Sito on the outskirts of Nola, uncovered a Bronze Age village some 20 feet below the modern ground level. The village had been overcome by an eruption of Vesuvius, around 1780 BC, even more massive than that of AD 79. Further investigation revealed many artefacts: three huts, a kiln, many items of pottery and a pen holding pregnant goats. Unlike Pompeii, however, there were no bodies on the site, although two skeletons of a young woman and an older man had been found nearby in 1996, their postures indicating that they had died of suffocation. What was found, though, were the footprints of humans and animals, fleeing the source of danger in a panic-stricken dash to who knows where? Could the 1996 skeletons have been those of a dutiful daughter trying to help her aged father escape the destructive forces about to destroy their world? We shall never know.

Apart from the great archaeological significance of this exciting discovery, there was a more sombre aspect. This Bronze

Age eruption had devastated an area far beyond the 2.7 kilometre 'Red Zone'. San Paolo is about 15 kilometres north-north-east of the cone of Vesuvius so a revised 'Red Zone' looking at a 'worst-case' scenario would need to encompass an area out to 10 kilometres from the foot of the volcano. This would place most of the city of Naples in the danger zone and any evacuation plan would need to deal with three million people rather than the 600,000 planned for. The civil authority's task had suddenly moved from the improbable to the impossible. Perhaps the inhabitants of the Vesuvius area have it right after all.

26

MY OWN VILLA

I mentioned above that I dreamed of having my own villa to explore. Well, one hot Sunday afternoon I was lying on a sun lounger, glass of wine in hand, after a splendid barbecue at a friend's house close to the slope of Monte San Angelo, the volcanic hill overlooking Monte Rusciello. He remarked that on a recent walk with his dog, an energetic spaniel, he had come across a piece of mosaic up in the woods. Would I care to take a look? Despite a certain Mediterranean lethargy, I thought the opportunity too good to miss, so off we went, leaving our wives to enjoy a restful afternoon.

The wooded slopes of Monte San Angelo were criss-crossed with paths at all levels and it was quite easy to become lost – except that if all else failed you could just keep walking downhill until clear of the trees. After some searching my friend found the place we were looking for: a flat piece of ground with a stand of trees closely spaced such that the undergrowth was not too thick. And there, standing on its side, was a piece of black and white mosaic about two feet square, obviously having been dug out of the ground nearby. We looked around and discovered signs of walls as well as a number of pieces of pottery. I felt a surge of excitement but, our exploration over for the time being, we returned home to a welcome cold Nastro Azzurro.

Over the next few months my feeling of excitement grew as I returned time and time again to carry out a survey of the site, sometimes alone, sometimes with my wife and sometimes with my American friend, Dick Barnum. We did not dig but cleared as much of the undergrowth as we could, a painful activity as the undergrowth consisted of particularly spiky plants. Every so often a local farmer would approach to see what we were up to and it was interesting that, after some of these visits, a certain amount of excavation was carried out, although we never saw who did it. However, thanks in part to these local clandestine diggers we found many Roman walls, mostly in the style known as *opus reticulatum*, in which pieces of volcanic tufa stone were set in cement to make a net-like pattern that was the most common building technique of the 1st century BC and 1st century AD.

We discovered that the main building, built on an artificial terrace 30 metres in depth, had a frontage of some 100 metres and comprised a number of rooms. The internal walls still had remnants of wall painting, mainly in white, blue, red and green, and there were also pieces of painted stucco and coloured marble decoration. The presence of flue tiles and hypocaust pillars indicated that the villa had possessed a baths suite. Not surprisingly we found a lot of pottery, some clearly used for cooking, some for storage and even some finer pieces that might have been part of a dinner service; according to my friend, Dr Paul Arthur, these items covered a period from the 2nd century BC to the 5th century AD. We also uncovered a coin of Constantius II dating from around AD 360. The evidence we found showed that this was a Roman villa of some distinction with high status decoration of what we assumed was the residential quarter. We decided we would look a little further afield for signs of the 'working farm' element. It didn't take us long to find them.

On a higher terrace we found two large water cisterns – one on the surface and one underground, the latter being discovered by my almost falling into it through a hole in the ground hidden beneath a cover of vegetation. We were not the first to locate the underground cistern as a rickety home-made ladder had been propped up on its floor some 20 feet below. There did not seem to be anything inside worth risking life and limb for, so we gave the ladder a miss. However, we did find the remains of a number of substantial Roman buildings within five hundred yards or so of the one we had surveyed. Most interesting was a Roman tomb comprising four separate chambers in a single structure of *opus quasi recticulatum*, the forerunner of *opus reticulatum*, and therefore likely to date from the 1st century BC. A little further beyond the tomb were the remains of a wine press; the wooden parts had, of course, disappeared but the stone elements were in an almost pristine condition. From these and other small finds it would appear that, as in the 20th century, the slopes of Monte San Angelo were farmed just as extensively in Roman times.

Now, had we discovered such a site in the UK there is no doubt that it would have figured largely in the national news and my amateur survey would have been followed up with a professional excavation. I was somewhat disappointed, therefore, when I reported 'my' find to the local Italian archaeological authority. Although a couple of its staff deigned to visit the site they rather dismissed it as just another villa, of which they had plenty. I could almost hear their yawns. Despite this apparent lack of interest the three of us had thoroughly enjoyed the challenge. But the villa still had one surprise up its sleeve.

Some time after our survey had been completed I decided to see if any more clandestine digging had been carried out. It was late afternoon when I arrived, the sun already low in the sky, the atmosphere under the trees quite gloomy. Overhead the leaves whispered in the last of the onshore breeze. Were I superstitious I might have imagined that the spirits of the ancient inhabitants were abroad. Actually, I am superstitious and I felt the hairs on the back of my neck stand up as I climbed the few feet up to the villa site to take a look round.

As soon as I reached the terrace I could see that, at the far end of the site, a considerable amount of digging had been done. Part of a wall had been demolished and below it was a spoil heap in which a large number of pieces of pottery and broken roof tiles were visible in among the stonework from the wall. Climbing the spoil heap, my attention was caught by what looked suspiciously like a skull jutting out of the debris in amongst the pottery sherds.

On even closer examination I could see that this is exactly what it was. I picked it up and turned it in my hands. It felt both strange and exciting to be in such close contact with an ancient human. Archaeology usually involves the uncovering and study of ruined structures and artefacts; now I was face to face with a probable owner of this very villa. I placed the skull gently on one side and started to sift through the pile of spoil. Before long I had uncovered not only the skull but also the jawbone and several other bones, both large and small, not quite enough to assemble a full body but certainly the remains of at least one person.

Darkness was now almost upon me so I gathered up the bones I had uncovered and returned home. The next morning, bright and early, I returned to the site and continued to sift through the spoil. I collected several more bones and some 75 pieces of pottery I believed belonged to a single vessel as well as some that obviously did not. Investigating further I found that on the far side of the demolished wall was a tomb in the form of a stone-lined tunnel about six feet long, built against the outer wall of our villa. Inside the tomb, at the far end, was an almost intact globular-shaped pottery jar with a single handle and the upper part covered in a reddish slip. There would have been a coin in the mouth of the deceased to pay the ferryman to cross the Styx; unfortunately I could not find it and assumed that the tomb-robber had departed with his treasure.

The next day I took the bones to my friend, Dr Sara Bisel who, you will recall, was working with the newly discovered skeletons in Herculaneum. She kindly analysed the bones and, a few days later, gave me a written report of her findings. To my surprise the tomb had contained not one but two skeletons, one of a man aged around 45 and one of a three-year-old child. The man was quite tall for the period being about five foot seven inches. He was well nourished and had not done any hard physical work. His teeth were in good condition although there were some signs of decay. Sara was unable to learn much from the child's bones however.

The other elements in the spoil heap also proved interesting. I managed to piece together all 75 pieces of pottery and ended up with an *amphora* from Tunisia, without its neck. Almost certainly this had been used as a funerary container for the child, a not unusual use for such vessels. The roof tiles had probably been arranged to form a V-shaped roof over the man's body, a technique known as a *capuchin* burial. The jar and other pieces of pottery were the grave goods that accompanied the deceased. Taken together the evidence from this burial indicated that it had taken place in the late Roman period, perhaps the 4th or 5th century AD.

Although I did visit the site several more times nothing more of interest was uncovered, as far as I could see. It was a shame that the Italian authorities would not countenance a proper excavation; they did not have the money to spend on, what to them, was not a priority site and they were not inclined to let foreigners have a go. However, I did publish and present them with a report on our survey, which was translated into Italian. So I felt our work had not been entirely in vain; and, anyway, it was not a little educational and great fun besides.

27

DIGGING AT THE GLORIOUS ROCK

Although I hadn't done any digging at 'my' Roman villa site the opportunity to excavate did arise. As a spin-off from membership of the International Archaeological Society my wife and I – not forgetting Katie, the dog – were invited to join an excavation of a pre-Roman, Lucanian, site in Campania, south of Salerno. The Lucanians were an Oscan-speaking hill tribe who, at one point in their history, decided that quality of life on the plain by the sea would be preferable to that in the rather bleak mountain fastness of Lucania. So around 350 BC they descended on the Greek colony of Poseidonia and took control of the city. Apparently they achieved this without the mass shedding of blood common in those times; it was more of an enforced assimilation. The archaeological record illustrates this takeover quite dramatically through changed burial practices: in place of the boring, plain graves of the Greek great and good we find plastered and painted tombs of a Lucanian warrior aristocracy. The inner sides and roofs of these tombs reveal mounted warriors being bid farewell by anxious-looking wives, bloody boxing bouts, fierce gladiatorial contests, exciting chariot races and poignant scenes of Lucanian funeral rites. It is worth travelling to Paestum, the Roman and modern name for Poseidonia, just to see these unique works of funerary art well displayed in the modern museum.

But to return to the excavation, a team of Canadian students under the directorship of Maurizio Gualtieri and his American wife, Helena, were investigating a small, walled Lucanian settlement near the grandly named town of Roccagloriosa. To reach this rather isolated venue Monica and I left the *autostrada* 60 miles or so south east of Salerno and took the *Strada Statale 517* towards Policastro before taking to the narrow, winding, mountain roads into the middle of nowhere. Whereas Naples was always chock-a-block with traffic, here there was none at all and there was time to enjoy the magnificent scenery. We eventually drove into Torre Orsaia and a small but clean 2-star hotel, our base for the next two weeks in this neat little town that time had seemingly passed by. As a base Torre Orsaia suffered from one distinct disadvantage: the excavation site was an uphill walk of one and a half hours, and work started promptly at 7 o'clock! For Monica and me this was not too much of a problem as the site was only 15 minutes away by car. On the first morning we drove up alone. On the second two students were waiting outside the hotel hoping for a lift. On the third morning the number had grown to four. By the end of the first week I was running a shuttle service, so much so that on Day 6 my last delivery was 5 minutes late and I, along with my chastened passengers, had to suffer the director's reprimand.

The site itself was, not surprisingly, remote and surrounded by the same spectacular mountain scenery we'd recently driven through. More unexpectedly there appeared to be a farm nearby as our arrival was always welcomed by the frantic barking of unseen dogs. And it soon became clear why we started so early for as soon as the sun appeared above the eastern ridge the temperature rose dramatically. Fortunately the site boasted a stone-lined well some 20 feet deep providing a constant supply of pure, icy-cool water. We brought the water up in a bucket attached to a long bamboo pole; when the heat became unbearable, we drew up a bucket, drank a cooling draught then tipped the remainder over our heads. Fifteen minutes later it was time to do it again, and so on until the end of our day at 1 o'clock.

Our director, Maurizio, had begun his professional life as an economist but, finding this discipline tedious, had embarked on a second career as an archaeologist. He and Helena worked at the University of Alberta but also had connections with the University of Perugia and it must have been this association that led to the Italian State granting authority for the Roccagloriosa excavation. It is unlikely, however, that the Italian State could have foreseen the dramatic and early find of an un-robbed tomb of a cremated Lucanian aristocratic warrior outside the walls of this diminutive hilltop city. Three years on from this remarkable event we were excavating within these walls in an area beside a small, handsomely paved square bounded by stone buildings. No doubt this was the Lucanian equivalent of a Roman forum, the town square. As we trowelled away, Katie found a patch of shade in one of the trenches and either watched us workers or, more usually, snoozed with her head resting on her front paws. At first she had been nervous of the farm dogs around the site but, after just one day, she had taken control of what she now considered her territory and defended it with fierce barking if any person or another dog approached. She proved to be an excellent early warning system.

While Katie dozed we toiled. The work was painstaking, dusty and hot but, bit-by-bit, we were revealing this long-forgotten Lucanian town. In addition we were coming across a variety of artefacts, nothing extraordinary but pottery and everyday items once used by the ancient inhabitants. Thus does archaeology link the past with the present and bring the ancient people almost within touching distance. The mid-morning break, with refreshments collected by Maurizio from the nearby village, was very welcome. The entire team sprawled around the well, tired, dusty but exhilarated by the dramatic scenery and the thought of discoveries still to come. Our director was a hard task-master though. Thirty minutes only were we allowed; then it was back to work until one o'clock when the band of weary and grubby workers made its way back down the hill to the luxury of a shower and a well-earned afternoon nap.

One afternoon, when all sensible people were escaping the heat and enjoying a little *riposo*, the peace of Torre Orsaia was shattered by the penetrating sound of the church bell echoing around the deserted streets. The good citizens of the town stumbled out of their slumbers to see what great news was being announced. In fact, two of the students had scaled the imposing medieval campanile of *San Lorenzo* and tried their hand at bell ringing. When Maurizio learned of this he promptly banned them from the dig and it was only through the intervention of the mayor who said, perhaps exaggerating a little, that it was the most exciting thing that had happened in Torre Orsaia since the end of World War Two, that the miscreants were reinstated.

A couple of days later I was approached by a delegation of fellow diggers who told me that it was Maurizio's birthday and that they had arranged a surprise for him. My part in the plan was to collect, during Maurizio's trip for the morning refreshments, a birthday cake, sparkling wine and balloons. This I did and, while Maurizio was absent, we decorated the site with balloons, erected a huge 'HAPPY BIRTHDAY' banner and mounted the cake in a place of honour on an ancient plinth. The *piece de resistance* awaited Maurizio's return: we presented him with a gleaming white, colonial-style pith helmet decorated with a red and a blue balloon. The scene was set for a pleasant birthday party. However, what we had not bargained for was a visit by State officials, their arrival being heralded by Katie. To give him his due, Maurizio did not turn a hair. He strode over to greet the visitors, balloons bouncing either side of his helmet, and proceeded to give them a tour of the colourfully decorated site before inviting them to join us in our small celebration. What the officials thought we never learnt; maybe they assumed that all archaeologists were eccentric; for those of us who've followed *Time Team* there might be something in that.

At the end of our two weeks' labour we were sad to leave the excavation and our new-found friends but felt that we had in some small way contributed to its success. And, on the day of our departure, the temperature topped one hundred degrees Fahrenheit; somehow the air-conditioned comfort of the car seemed preferable to another day on the sun-scorched site.

28

NIGHTS AT THE OPERA

In terms of cultural enlightenment no visitor to Italy, nor one who is living there, should miss a trip to the opera. Even the name is Italian. In Naples we were fortunate in having the *Real Teatro di San Carlo*, the Royal San Carlo Opera House, founded by the Bourbon King Charles VII in 1737 and the oldest continuously active such venue in Europe. A performance there is much more than just the opera; all levels of Neapolitan society are represented, for in Italy opera is not regarded as an entertainment solely for the musical elite. Bejewelled, designer dressed ladies and their Armani-suited escorts sweep in on a cloud of expensive perfume while, from lower down the social scale, faded but elegant fur-clad widows stroll among the crowd accompanied by the faint odour of mothballs. And between these extremes can be seen every other fashion from faded jeans and jumpers to posh frocks and dinner jackets.

The interior of the theatre is almost overwhelming, a riot of gold, crimson and magnificent frescoes. Five horseshoe-shaped levels rise from the stalls, a scarlet sea of seats, each level comprising a series of private boxes. Each box has a large mirror on the wall nearest the stage; this is now used by the ladies to freshen-up their make-up but was there, in times past, to ensure that the occupants would not miss the arrival of the king in the magnificent Royal Box above the main entrance at the rear of the auditorium. All could then, as one, rise deferentially; no doubt Mussolini would have expected the same mark of respect. My wife and I were fortunate to attend a number of performances at the San Carlo; all were of the highest quality – faultless music, superior singing and splendid stage sets.

This being Italy, opera was not confined to the grand opera

houses though. While staying with our friends Italo and Mimma Marinari we enjoyed performances in the Greco-Roman theatre of Syracuse, Sicily's oldest and largest theatre where some of Aeschylus' most famous works had their premiere. Originally built in the 5th century BC it was 'modernised' in the 3rd century BC and is still used extensively today. Seating, arranged in a horseshoe shape, is on the original stone seats, so a cushion is more of an essential than a luxury. Beyond the stage is a backdrop of dark green pine trees above which the sea can just about be seen. Opera under the stars in the warmth of a Mediterranean evening was certainly one of the delights of a NATO posting.

And we will never forget a grand performance of Verdi's *Aida* in the amphitheatre of Pompeii, perhaps an unusual venue given the original entertainment that used to take place here. Sadly we never saw the end of this performance as it fell victim to a violent Mediterranean rain storm; even we British had to flee, although I am proud to report that we were the last to leave the arena! My abiding memory is of Aida, the Ethiopian princess, and Radames, Captain of the Pharaoh's Guard, having decided to flee into the desert, standing on stage with water pouring off them, no doubt thinking that this would never have happened in Ancient Egypt.

My favourite opera experience, however, was in the Baths of Caracalla in Rome. Monica and I joined a group of Americans from the United States Naval Hospital in Naples for this cultural trip. We thought we were to see Verdi's *Nabucco*; however, on arrival at our hotel in Rome we learned that the programme had been changed and that instead of following the Jews into captivity we were to journey to China with Puccini's *Turandot*. Unfortunately this rather negated all the preparatory work the Americans had done for the trip. As luck would have it my boss, Captain Paul Pedisich, was something of an opera buff and he had lent me a book giving the storylines and *libretti* of all the well-known operas. After a quick read of the book I was able, en route to the Baths, to relate the story of the Prince of Tartary and the cold-hearted Princess Turandot, adding, tongue in cheek, that, of course, all English people were knowledgeable about opera.

We arrived at the Baths in good time and were even able to tour what, in Roman times, must have been an extraordinarily magnificent building, its massive walls now given a golden glow by the floodlights. Having wandered all around the site my wife and I happened on a bar and decided there was still time for a drink before the performance started. Surprisingly, Monica seemed oblivious to the fact that almost everyone except us was dressed in somewhat bizarre, theatrical-Chinese fashion; clearly they were members of the cast. Before I could quietly point this fact out to Monica a young man dressed in a dinner jacket and carrying a violin case approached us. He advised us, most politely, that we were in the performers' bar but, as we already had drinks, he decided to join us rather than have us ejected. It turned out that he was English and part of the orchestra. More importantly he was a most useful source of information. He told us that the whole cast was on strike, for reasons that were not immediately apparent. However, this being Italy, they would make only a token gesture: the opera would start 45 minutes late. He also told us that the opera was incomplete at the time of Puccini's death in 1924 and was completed by Franco Alfano in 1926. To mark this sequence of events our first conductor for the evening would step down at the point where Puccini's work ended; there would then be a short interval and the work would be concluded under a second conductor. We continued talking for a while before returning to our seats, about 30 minutes after the advertised start time. Needless to say we were able to explain everything to our American friends, so further enhancing the cultural credentials of the British.

The performance did proceed exactly as our informant had forecast – and a very good performance it was too, under a sea of stars amid the atmospheric ruins of a great and ancient culture. There was only one complaint: our seats were a long way from the stage. And thereby hangs a particularly Italian tale. The organiser of our event was unable to accompany us as she had to travel to Germany. However, she had passed a sum of money to our hotel proprietor sufficient to book the best seats. A young employee had been despatched to the booking office but instead of buying the most expensive seats he bought the cheapest. He put the tickets in an envelope, handed them to the hotel proprietor, pocketed the cash difference – and has not been seen since!

29

LIFE IN THE BAY OF NAPLES – CAPRI

By now you've probably realised that working for NATO was not exactly taxing and trips away from the office were pleasant interludes in the usually rather tedious daily routine. In fact, one characteristic of the Cold War was that, from a military perspective, little changed; the cycle of activity – in my case the review of war plans and the planning and running of exercises – came around with the same regularity as events in the film *Groundhog Day*. In addition to working visits outside Italy there were opportunities to see something of southern Italy and I've already described some of my adventures. But I also wanted to see something of life in the Bay of Naples: was it the same as on the mainland or was it quite different?

Guarding the Bay of Naples are three islands: Ischia and Procida to the north and the better-known Capri to the south. Despite their proximity, one to another, each has its own topography, character and charm and all seemed to offer a welcome refuge from the hustle and bustle of chaotic Naples. I resolved to find out if this were true.

First on my list was Capri, the most famous and by far the most expensive. My wife and I chose to travel by ferry from Naples, not the quickest journey – the hydrofoil takes only half the time – but a more sedate one of just less than an hour and a half. The main ferry terminal of Naples is at *Molo Beverello*, in the shadow of the Royal Palace, *Palazzo Reale*, and the New Castle, *Castel Nuovo*, not quite so *nuovo* as it dates back to the 13th century. Somewhat to our surprise, this being Naples, buying tickets, finding the right ferry and boarding went without a hitch and we were soon on our way. Soon we were leaving Naples behind, the imposing peak of Vesuvius/Somma on our left becoming less menacing as we steamed out into the bay. Twenty miles ahead lay Capri, looking to me like a sleeping dragon, its head pointing towards the Sorrento Peninsular that formed the southern arm of the bay. The ferry docked at the *Marina Grande*, the main port of Capri where we disembarked to join many others, most of whom were mere day-trippers. Of interest, Capri's population of about 12,000 is swelled daily by about the same number of tourists.

The narrow waterfront was a hive of activity with white, open-top taxis touting for business, agents extolling the virtues of their hotels and a multitude of multi-national tourists milling about or patronising the many bars and cafés. On the landward side the land rose steeply to Capri's main town, also called Capri. To our right loomed the sheer limestone cliffs of Monte Solaro, the highest point on Capri at nearly 2,000 feet.

We had already booked our accommodation so we ignored the touts and made our way to the funicular railway just a few yards from the quayside. The ride up to the town, although only five minutes in duration, must be one of the most scenic anywhere as the railway climbs steeply through the terraced vegetable gardens and lemon groves of picturesque whitewashed villas each splashed with the vivid purple of bougainvillea or crimson of hibiscus. Looking back down the narrow track we enjoyed an ever-expanding view of the whole Gulf of Naples and, immediately below us, the harbour with its collection of ferries, hydrofoils, fishing boats and private yachts. Yes, Capri is indeed a popular place!

The upper station of the funicular sits snugly alongside the *Piazzetta*, or *la Piazza Umberto Uno* to give it its proper name. This small and intimate square, the social centre of Capri, is dominated by the impressive clock tower while opposite, at the top of an impressive flight of flower-bedecked steps, is the former cathedral of Capri, the 17th century Baroque *Santo Stefano*. We climbed the steps to the square, pausing to admire again the magnificent view across the bay and towards Monte Solaro, then slowly made our way through the crowded square past the packed pavement cafés, one in each corner, that funnelled pedestrians through a single narrow channel.

We left the square and headed down the Via Vittorio Emanuele, past elegant shops of the type that don't have any prices on their wares, until reaching Capri's grandest hotel, the *Qui si sana*. The name 'Here we heal you' gives a clue as to its origins: it was built in 1845 by a Scottish doctor, George Clark, as a health centre. Now it is patronised by the great and the good – and the not so good, provided they are wealthy. Needless to say, we continued past this impressive example of Victorian benefaction, its grandeur enhanced by colourful window boxes and the ubiquitous bougainvillea, and continued downhill. Our destination was not far beyond: the Hotel Villa Krupp. The name records the presence of the German industrialist, Friedrich Krupp who, in 1900, commissioned the amazing zig-zag footpath overlooked by the hotel, the Via Krupp. This beautifully paved path takes the form of a series of continuous sharp hairpin bends cut into the cliff face and links this part of the island with Capri's second harbour, the *Marina Piccola*, several hundred feet below. According to Herr Krupp the footpath was built so that he could more easily travel between his room in the *Qui Si Sana* hotel to his marine biology research vessel moored at the *Marina Piccola*. However, it was said that he used it to visit a cave to indulge in sex orgies with local youths. Whether true or not Krupp was asked to leave Italy in 1902, the year the path was completed.

The hotel that bears his name, a modest 3-star establishment, was built as a private residence in 1900. It found a degree of fame as the residence of Maxim Gorky who entertained Lenin here in 1908. Our room was light and airy with pastel-coloured walls and a floor of beautiful hand-painted floral tiles. The *piece de resistance*, however, was the spectacular view from our small balcony: below us the colourful and well-tended Gardens of Augustus (despite the name, nothing to do with the Emperor);

beyond, the famous *Faraglioni* rocks set in the azure blue Tyrrhenian Sea. It would be difficult to tear ourselves away from such an idyllic setting.

That evening we strolled into town. What a change! The hordes of day-trippers had gone and the narrow streets – more like alleyways, really – were lively but uncrowded. And, an added bonus: no traffic; there are no cars in Capri town. Moon had ousted Sun and the harsh heat of the day had been replaced by the warm and fragrant air of a summer's evening. We strolled past the *Qui Si Sana* hotel along the Via Camerelle. Lantern-shaped street lights cast pools of soft light that were interspersed with areas of more brilliant light spilling from the windows of the elegant shops on either side. Restaurants, their diners sitting outside at candle-lit tables with gleaming white tablecloths, added to the relaxed atmosphere. But, enchanting though the scenery was, it does not feed the inner man, so we looked for a suitable place to dine ourselves. We did not have to look far before we found a smart *trattoria* with a magnificent view across the Bay of Naples. And the food matched the view: an *insalata caprese* (alternating slices of buffalo-milk cheese and tomato topped with basil), *dentice alla griglia* (grilled sea bream) with *patate fritte* (chips – well, we are British) washed down with a carafe of local wine, *Capri Bianco*. Across the bay the lights of Naples twinkled alongside the distinctive silhouette of Vesuvius. What more could one want?

The next morning we decided to visit the famous Blue Grotto, known to the Romans but rediscovered only in 1826. We took the funicular to the *Marina Grande* and walked along the quay to a sign stating: 'To the Blue Grotto'. There we boarded a small motor launch that soon set off along the north coast to the grotto. What we hadn't realised was that our launch took us only to the entrance to the Blue Grotto; we then had to transfer to a rowing boat – and pay again – for the privilege of exploring this natural wonder. (So be warned!) The entrance was both narrow and low and we had to duck as the boatman pulled us inside the cave by a fixed chain. The transition into a different world took our breath away. The water inside the cave was crystal clear and a most beautiful royal blue in colour that shimmered as our boat disturbed the surface. The dark rock of the grotto formed a perfect setting for this display of liquid colour, almost too blue to be real. Our time in the grotto was all too short; an expensive but thoroughly worthwhile visit.

For lunch we bought a couple of *panini* (not *paninis* as British cafés are wont to call them) and sat on the cliff overlooking the *Faraglioni* rocks, watching the succession of tourist boats making their way around the island. Lunch over, we decided to step back in time – to the era of the Roman Empire and, in particular, to the reign of Rome's second emperor, Tiberius. Tiberius ruled from AD 14 to AD 37 but spent the last ten years of his life on Capri. Here he lived at his magnificent, palatial villa, now known as the *Villa Jovis*, the largest of 12 Imperial villas on the island. It is located high up the eastern end of the island on Monte Tiberio, at 1,095 feet the second highest point on the island. Here, according to Suetonius, Tiberius got up to all sorts of mischief. Listen to this: *'On retiring to Capreae he made himself a private sporting-house where sexual extravagances were practised for his secret pleasure. Bevies of girls and young men, whom he had collected from all over the Empire as adepts in unnatural practices, would perform before him in groups of three to excite his waning passions.'* We have to bear in mind, however, that Suetonius was writing at least 60 years after Tiberius' death so these accounts are all hearsay.

The walk from Capri town to the villa, about 40 minutes all uphill, was very scenic with views across the Bay of Naples and, closer at hand, the gardens of luxurious white-washed villas filled with dramatic purple bougainvillea, bright blue morning glory, scarlet camellias and multi-coloured roses. Interspersed with this luxury were more everyday plots of vines, tomatoes and the popular *fava* beans. Eventually we sighted the ruins of the villa, seemingly growing out of the limestone that makes up the island, which is, in fact, an extension of the Sorrento Peninsular. Ten more minutes hard climb and we had arrived.

The villa is immense and built on a series of terraces, but only the shell remains. At its heart are four massive water cisterns, essential on an island without its own water supply. In fact, it was not until 1978 that an undersea pipeline was constructed to bring water from the mainland. The first attempt was thwarted by the *Camorra* who blew a large hole in the pipe, probably because of a lack of promised funding. Payment being made, the pipeline was repaired and, for the first time in its history, Capri had a reliable water supply.

Truth be told, the villa was rather disappointing. Only very minute elements of the original decoration were visible and much of the internal space had been reconstructed in the manner of our old Ministry of Public Buildings and Works, lacking any sympathy with the original construction. At the highest point of the villa we found the church of *Santa Maria del Soccorso* dating from 1610. Outside the church we admired – or rather didn't – the bronze statue of the Madonna and Child, lifted in place, so a plaque informed us, by a helicopter of the United States Navy. From this viewpoint we could see the ruins of the Roman lighthouse that guided ships into the only port of those days, now the *Marina Piccola*. Apparently the lighthouse collapsed in an earthquake shortly after Tiberius' death but was rebuilt by the Emperor Domitian and remained in use until the 17th century.

More interesting was the promenade at the foot of the villa to the north. A large dining room faced onto the promenade, which in Tiberius' day would have enjoyed a splendid panoramic view towards the mainland; today the view is masked by trees. At the extreme eastern end we were able to look down more than one thousand feet to the rocks at sea level. According to Suetonius this is where Tiberius cast those who had displeased him. However, Suetonius had clearly never visited this spot as he reported that soldiers were stationed at the foot of the drop to finish off those who had survived the one thousand foot fall! Suetonius obviously liked a good story, true or not.

The walk back into Capri town was equally scenic, but a good deal easier as it was all downhill! So ended our first full day on Capri.

The next morning, after a leisurely breakfast enhanced by the spectacular view, we strolled up to the *Piazzetta* and enjoyed an expensive coffee in the *Al Piccolo* bar. We had decided to have a look at Capri's other town, Anacapri, the *ana* reflecting its Greek heritage, meaning 'up' or 'above'. From the terrace in the shadow of the 17th century *Torre dell'Orologio*, said to be the bell tower of the former cathedral of *Santo Stefano*, we could see over towards Anacapri, though not the town itself. That end of the island is more mountainous and is dominated by Monte Cappello and Monte Solara. We could just make out the famous *Villa San Michele*, shining white against the darker rock, apparently clinging somewhat nervously to the side of the mountain, a sheer drop in front of it. We considered taking the funicular down to the *Marina Grande* then walking up the so-called Phoenician Steps but, having assessed the steepness of this route and learnt that there were 800 steps, we decided on the bus! At least we had a choice; at the beginning of the 20th century there was no road and the steps, probably Greek rather than Phoenician, were the only means of access to Anacapri. There are few roads on Capri and those that exist are narrow and winding; the buses, therefore, are miniature versions of the standard yellow Italian bus. The bus station of Capri, not far from the *Piazzetta*, is also in miniature, like the start of a children's ride at Disney World. We bought our tickets and crammed on to one of these miniature buses. The buses may be small but the same number of passengers as you might expect for a normal sized bus seemed to board; it made for a friendly experience but not a particularly comfortable one.

Fortunately the journey was not a long one and we were disgorged 15 minutes later at the *Piazza Vittorio*. Although not as stylish as the *Piazzetta* in Capri, this was larger and greener having both trees and a small but colourful garden. Clearly this was the nerve centre of the town; buses, taxis and people filled the square, which was bordered by the ubiquitous tourist shops and stalls. However, having read Axel Munthe's rather strange but famous book, *The Story of San Michele*, we decided that this villa should be our first port of call so we made our way along a narrow street lined with yet more touristy shops and stalls to the villa itself.

Axel Munthe, a Swedish doctor, was a remarkable man. Although he was personal physician to and friend of Victoria, the Queen of Sweden, and had medical practices in Paris and Rome, he also chose to work with the poorest of people, most notably in Naples where in 1884 a serious cholera epidemic was decimating the population. He married a British woman, became a British citizen in the First World War and served with the French Ambulance Corps. In 1887 he bought the ruined chapel of *San Michele* and subsequently spent much of his time on Capri building the villa and filling it with antiquities. Munthe wanted his house 'to be open to the sun to the wind, to the voice of the sea', and so it is. It is built on several levels and many of the spaces are open to the sky with grand views across the Bay of Naples. We particularly enjoyed the splendid *loggia* where we walked between gleaming white pillars with wisteria overhead and borders of geraniums, hydrangeas and other flowers whose names I can never remember. And, throughout the garden and inner rooms, Ancient Egyptian, Roman and Medieval statues and other artefacts to surprise and enlighten. We spent a very pleasant two hours wandering through this testament to one man's vision and, by the end of our visit his book began to make a little more sense.

Finding somewhere for lunch was not a problem as Anacapri, like Capri, has no shortage of cafés and restaurants. We ate well but drank sparingly as our afternoon plan was to scale Monte

Solaro. Originally we intended to walk up but, on reflection, decided it would be more fun – and considerably less strenuous – to take the chairlift. We made our way to the chairlift station, just off the *Piazza Vittoria*, bought our tickets and prepared for the ascent. Boarding the single chair was a little challenging as the chairs are on a continuous loop so are moving when they arrive. However, we both managed this without injury and moved out into the open air. The route was very scenic, initially over villas and gardens then through an avenue of mature trees and over vineyards and areas of old terracing, our feet never far from the vegetation. We had definitely chosen well, no huffing and puffing with the threat of a heart attack but instead a gentle ride with the added benefit of grand views, to Anacapri below us and out across the western part of the island with its scattering of whitewashed houses. Twelve minutes later we were at the top.

From up here the views were even more impressive, especially towards the opposite end of the island. We could look down on Capri town and, beyond, Tiberius' villa on its crag; further on, softly veiled in the afternoon haze, we could make out the end of the Sorrento Peninsular. Below, to our left, we could just see the outer part of *Marina Grande*, while on the other side of the island the *Faraglioni* rocks rose majestically out of a sea of the deepest blue.

A short stroll through the wooded slopes took us to the small valley of *Cetrella*, named so it is said after the lemon-scented plant known locally as *cedronella*. Here we came across the small 15th century monastery of *Santa Maria di Cetrella*, a holy but somewhat austere contrast to the surrounding colourful carpet of flowers. Entering the enclosure we were able to visit the sacristy, kitchen and the cells of the original Franciscan and Dominican friars, now long gone. The beauty and splendid isolation of this spot must have been a real joy to the friars, despite their spartan lifestyle. Now, of course, there are the tourists! The most significant building is, of course, the church, which stands next to the simple bell tower – a later addition. Over the entrance we noted the painting of the Madonna; surely her mother would not have approved of the scarlet lipstick she was wearing? Inside, however, the two naves are simply decorated with an altar at the end of each; that dedicated to *Santa Maria* is ornate with a painting of the Virgin and Child within an elaborate marble, architectural frame. The second nave has to make do with a painting of *San Domenico* in a very simple wooden frame. At the back of the church we found a small terrace shaded by a magnificent wisteria, an ideal place for rest and contemplation. However, we thought that even the friars might have considered the knee-high wall a somewhat insubstantial barrier to the 1,200 foot fall to *Marina Piccola*.

Suitably refreshed by the tranquillity of the monastery, the view and the lush nature of this secluded spot – happily not overrun with visitors – we made our way back to the chairlift passing, en route, a house where Compton Mackenzie, the Scottish author of *Whisky Galore* (among more than 90 other books), lived for a short time before the First World War. It is now a museum. After enjoying another restful descent of the mountain we just had time back in Anacapri to visit her two main churches: *Santa Sofia* and *San Michele*. The parish church *Santa Sofia* dates from 1510 and is on the site of the original 11th century parish church of *Santa Maria di Constantinopoli*. We thought the Baroque façade rather grand, gleaming white pilasters rising two storeys, the walls between painted a pleasing shade of yellow. Against this sophisticated face the bell tower, to the rear of the church and constructed of rough-looking stone, looked out of place. The most unusual element within the church, we thought, was the massive organ at the east end above the altar.

A few yards away is the church of *San Michele* dating from the early 18th century. Its white Baroque façade is simpler than that of its near neighbour but this belies the artistic treasure within. Although we had read about the majolica floor decoration we were not prepared for the sheer expanse of beautiful hand-painted tiles. The entire floor is covered with the story of Adam and Eve being expelled from the Garden of Eden. Everything is there: the apple tree, the snake, the archangel perched on a cloud and pointing to the exit, and a wonderful collection of animals and plants in an idyllic setting. We could only wonder at the detail, the colours and the brilliant composition of its creator, Leonardo Chiaiese.

And so ended another splendid, albeit tiring, day on Capri. We were ready for the bus back to Capri, a shower, a spot of *riposo* and another excellent dinner. Tomorrow we were to return home.

30

FRIENDS AND ALLIES

A rather less peaceful episode later took place on another Italian island I knew well: Sicily. While not directly involved in this extraordinary event I certainly experienced the tensions it caused between two NATO allies: the Italians and the Americans. The affair took place at the airbase of Sigonella, an Italian Air Force base but one tenanted by the United States as Naval Air Station Sigonella. Several thousand American sailors and civilians lived and worked at two separate sites, one operational the other domestic. Although the location was in Italy, an Italian presence was hard to spot. The only resident Italian unit was a squadron of Italian Atlantique ASW aircraft one of whose former pilots was Commander Italo Marinari, my MARAIRMED colleague and close friend. To all intents and purposes, therefore, Sigonella was a very busy operational American base with all the supporting domestic, social and entertainment facilities that can be found wherever the United States puts down roots.

On 7th October 1985 four young terrorists from the Palestine Liberation Front (PLF), an offshoot of the Palestinian Liberation Organisation (PLO), hijacked the Naples-registered cruise ship, the *Achille Lauro*, off the coast of Egypt. Armed with the ubiquitous AK-47s they forced the captain to sail to Tartus in Syria and demanded the release of Palestinians held by Israel. As many of the ship's passengers were American citizens, President Reagan ordered US Special Forces to prepare for a rescue mission.

The following day, after being refused permission to dock at Tartus, the hijackers murdered the disabled American, Leon Klinghoffer, throwing him and his wheelchair into the sea. The ship then continued to Port Said where negotiations began between the four terrorists, Abu Abbas – the mastermind behind the hijacking – and President Mubarak of Egypt. After several hours the hijackers agreed to give up the ship in return for safe passage to Tunisia, then the headquarters of the PLF. The four, together with Abu Abbas, duly boarded an Egyptian commercial airliner bound for Tunis on 10th October.

Incensed by the murder of an American citizen, President Reagan ordered fighter aircraft from the USS *Saratoga* to intercept the airliner. After tailing the aircraft for some time the fighters eventually forced it to land at Sigonella where heavily armed American Special Forces were awaiting its arrival. However, despite being a Naval Air Station, Sigonella was on Italian soil and therefore, according to Italian President Bettino Craxi, the hijackers were now under Italian jurisdiction. For that reason he ordered the *carabinieri* to prevent the Americans from boarding the Egyptian aircraft and apprehending the terrorists, using lethal force if necessary. A tense stand-off then ensued: armed NATO allies facing each other under the glare of the airfield's arc lights. This situation continued throughout the night while top-level talks took place between Reagan and Craxi. Who knows what was said? But on the ground at Sigonella a mistaken gesture, an accidental shot or a misunderstood word of command could have precipitated perhaps the most serious international incident between these two member nations, with far–reaching implications for NATO.

Fortunately, Reagan saw sense and finally ordered his forces to stand down. The four hijackers were taken into Italian custody and were eventually put on trial and given prison sentences of between 15 and 20 years. Somewhat surprisingly, Abu Abbas was not put on trial but was permitted to leave Italy for Yugoslavia.

Italo learnt of this incident from an Italian friend at Sigonella. He, like many Italians in the forthcoming days, felt very aggrieved that the Americans had felt that they could ride roughshod over international conventions concerning sovereign territory. Needless to say, my American colleagues took a rather different view and this led to some interesting and heated discussions among our NATO staff.

Another potentially dangerous stand-off between NATO allies arose during my last year in Naples, this time involving Greece and Turkey. In March 1987 the Turkish seismic survey ship *Sismik*, accompanied by Turkish warships, set sail to conduct an oil exploration survey in the disputed waters around the islands of Lesbos, Lemnos and Samothrace in the north-east Aegean. In response the Greek Prime Minister, Andreas Papandreou, considering these waters to be Greek, gave orders for the ship to be sunk were it to be found within Greek waters. An armed clash was only avoided when the Turkish Prime Minister, Turgut Özal, under pressure from the United States and other NATO allies, ordered the *Sismik* to withdraw. I was interested to learn that America's actions may not have been entirely altruistic as Prime Minister Papandreou announced shortly after the incident that the United States Naval Base at Nea Makri near Athens would not, after all, be required to close!

What these episodes illustrated is that, while it is mutually convenient for nations to be allies, this does not mean that they will always be friends. We, too, learnt this lesson during our two Cod Wars with Iceland, one of the reasons why cod and chips is no longer the cheap meal it once was.

31

LIFE IN THE BAY OF NAPLES – ISCHIA

The year 1986 was the last time Halley's Comet appeared in our skies and I thought we would have a better chance of seeing it if we forsook the light pollution of the mainland and went to Ischia. After all, this was a once-in-a-lifetime opportunity to observe this heavenly wonder so I booked a hotel in the small town of Serrara Fontana in the hills above the fishing village of Sant'Angelo.

Ischia, standing guard at the northern end of the Bay of Naples, is a larger island than Capri at the opposite end measuring about six miles by four and cars are as ubiquitous as anywhere else. However, there are not many roads, the main one circumnavigating the island running along the coast on the north and west and climbing high into the mountains on the south and east. Minor roads, some more like tracks, look down on the sea from on high.

We boarded the car ferry at Pozzuoli and one hour later disembarked at Ischia Porto, the main town of the island. The port itself is interesting as it was once the crater of a volcano that had filled with water to form a lake. In the mid-nineteenth century Ferdinand II had a canal dug between two hills to connect the lake to the sea and created what was an attractive and safe harbour. As we drove away from the ferry, inching our way through crowds of pedestrians and a phalanx of taxis we noticed that the reception committee of taxi drivers and hotel representatives all held signs in German. Later we learned that the island's many thermal spas were especially popular with German tourists. Clearly the British preferred Capri. We set off westwards along the main road with the sea on our right and were soon passing through the attractive towns of Casamicciola – the island's second port – Lacco Ameno and Forio. On our left loomed the towering bulk of Monte Epomeo, at 788 metres the highest of Ischia's seven volcanoes that are the source of the many hot mineral springs. We were pleasantly surprised to find that the cars, despite having the dreaded 'NA' plates, were driven far less aggressively than those on the mainland; Ischia's motorists definitely had a more laid-back attitude.

Once through Forio the road began to climb inland, becoming narrower as it twisted and turned round many blind corners. Occasionally we were warned of an approaching bus by the blast of its horn just before the small orange vehicle swept round the bend. Serrara Fontana is today considered one small town but in fact it is two separate villages. The road here was hemmed in by houses and shops painted in pastel shades of green, pink and yellow – some in urgent need of repainting – and opening straight onto the narrow road.

We drove through Serrara, passing under an arch that seemed to be part of the village church and continued to Fontana and our small hotel. There we found that our room was in an annex a couple of hundred metres up the hill. We collected our key and walked back up to the picturesque main square overlooked by the elegant church, white painted with contrasting yellow pediment, pilasters on the façade, surrounding the central round window and frame of the central doorway. On the ground just outside the church was a large star-shaped mosaic in white stone showing the cardinal points and to one side a gleaming statue of Christ, arms upraised. Colourful flowers in two small gardens and shrubs in terracotta urns brought a pastoral air to the scene while pine trees shaded tables and chairs. Beyond Christ was a viewing point – and what a view! Over one thousand feet below lay Sant'Angelo, its two small harbours either side of a narrow causeway that linked the main village to a conical island rising from the azure sea like an ancient green-clad pyramid. On the horizon we could see Capri stretched out as if enjoying the sunshine. Inland, green-clad Monte Epomeo towered more than one thousand feet above the village, this being the closest we could be to the summit without going on foot. The views were too good to pass by so we sat and ordered coffee. Old men sat at tables by us quietly smoking and watching the world go by while young mums chatted animatedly to each other as their children raced around Christ. Given the frenetic character of Naples this was tranquillity indeed.

Later, having eaten an excellent pizza at the local pizzeria we retired to our room and, as darkness fell, sat on the small balcony binoculars in hand and searched the skies full of confidence that we would see this astronomical marvel. The sky was crystal-clear and there was no light pollution. However, we were not to know that the 1986 appearance of the comet was the least favourable on record and even with the help of our binoculars we were not certain we had identified it. Disappointed we went to bed to be woken at intervals by Katie who, unusually, barked at everyone who walked past our apartment.

The next morning we had the usual insubstantial Italian breakfast and decided to do a bit of exploring. We retraced our route as far as Lacco Ameno where we knew there was a museum beneath the church of *Saint Restituta*, a lady martyred under Diocletian in the third century AD and whose church adjoining the cathedral I had visited on my first trip to Naples. According to legend she was born in Carthage but was tortured for her Christian beliefs before being placed in a burning boat and cast adrift from the African shore. The boat landed on Ischia where a Christian lady who'd dreamt of Restituta's fate found the boat and its occupant, dead but otherwise untouched by fire. The local people carried Restituta to the nearby town and buried her there, a site on which a paleo-Christian church was later built. As well as having the remains of this early church the museum contains items from as long ago as the 8th century BC when Pithekoussai was a thriving Greek settlement pre-dating the first Greek colony on the mainland at Cuma.

We learnt that the present church dates from the 16th century and has an attractive neo-classical façade in pink with white pilasters supporting a plain white architrave and a pediment. We entered to pay our respects to the saint who was crowned and magnificently dressed, and standing in a crimson-lined shrine next to the High Altar. At her feet was the boat in which she had sailed from Africa.

The museum is in an architecturally matching building attached to the church where we found an interesting collection of Greek and Roman artefacts: vases, statues, toys and other items from tombs in the vicinity. At a lower level there were a number of ancient furnaces, the original 8th century BC Greek industrial district, over which lay Roman walls and the ruins of the paleo-Christian church.

Just before leaving the custodian told us that we should return in May when the statue of Saint Restituta is carried amidst much ceremony to the beach where she was originally found. Such is her popularity that the entire population of the town accompanies her. He also told us that we should visit the nearby Villa Arbusto and, in particular, seek out the famous 'Cup of Nestor'.

The villa was only a ten-minute walk away and we were delighted to find that, in addition to housing a museum, there were extensive colonnaded walks with overhead wisteria-clad trellises through lovely gardens among numerous pine trees and with splendid views across the town to the sea, and along the coast to Casamicciola and the mainland far beyond. After the relative gloom of the underground museum the air was most refreshing and we enjoyed a stroll before entering the villa itself where we soon found 'Nestor's Cup'. So why is it so famous? Because it has on it one of the oldest example of alphabetic writing. The cup is a drinking vase and was part of a rich funeral treasure in the tomb of a ten-year-old boy dating from around 720 BC. The inscription reads:

I am the beautiful cup of Nestor
He who shall drink from this cup will immediately desire
Aphrodite of the beautiful crown

Those with a Classical background will recall that Homer refers to the famous cup of Nestor, King of Pylos, in the *Iliad* so the lines above are contemporary with those of Homer's time. Furthermore, this alphabet was passed by the Greeks of Pithekoussai to the tribes of the nearby mainland and the Etruscans with whom they traded and thence to the Romans. With modifications this is the alphabet we use today.

While the museum under the church had many items still in situ those in the villa, mostly from Greek and Roman tombs, were displayed in a more traditional museum style. There was a fine selection of artefacts from the Neolithic and Bronze Ages through the Greek and Hellenistic periods to the coming of the Romans. We decided that we would have to return. Now it was time for lunch.

There was no shortage of eating places in Lacco and we found an excellent one with a sea view onto a strange mushroom-shaped rock, *il Fungo Di Lacco*. Tired out by the ancient world we enjoyed a long and leisurely meal before returning to Fontana.

While in the restaurant we'd seen a news programme on the TV showing a clip of Halley's Comet. Rather than the well-defined comet shape we'd been seeking the image showed it to be a sort of diffuse and blurry snowball. Thus enlightened we searched the night sky with greater confidence and were rewarded with seeing, after a lengthy search, the rather faint, indistinct and hazy patch of light that we identified as Halley's Comet. Our mission had been successful!

There was of course much more to see on Ischia but, sadly, next day it was time to go home. We left Fontana and continued anti-clockwise around the island. Initially the road remained well inland and high on the slope of Monte Epomeo, the blue waters of the Tyrrhenian Sea sparkling in the distance. A few minutes later the road almost doubled back on itself and began to descend and take us back towards the coast through pine trees and olive groves. Lower down we found a more agricultural landscape and we drove past vineyards and lemon groves on extensive terraces before coming into the town of Barano, the third largest after Ischia Porto and Forio. We caught glimpses of the famous Maronti Beach below the town stretching almost to Sant'Angelo, barely a mile and a half away despite our lengthy drive in the hills. The beach is famous because of its volcanic fumeroles and stretches of sand so hot from thermal activity that it is not possible to walk on them in bare feet. Unlike the other towns we had seen Barano appeared much less crowded and more tranquil. My abiding memory is of the lovely church of *San Rocco* at the end of an avenue of palm trees with its imposing Palladian-style double register façade of the palest yellow with architectural details – pediment, pilasters and architraves – in the purest white.

Leaving Barano the road remained inland and eventually arrived at flatter and more crowded terrain. We decided to take a short detour for some views of the Aragonese castle at Ischia Ponte, the second district of Ischia town. We found a place to park and admired the massive medieval fortress standing proudly on a rocky islet connected to the mainland by a stone causeway built by Alfonso V of Aragon in 1441. Around the turn of the 17th century more than two thousand people lived on the islet, which in addition to the fortifications and military garrison had a Poor Clares convent, an abbey of Greek orthodox monks and no less than 13 churches. Sadly, in 1809 we British shelled the French-held islet and caused an immense amount of damage. Now the castle is perhaps the most visited site on the island and we agreed that we, too, would visit before long.

We were now close to Ischia Porto and 20 minutes later we were boarding the car ferry, the return to Pozzuoli and home. We had really enjoyed our short stay on Ischia, a green and mountainous island with its own character and a host of fascinating historical sites to visit, interesting towns to explore and dramatic and beautiful scenery to enjoy. And we had seen Halley's Comet! We would be back.

32

EXERCISE ABLE ARCHER

Now that the Cold War is behind us we are wont to forget that, during five decades of mutual distrust and tension between West and East, nuclear devastation was never far away; indeed, there were a number of incidents that could have precipitated a nuclear exchange between the so-called Super Powers. The best known was the Cuban Missile Crisis of 1962 I described above. But unbeknown to most people there were others and, although they did not receive any publicity at the time, NATO was in the forefront – and I was, unknowingly, a part of them.

I mentioned above that the use of simulated nuclear weapons was rarely a significant element in the long Command Post Exercises. There was, however, one significant exception: the series of CPXs code-named Able Archer. These involved a relatively small number of action officers and were unusual in that they included the participation of high-level national politicians. The aim of the series was to exercise the necessarily complicated procedures associated with releasing nuclear weapons for use, bearing in mind that such weapons were, and are, under political rather than military control.

The year before I was posted to Naples I attended the Nuclear Weapon Release Procedures course at the NATO School in Oberammergau and subsequently participated in Exercise Able Archer 83. The NATO script, on which the exercise was based, envisaged a period of conflict escalation between NATO (Blue) and Warsaw Pact (Orange) forces culminating in a co-ordinated nuclear release. In detail, the scenario presupposed a change in leadership of the Soviet Union leading to growing unrest in Eastern Europe. Concern about this threatening development on its borders led Yugoslavia to request military assistance from the

West. In response to this perceived provocation, Orange forces invaded. So began, hypothetically, what would have been World War III.

According to the exercise scenario Orange land forces also crossed into Finland and then into Norway and West Germany. Orange air forces also attacked airfields in the UK. Blue forces were quickly overrun and, in consequence, NATO's military leadership – SACEUR in this case – requested initial, limited use of nuclear weapons. Authorisation was duly given by NATO's political leaders (the USA and the UK held nuclear weapons for NATO use; France's Force de Frappe was held nationally) and pre-selected Orange targets were attacked. However, even this drastic action failed to halt the Orange advance; furthermore, Orange forces responded in kind.

Having failed to stop the Orange forces SACEUR requested the more extensive, follow-on use of nuclear weapons. This was duly authorised, no doubt after a lot of discussion amongst NATO's political players, and the second nuclear phase began. Retaliation was inevitable and, mutual nuclear devastation having become a real possibility, Able Archer 83 was terminated. Who won? The answer is 'nobody' for the exercise was not meant to reflect the real world but, as I said earlier, was purely to practise NATO's procedures for the release of nuclear weapons, 'release' in this case meaning the transfer of the weapons from political to military control and the subsequent authorisation of military commanders and nuclear-equipped units to deliver their weapons.

Unbeknownst to us, while we in NATO were participating in what we considered to be a routine, and somewhat tedious, procedural 'war game', the Soviet leadership was seeing it in a quite different light as they detected several non-routine aspects not seen previously in a NATO exercise. Firstly, NATO's new nuclear weapon release procedures (NWRP) involved a revised format of coded communications and included political input at a high government level in both London and Washington; indeed, the United States even adopted a simulated DEFCON 1 alert indicating that hostilities were imminent. Secondly, a simulated reinforcement of 19,000 US troops was conducted in radio silence. Thirdly, military commands were moved from Permanent to Alternative War Headquarters. Finally, to add to Soviet concerns, some communications between exercise players could easily have been interpreted as referring to real life rather than simulated incidents. Not surprisingly, therefore, the Soviet leadership began to fear that Able Archer was not an exercise at all but a means of disguising preparations for a real nuclear first strike. Accordingly, Soviet aircraft in East Germany and Poland were fitted with nuclear weapons, nuclear missiles were placed on heightened alert and ballistic missile submarines were deployed under the Arctic ice. These measures indicated that the Soviet Union was preparing for a NATO pre-emptive strike and its finger was on a hair trigger. The danger had been averted but had not gone away.

Being familiar with NATO's new NWRP and having had experience of their use in Able Archer 83, I was involved in the similar exercise, Able Archer 84, in the autumn of that year. Once again, the aim was to practise and exercise the complex procedures that would be involved in any NATO use of nuclear weapons. The exercise scenario was similar in most respects to that in Able Archer 83. Although the exercise was focussed on land operations, there was a continuing requirement for us in COMARAIRMED to be familiar with the procedures as several of our maritime patrol aircraft types were capable of carrying, and their crews were trained in the use of, nuclear weapons. As in 1983, while we NATO staff officers read and decoded incoming nuclear messages, and sent the appropriate coded replies, the Soviet leadership was busily raising the alert level of their forces and increasing air and sub-surface surveillance operations throughout the NATO area. No doubt, also, the Soviets monitored NATO communications with an added intensity of effort. Of course, we in Naples were largely unaware of the effect our NATO CPX was having on our potential enemy; there was none of the tension that accompanied the Cuban Missile Crisis, which was played out in the spotlight of the world's media. Nevertheless, recent analysis has concluded that we came closer to mutually assured destruction as a result of Exercises Able Archer 83 and 84 than at any time since 1962. As one American journalist has put it: 'The entire Cold War was really one bad day away from the end of civilisation as we know it.' In 1983 and 1984 we perhaps came close to that bad day – and I was there!

The German TV series *Deutschland 83* gives a very dramatic and believable interpretation of events similar to those describes above and is well worth watching. In addition the two novels by General Sir John Hackett *The Third World War – August 1985* published in 1978 and its updated version *The Third World War – The Untold Story* published in 1982 cover in detail what events could have conceivably precipitated a disastrous nuclear exchange of strategic nuclear weapons.

33

BEWARE GREEKS BEARING GIFTS

As we've seen NATO was, and is, primarily a political alliance. This has led to some convoluted political manoeuvring in cases where a straightforward military solution was staring us in the face. An example of this came towards the end of my tour in Naples and led to an interesting and, I have to say, enjoyable trip.

In 1987 CINCSOUTH received an offer from the Greek Ministry of Defence of an airfield on Crete to use as a base for American maritime patrol aircraft assigned to NATO. On the face of it this was a generous offer and I was tasked with investigating the proposal. My first action was to consult the various documents that listed facilities at Kastelli, the airfield in question. I quickly concluded that it would not be suitable: the taxiways were too narrow, there were hardened aircraft shelters suitable only for small fighter aircraft and there was a distinct paucity of any support facilities. I reported my conclusion to my boss who passed it up the chain of command. The response was duly communicated to the Greek authorities who, needless to say, were not amused. They responded that, in their opinion, the airfield would be ideal for United States Navy P-3s to be based there at the appropriate time should Transition to War measures be implemented. In fact, we did not need another airfield on Crete as the aircraft referred to by the Greeks already had an excellent base at Souda Bay in the west of the island. There was, of course, a hidden agenda here. Were the Greek offer to be accepted the shortfall in requirements at Kastelli would have to be made up using NATO funds; in other words an improved airfield would be obtained without any national expenditure!

This being NATO the CINC was prevailed upon by the NATO hierarchy to send a team to Kastelli to review and report on the airfield's suitability. Being a mere wing commander I was not deemed senior enough to lead such a team; a Royal Navy officer, Captain King, a communications specialist, was duly appointed to this role. Making up the team were an American commander, who would look at the logistics side, and my colleague, Captain Stinis of the Hellenic Navy, who would be our liaison officer with the Greek authorities. I was to look after the operational aspects of the survey.

We set off in February, taking a commercial flight from Naples to Athens. Our onward flight to Crete was not until the following day so we spent the evening in the *Plaka* district. Always a lively place, on that particular night it was heaving. Many in the crowd carried plastic hammers and took great delight in hitting each other, and us, on the head. Our leader came in for particular attention as he was partly bald, a magnet for these apparently crazy people. In fact we were experiencing one of the customs of the carnival known as *Apokries*, the Greek form of *mardi gras.*

The next morning, still suffering from the after-effects of head bashing – or was it the ouzo? – we were taken to Athens' military airfield at Eleusis where we boarded a Hellenic Air Force C-130 for the flight to Kastelli. This aircraft was on a round-robin flight delivering and collecting Greek service personnel and families to and from airfields scattered around the Greek mainland and islands. We took our place in the spartan interior of the aircraft in webbing seats against the side of the fuselage. Shortly after take-off we realized that the heating system, never very efficient in an aircraft designed for freight rather than passengers, was not working, a fact confirmed by a crew member coming to apologise. Sitting with us was a young Greek wife not equipped for the fridge-like temperatures we were experiencing; after all, Greece is a place of Mediterranean sunshine is it not? She reminded me of the British wives, ex-Singapore, arriving at RAF Brize Norton in winter wearing the cotton frocks suitable for the heat and humidity of Singapore. Anyway, as a gesture of NATO gallantry we wrapped her in our coats and thus condemned ourselves to a chilly, but fortunately short, transit.

On landing at Kastelli we were greeted by the Base Commander, a lieutenant colonel of the Hellenic Air Force. He and his deputy, a major, were very welcoming and took us to the mess where we enjoyed an excellent lunch; the oranges we had as dessert were, and still are, the best I have ever tasted. After lunch the Base Commander took us on what the Americans call a 'windshield tour' of his empire. He was particularly proud of his kennels in which were a number of hounds; the colonel enjoyed his hunting and, on an airfield without any aircraft based there, he had plenty of opportunity to indulge his passion.

We did not stay on the airfield – there were no domestic facilities – but were driven down to Iraklion about 20 miles away. That evening we were hosted by a group of Greek officers at a restaurant just out of town. It was cavernous, and totally devoid of patrons. This did not bode well. We ate our first course – or courses as it was in the form of a mini-*meze* – in splendid isolation. Not until well into the second main course, at an hour when most decent folk back home would be thinking of bed, did the place start to liven up. Soon it was crowded, mostly with youngsters, and by 11 o'clock when we were leaving they were just starting. I wondered at what time their working day began?

We returned to Kastelli the following morning and began our survey. The Base Commander told us that the only aircraft permanently on site were a couple of crop sprayers; the C-130 came in most weeks but the hardened aircraft shelters, designed for fighter aircraft, were empty. In its favour the airfield had a single, long runway with a parallel taxiway. However, the sole dispersal area was small, designed for fighter-type aircraft, there was no hangarage suitable for maritime patrol aircraft and there was a distinct lack of technical, operational and domestic accommodation. We never learnt about the communications facilities as Greek national sensitivities precluded our inspection of them. In short, the information we had gathered was the same as I had extracted from the publications back in Naples. We did, though, enjoy another excellent lunch, during which Captain Stinis disappeared. He returned a little later and informed us that he had some good news and some bad news. The good news was that we had an aircraft to fly us to Athens; the bad news was: 'It is not a very good aircraft!' This did not bode well!

We took leave of our excellent hosts and drove onto the airfield. There, awaiting us, was a C-47, the military version of the DC-3 Dakota that first flew in 1941. On climbing aboard we found that this particular aircraft had been modified for target towing; in the centre of the fuselage was a massive winch assembly. Our seats, of polished wood, were along the sides of the fuselage so there was not much legroom. Furthermore, as the DC-3 is a tail-wheel aircraft there was a tendency to slide towards the rear of the cabin, our bodies only being held in check by flimsy seat belts. However, this type of aircraft had enjoyed a long and distinguished career and was renowned for its ruggedness. Consequently, I was relatively relaxed about the forthcoming flight despite the apparent absence of lifejackets; not so my naval colleagues, and especially not Captain Stinis who felt that the Hellenic Air Force had let him down. The crew of two pilots soon climbed aboard and we were off. Our return flight was longer than our outbound trip – the C-47 flies at only around 150 knots – but at least we were at a much lower altitude so temperature was not a problem. And, as I expected, we arrived safely at Eleusis just over one and a half hours later.

After another night in Athens, this time without the head bangers putting in an appearance, we left on a commercial flight to Naples, a flight much more to the liking of the fish-heads.

The report on our survey did not take long to complete but the normal NATO staffing process, in which every man and his dog has an opportunity to read and comment, took rather longer. Some weeks later Captain Stinis asked why no official reply, based on our survey, had been passed to the Hellenic authorities. I told him that the answer was quite simple: 'NATO has no word for "*No*".' I don't think he appreciated the irony of this remark, an irony though that had its basis in fact. I don't know whether a formal answer was ever given to the Greeks as I left Naples some months later. I do know, though, that Kastelli did not receive the massive funding it would have needed to make it a suitable deployment base for maritime patrol aircraft. It remained a sometime base for Hellenic Air Force fighters.

34

FINAL THOUGHTS

As I noted on my first visit to Naples all those years ago, all good things must come to an end; so eventually did my adventure in Italy. Unusually I was dined-out twice: once by the British community in the Allied Officers' Club and once by my MARAIRMED colleagues at the Italian Officers' Club in Naples hosted by my great friend Commander Italo Marinari. Sitting among friends from the UK and this region of NATO brought home to me what a privilege it had been to serve in Naples. It had been professionally rewarding and had given me a deeper understanding of the Alliance and our part in it. It reinforced my awareness that America was more than just the cornerstone of NATO; it provided by far the greater part of the funding and the majority of the advanced high-tech equipment. In the Mediterranean the US Sixth Fleet with its Carrier Battle Groups and nuclear submarines together with its naval and air force aircraft dwarfed force contributions from the other regional nations. However, I was impressed with the professionalism of those Southern Region officers with whom I worked and met and I was certain that the UK, though neither a Southern Region nation nor a major contributor of forces, more than pulled its weight in the form of experienced and well-trained staff – NCOs and officers – at all levels within ASOUTH.

Away from the office I had enjoyed being part of the close-knit British society and being able to participate in the sporting and social activities as well as contributing to the fun-filled charitable events. I'm not sure I want to see another ploughman's lunch though! My wife had also played a full part and her stories of driving through Naples to visit the various markets and hurling abuse back at locals impatient as her team were delivering essential food supplies to Neapolitan widows have to be heard to be believed. Above all we made international friendships that are still thriving as I write this.

We had certainly learnt much about southern Italy, its people and its cuisine and we had delved enthusiastically into the fascinating history of the region. Particularly rewarding were the many visits to Naples, the surrounding area and the beautiful nearby islands. We had also visited most if not all of the archaeological sites around Vesuvius and many further afield and been especially fortunate in seeing excavations not open to the general public. Overall it had been a hugely enjoyable and interesting experience.

I returned to the UK towards the end of 1987 confident that I'd played at least a small part in maintaining the success of NATO in the Cold War. Little did I know then that I would be the last RAF officer to serve a full tour in Naples under the same circumstances: the Cold War was soon to be won. However, deterrence was still to be based on strategic nuclear weapons and, almost unbelievably, former Warsaw Pact states were to become NATO members. For my part I was to return to Naples in a few years at a time when NATO, for the first time in its history, was at war. But that's another story – and another book.

PRINTED AND BOUND BY:

Copytech (UK) Limited trading as Printondemand-worldwide,
9 Culley Court, Bakewell Road, Orton Southgate.
Peterborough, PE2 6XD, United Kingdom.